RADICAL GRACE

Anyone who wants to know the human psyche will learn next to nothing from experimental psychology. He would be better advised to abandon exact science, put away his scholar's gown, bid farewell to his study, and wander with human heart throughout the world. There in the horrors of prisons, lunatic asylums and hospitals, in drab suburban pubs, in brothels and gambling-halls, in the salons of the elegant, the Stock Exchanges, socialist meetings, churches, revivalist gatherings and ecstatic sects, through love and hate, through the experience of passion in every form in his own body, he would reap richer stores of knowledge than textbooks a foot thick could give him, and he will know how to doctor the sick with a real knowledge of the human soul.

—Carl Jung, *New Paths in Psychology*

The central problem with which we are perpetually faced throughout the world today…is rooted in the core metaphor of a violent cosmic contest between good and evil…This metaphor appeals to our primal communal survival instincts and feeds…aggressive drives, giving form to unconscious psychological archetypes regarding us versus them, those on the side of God and the good versus those on the side of evil and the demonic.…This is a particularly obscene state of affairs, since the root hypothesis is erroneous. There is no reason to claim that there is such a thing as ontological evil in this world, and there is no evidence for a transcendental cosmic conflict. There are just communities of inadequate, ignorant, and sick humans trying to find their way to meaning in a world of radical freedom, constant growth,…perpetual change, and the pervasive pain that accommodating change always brings.

—J. Harold Ellens, *The Destructive Power of Religion*

I had sent him [my friend] a small book that treats religion as an illusion, and he answered that he entirely agreed with my judgement upon religion, but that he was sorry I had not properly appreciated the true source of religious sentiments. This, he says, consists in a peculiar feeling, which he himself is never without, which he finds confirmed by others, and which he may suppose is present in millions of people. It is a feeling which he would like to call a sensation of "eternity," a feeling as of something limitless, unbounded—as it were, "oceanic." This feeling, he adds, is a purely subjective fact, not an article of faith; it brings with it no assurance of personal immortality, but is the source of the religious energy…One may, he thinks, rightly call oneself religious on the ground of this oceanic feeling alone, even if one rejects every belief and every illusion.

—Sigmund Freud, *Civilization and Its Discontents*

Freud…learned avidly from his patients and made their truths the basis for his large statement with respect to human affairs. Psychoanalysis did not emerge from lecture halls and seminar rooms, but rather from the offices of clinicians who were sought by exceedingly troubled, confused, vulnerable people. It was Freud's genius to learn from them, to connect their seemingly eccentric, turmoil-ridden, even bizarre and endangered lives to those the rest of us live. In a sense, he restored their humanity, and as a consequence, enlarged our own collective human imagination. It was also Freud's genius to envision psychoanalysis as…a way of being, really, between two humans: the analyst and the analysand as partners, as companions even, in an effort to learn from one another.

—Robert Coles, "Introduction," *Selected Writings (of Sigmund Freud)*

RADICAL GRACE

How Belief in a Benevolent God
Benefits Our Health

J. Harold Ellens

Psychology, Religion, and Spirituality

Westport, Connecticut
London

Library of Congress Cataloging-in-Publication Data

Ellens, J. Harold, 1932–
    Radical grace : how belief in a benevolent God benefits our health / J. Harold Ellens.
        p. cm. — (Psychology, religion, and spirituality, 1546–8070)
    Includes bibliographical references and index.
    ISBN 978–0–313–34816–7 (alk. paper)
    1. Health—Religious aspects—Christianity.   I. Title.
BT732.E453 2007
261.5'15—dc22   2007026341

British Library Cataloguing in Publication Data is available.

Library of Congress Catalog Card Number: 2007026341
ISBN-13: 978–0–313–34816–7
ISSN: 1546–8070

First published in 2007

Praeger Publishers, 88 Post Road West, Westport, CT 06881
An imprint of Greenwood Publishing Group, Inc.
www.praeger.com

Printed in the United States of America

The paper used in this book complies with the
Permanent Paper Standard issued by the National
Information Standards Organization (Z39.48–1984).

10 9 8 7 6 5 4 3 2 1

This work is for Mary Jo (Lewis) Ellens,
diligent mother of our four daughters and two sons,
durable companion for 52 years,
and, hopefully, for "the duration,"
as we say in "army speak."

Thoughts on Reading Blueboard's Bloody Chamber

Beuna Coburn Carlson
June 1, 2007

> There is a bloody chamber in my soul.
> There have I hidden
>> Thoughts, unbidden, but not dismissed,
>> Thoughts, shadowed and dark,
>> Thoughts I would erase.

> There is a bloody chamber in my soul.
> There have I hidden
>> Words, harsh words, spoken in anger,
>> Words, mean and meant to hurt,
>> Words, I would take back.

> There is a bloody chamber in my soul.
> There have I hidden
>> Deeds, careless, long regretted,
>> Deeds, unknown to those I love,
>> Deeds I would forget.

> There is a bloody chamber in my soul.
> But it is not hidden
>> From God's unending grace,
>> From God's forgiveness and healing,
>> From God's love that makes all things new.

Contents

PREFACE

My main professional life-interest has been understanding the interface and mutual illumination of psychology and spirituality. To that end, I have endeavored to master both the psychological and theological sciences. This book is a heuristic and phenomenological distillation of that inspiring interest and long labor. Now it remains for the reader to decide whether my way of casting the matter is interesting to and useful for (1) the earnest and informed local community library borrower; (2) the undergraduate and (3) graduate student in psychology, (4) theology, and (5) spirituality; and to (6) professors of psychology and (7) religious studies, (8) theological seminary professors of pastoral care, (9) clergypersons, (10) lay-counselors, (11) social workers, and (12) the like. This is the broad audience for which the volume was written.

It is my intent in this work to express a specific perspective on the field of the Helping Professions. I wish thereby to illumine as wide a range of conceptual issues as possible in the fields of psychology, theology, and spirituality. The outlook I will express is that of human personhood fashioned in the nature, and for the work, of God; and viewed in terms of the biblical notion of God's radical, unconditional, and universal grace. To accomplish that, I wish to develop a model of the interface and mutual illumination between psychology and theology. Psychology brings with it all the natural and social sciences that apply to it. Theology likewise, carries with it the historical, philosophical, linguistic, and literary sciences that apply to it. I will attempt to bring them to bear on some of the main themes and current problems of the Helping Professions, so as to lead the earnest reader across some new psychospiritual frontiers of insight and vision.

   The objective of this work will be, therefore, to emphasize the urgent need for a thoroughly holistic and integrated model of people-care, in all facets of the Helping Professions. Human health and wholeness requires a unity in body, mind, and spirit. In that psychospiritual direction lies the future of all healing ministry, and the only hopeful future for humankind.

ACKNOWLEDGMENTS

I am grateful to Dr. Alfred J. Eppens, a deeply thoughtful colleague, who earnestly encouraged the preparation of this work. I want to express great esteem and appreciation to Frank Shiffett for his intricate technical work on the figures that illustrate the text, and for keeping my computer operating well. Buena Carlson read every word with the careful eye of a line editor and helped me avoid typographical errors and other infelicities. In this way, she has been my guardian angel, and enthusiastic cheerleader, and while it is impossible adequately to thank such heavenly visitors, this is my feeble attempt to do so.

Introduction: Grace and Health

My mother's name was Grace. She was also a fine example of that virtue. Grace is an important word, with great depth of meaning. It means unconditional goodwill of one person toward another. Usually it refers to God's unconditional love and forgiveness toward us. Derived from that divine notion, it also describes such cherishing of one human for another. It can also be used to describe our attitude and care for the rest of the created world. It is surely the case that all of us are intended to be persons of grace and graciousness.

Grace has everything in the world to do with health. Health comes in many forms, health of body, mind, psyche, or spirit. All these domains of health are directly influenced by the degree to which the atmosphere in which we live is full or empty of grace. Carl Rogers referred to the grace humans express to each other as unconditional positive regard. He claimed that it was the main factor in whether people are psychologically healthy or sick. He said that this unconditional positive regard in the therapist was the main virtue which assisted patients in developing unconditional positive regard for themselves, and so get well from most of the mental illness that troubles fifty percent of persons in every human community.

Thinking about human health is stimulating and mysterious. It is stimulating because it draws us into exploring the rather amazing scope and variety of human life. It focuses our attention on the surprising ways in which humans function. It also makes us realize that the issues of health touch every experience of being human. To explore what health really means makes us immediately aware that we are always either healthy or unhealthy, in body, mind, psyche, and spirit. Moreover, such an inquiry suggests to us the incredible number of ways in which one can be sick or well.

Nonetheless, it is impressive that those ways in which humans get sick tend to fall into a relatively few very stereotyped patterns. From that point of view, the number and variety of ways people can be ill seems finite, typical, and predictable. However, we all have our own individualized style of being ill or well, that is, of reacting to or managing and carrying our health and our illness. We are so typically human and yet so surprisingly unique, for better or worse, in sickness and in health.

Likewise, getting well can usually be achieved in surprisingly predictable and prescribed ways, yet each human does it with an intriguing distinctiveness. That is why it is also mysterious to speak of human health. Humans are healthy or ill so remarkably variously. Moreover, that already sufficiently complicates the matter of what health is and how it is achieved. Then the variety of *definitions* of health used by scientists, physicians, and in our daily speech, is almost beyond our ability to count them.

I remember that I was 14 when I first came genuinely to grips with the issue of what health is. It was during my sophomore year in high school. The quest was stimulated by a rather wide-ranging course in general biology. I was a small, rather neurotic, withdrawn, intense, anxiety laden, and shy pubescent boy. I was, obviously, and at least semiconsciously, maturing extremely late. I am not certain whether the painfulness of body and psyche that seemed to dominate my experience is typical for early adolescence. I am not sure whether it was mainly physical or psychological. I did not understand whether it was a sign of health or illness, at the time. I remember, however, that this experience stimulated my thinking about health at the same time that it mystified me.

The quest came rather quickly to something helpful: an applied definition of health. I have no idea which supplemental text we were using. It may have been one of those weekly student journals so popular at the time. In any case, it simply said that health is the state or condition in which a person can carry out a normal pattern or program of work without experiencing inappropriate pain. The teacher was impressed that I had caught that. I was astonished that no other student had. The teacher was suffering from a chronic illness, and the other students were rather beyond puberty. Perhaps my own personal need prompted me to fix on that issue, which for others was routine.

Since then I have found that two things are true about health: first, most of us take it for granted when we have it; second, this elementary definition is the best place to begin thinking about health. In this day of increasing emphasis on holistic health care, the old positivist notion that health is essentially, if not exclusively, a matter of physical well-being seems to be receding. Few professionals would now argue with the notion that health is more than physical well-being, involving also the interrelatedness of physical, mental, and social well-being. Even in the popular mind, the holistic notion is genuinely gaining ground. These gains have been a long time in developing.

In ancient societies of the Near East, from 3200 B.C.E. to 1000 C.E.—the cultures from which the West draws its sources and resources: Egyptian, Mesopotamian, Hebrew, Greek, and Roman—the stress was on physical well-being and prescriptions for physical hygiene. Matters that would be referred to today as mental hygiene or psychotherapy were largely relegated to the realm of religion. Emphasis on physical health continued through the Renaissance and well into the eighteenth century. Horace Mann, first secretary of the board of education in the United States, emphasized as late as 1840 that educating for health as physical well-being was crucial. In 1850, A. M. Shattuck, in his *Report of the Sanitary Conditions in Massachusetts*, emphasized the need for preventive programs of disease control, indicating that health was more than the absence of disease. However, his orientation remained essentially shaped by the physical emphasis.

There were notable exceptions to this over the centuries. Already in Homeric times Asklepios, and more pronouncedly Hippocrates in fifth-century Athens, placed considerable emphasis on both physical and spiritual well-being, that is, the health of *soma* and *psyche*. This emphasis is weaker in the Roman, Galen. In the early modern period, it raises its head briefly: John Locke considered "a sound mind in a sound body" to be essential.

It is only after the two world wars of the twentieth century that notions of health as optimal well-being of body, mind, and relationships began to take palpable form. Out of that development came such definitions as the following.

1. Health is a state of complete physical, mental, and social well-being and not merely the absence of disease or infirmity.
2. Health is that complete fitness of body, soundness of mind, and wholeness of emotions that make possible the highest quality of effective living and service.
3. Health is the quality, resulting from the total functioning of the individual, that empowers him or her to achieve a personally satisfying and socially useful life.
4. Health is the condition under which the individual is able to mobilize all his or her resources—intellectual, emotional, and physical—for optimum living.

Such holistic axioms take seriously the health-impacting significance of total personhood and do not underestimate the role that social relationships play in enhancing or defeating health. By the mid-twentieth century the goal of health was perceived to be not only the cure or alleviation of disease. It called for even more than prevention of disease; rather, it looked beyond, to strive for maximum physical, mental, and social efficiency for the individual person, for the family, and for the community.

The value of this perspective, as is generally recognized today, lies in the fact that it considers health in positive, rather than negative, terms. Health is not merely disease control, cure, or prevention. It is the achievement of a high level of wellness. Health is dynamic process, not a static state. It is a life of quality into which humans grow on a continuum that reaches ever forward and upward, rather than a status which people can achieve and at which they can then lie dormant or quiescent. Hence it becomes less significant to speak of being healthy or unhealthy and more meaningful to speak of relative levels of wellness or well-being. Physical, mental, and social well-being interact causatively and dynamically on the continuum from minimal to optimal wellness, as seen by most professionals and laity in the helping professions today.

A simple and direct link may be seen between the definition of health I encountered as an adolescent in 1946 and this holistic notion of health. Health as freedom from disease or pain is a notion that has in it the seeds of the definition of health set forth by J. F. Williams. He asserted that health is that quality of life that enables the individual to live most and serve best.[1] Such a quality of life, instead of mere quantity of physical freedom from disease, inevitably includes the holistic concerns of body, mind, and spirit. Williams emphasizes that the health needs of persons correspond to those of nations: vigor, vitality, progress toward a better way of life, and one's absorption in pursuit of objective causes that enhance growth in quality.

This emphasis on the intricate relationship between health and growth, physically and psychologically, is crucial for understanding the primary concern of this volume about God's health and human health. Since Francis Bacon's revival and elaboration of Aristotle's controlled scientific method, the modern era has thought about nearly everything, especially in the exact and applied sciences, in cause and effect terms. That outlook and its inherent confidence in the human ability to identify, analyze, and solve problems in the world of physical reality has been a great boon to the development of health care and the medical sciences.

The techniques for employing the causative perspective in health care have evolved rapidly. The nineteenth century saw a cause and effect model that largely identified a single effect in human health and illness with a single cause, and vice versa. By 1920, following World War I, a second model was in vogue, taking a more comprehensive approach and recognizing the multiplicity of cause and effect factors influencing wellness and illness in humans. A solid advance was evident in epidemiology in this recognition of the interactive forces in the multiple causes and effects at play. The social ecological model had been born. Disease came to be seen as the result of the condition of the host, the environment, and personal factors. The rise of Freudian psychology, replacing the old faculty psychology of the nineteenth century, was not insignificant in this development.

Since World War II and the rise of the World Health Organization (WHO), the multiple cause–multiple effect notion of illness and wellness has reached a relatively sophisticated level, taking with great seriousness the role of social, psychological, and physiological factors in shaping the health of humans and, incidentally, of most of the higher animals.

By the last quarter of the twentieth century in the United States, the effects of John F. Kennedy's emphasis on the high level of wellness model, implemented by individual responsibility for exercise, nutrition, stress management, and control of harmful substances, were well entrenched. The century ended and the new one began with clear movement toward the predictable and tangible consequence of that. An increasing emphasis is now placed on measurement of wellness quality and on efforts to calculate the manner and degree to which that quality of life is shaped by the environmental and social psychological issues of relationship, self-image, and will. The objective, obviously, is to quantify the variable factors and so enhance control of illness-inducing and wellness-inducing dynamics in human life.

Unfortunately, the recent progress toward a refined and sophisticated recognition of the function of the body-mind-spirit *(soma-psyche)* dynamo in human health has produced a seriously self-defeating side effect: the increasing preoccupation with the occult in some elements of the helping professions. This does not seem to be a fruitful avenue of pursuit for scientific understanding of how humans may achieve optimal wellness.

So we can now summarize our discussion thus far. It is clear that a considerable advance was made in health care with the recognition of the triad of interacting agents intrinsic to human persons: body, mind, and psyche. Then, another substantial step forward, beyond that simple triad, was achieved with the recognition that a triad of forces extrinsic to human beings also shaped human health: host factors, environmental social factors, and personal behavior factors.[2] Thereafter, with the rise of the WHO and its holistic influence in the world, emphasizing that health is a state of physical, mental, and social well-being, and not merely the absence of disease or infirmity, the social ecological model was elaborated fully into the environmental health model.[3]

Lalonde advanced the cause by proposing what he called the *field concept* of holistic well-being, in which he emphasized the influences of four factors: environment, lifestyle, biology, and organization of the relevant health care system.[4] Dever elaborated Lalonde's model into a complex and comprehensive proposal for a workable health care system and organizational policy.[5] He emphasized that health depends on complex internal and external factors: human biology, with its issues of maturation, aging, and genetic inheritance; environment, with its issues of social, psychological, and physical influences; lifestyle, with its issues of employment or occupation, leisure activities, and consumption patterns; and the health care system, with its measures for prevention, cure, and restoration.

These steps in the conceptualization of health and wellness have led to the current perspective in which health is defined less as the absence or elimination of diseases that cause illness and more in terms of increasing degrees and conditions of wellness. Travis devised a continuum model in which persons are assessed as always lying at some identifiable place on a line between premature death and a maximal level of well-being.[6] We have advanced significantly from my insight at age 14 to comprehensive holistic models. However, already in the notion that health is the state or condition in which a person can carry out a normal pattern or program of work without experiencing inappropriate pain lie the conceptual sources for the comprehensive definition of holistic health.

This volume urges one crucial additional dimension to the entire matter: the crucial significance for human health of a person's relationship with God. I mean to describe in detail the intricate interconnection between healthy spiritual clarity and human wellness in body, mind, and psyche. This requires setting forth what it means and how important it is to have an understanding of God that is healthy and wholesome. God's health and human health are crucially interactive. *Radical Grace* contends that a person's concept of God and actual ontological relationship with God as well as his or her *perceived* relationship definitively affect the quality or state of that person's health.

Sometimes the "posture before the face of God" is of such a sort that it creates or expands pathology. Sometimes that real or perceived relationship enhances health in body, mind, and psyche. The thesis of this book is not a new invitation to the self-defeating processes of mysticism, parapsychology, spiritism, or the occult. It is very much the opposite. It is a claim for the notion that holistic health involves the self-actualization of the full range of grand potentials for growth in body *(soma)*, mind *(nous)*, psyche *(psyche)*, and spirit *(pneuma)*, with which God has invested every human by creating us in his own image.

Health in this book, therefore, must be defined as that state or condition in which a person is achieving or has achieved the quality of life that arises out of a full-orbed realization and actualization of all the physical, spiritual, psychological, and mental possibilities with which God has invested humans and humanness. The crucial words, therefore, are *growth, dynamics, potential,* and *wellness,* which stand behind and are implied in that definition.

Radical Grace claims that both the science of the helping professions and the science of theology lead us uniformly to the recognition that the perception and experience of God as a God of grace is the central healing dynamic that moves us toward maximal well-being. There is no magic or mysticism in that. It does not require the peculiarities of the self-limited human fancies of Eastern religions. It urges, rather, a sound rational-empirical investigation of the measurable and manageable forces at play in the multifaceted human being, functioning spiritually, mentally, psychologically, and physically. Such an achievement, of course, requires a healthy God, that is, a wholesome inner image of God in each human being.

NOTES

1. J. F. Williams (1946), *Personal Hygiene Applied*, 8th ed., Philadelphia: Saunders, 2.

2. J. N. Morris (1975), *Uses of Epidemiology*, 3rd ed., Edinburgh: Churchill Livingstone, 177.

3. H. L. Blum (1974), *Planning for Health: Developmental Application of Social Change Theory*, New York: Human Sciences Press, 3.

4. M. Lalonde (1974), *A New Perspective on the Health of Canadians*, Ottawa: Office of the Canadian Minister of National Health and Welfare, 31.

5. G. E. Alan Dever (1976), "An Epidemiological Model for Health Policy Analysis," *Social Indicators* Research 2, 455–459.

6. Regina Ryan and John Travis (1981), *Wellness Workbook*, San Diego, CA: Ten-Speed Press.

CHAPTER 1

GOD'S HEALTH AND HUMAN HEALTH

For much of the last 4,000 years, God has been critically ill; that is, the reports on his nature and function indicate that his patterns of relationality, affect, and ideation have been outside of normal range. To be very specific, apparently, God has suffered from chronic paranoid schizophrenia or severe borderline personality disorder, with frequent erratic, unprovoked episodes of active psychosis. The dominant stream of reports, that is, human notions of God, indicates that he operates with the psychotic notion that he is caught in a cosmic battle with another god who threatens to thwart, corrupt, and undo his work. This is classic psychotic syndrome. According to the reports, it forms a global ideation shaping God's entire worldview. In point of fact, however, there is no empirical, heuristic, or phenomenological data to indicate that any such cosmic conflict or evil reality exists. His *notion* of reality has no reality to which it corresponds. Moreover, this pattern of ideation is specifically paranoid since it indicates that he thinks there are forces out there that are out to get him, whereas there exists no evidence that such forces exist. If the reports about him are accurate, these notions are figments of God's sick imagination. God is insane. The God of ancient Israelite religion, which produced Judaism, Christianity, and Islam, is diagnosably ill under the rubrics of the *Diagnostic and Statistical Manual of Mental Disorders (DSM–IV)*, published periodically by the American Psychiatric Association.

Sick gods make for sick people. To put it slightly differently, sick gods make people sick. As children and disciples model their parents and mentors, so individual humans and communities of humans create themselves in the image of their gods. Sick gods provide sick models, which produce sick persons and sick communities. To insure personal and communal well-being requires that one's god is well; or at least, the converse is so. If one's god is sick, one cannot achieve well-being, individually or communally.

Now you may feel that somehow, I am too severe in my clinical diagnosis. So let me recite a more palpable panoply of symptoms that, according to the dominant reports, constitute the syndrome of God's clinical disorder. He is reported to suffer from a perfectionistic need to have his world, and all who happen to wander through it, carefully conform to a prescribed set of thought forms and behavior. This sounds rather obsessive-compulsive, to say the least, particularly when you consider that the world he created is not a production factory or forced labor camp, but is designed by God to be more like a greenhouse, in which the primary style and objective is that of growth and development, thus necessitating a constant process of change and unpredictability. Perhaps you have not taken the reports of his demand for conformity so seriously as to have been much affected by this pathological symptom. But what about the fact that it is reported that God is so ticked off about human nature and behavior, human exploration and experimentation, that he simply cannot get his head screwed back on right until he has literally killed somebody?

Take all of Noah's community, for example, or Onan and his brother, or the Egyptian army at the Red Sea. Or think of the threatened genocide of the Israelites at Mount Sinai; the genocide of the Canaanites on the Israelite invasion of their land; the extermination of the Northern Israelite Kingdom; the exile of the Southern Israelite Kingdom; the sudden death of the man who tried to protect the Ark of the Covenant from falling off its cart into the mud; and the incineration of Sodom and Gomorrah.

Now if this does not sound to you like a pattern of consummate narcissism, chronic situation-inappropriateness, sadistic vindictiveness, impulsiveness and obsessive compulsive disorder, depressive and irrational rage, being out of touch with reality and out of proportion to the actual problematic events at hand in each case, you have not been paying attention. At least you have not been reading your Bible regularly. The behavioral syndrome I have just laid out is flagrant psychosis. Moreover, what about the fact that his furor was so intense toward you and me, innocent as we are, that he either had to exterminate us or slaughter his unique son, Jesus of Nazareth? If these reports are true, this God is one sick puppy, and dangerous. He solves all his ultimate impasses with ultimate violence. Don't you think that is sick? Any God who cannot behave at least as well as the average human would like to is a monster. Monster gods make monster people.

I referred to us as innocent. You may disagree. I concede that the only evil which exists in our world is the evil we do to each other. However, when I claim innocence, I mean to call attention to the fact that we humans did not ask to be born. We did not ask to be limited. We did not ask to be flawed. We did not ask to be developmental and therefore inherently and inevitably incomplete, growing, changing, achieving by trial and error, experimenting, exploring, and sometimes running down dead-end streets morally, relationally, psychological, and spiritually. We did not ask to be floated on the ocean of time and space with an inadequate database, immature judgment, and emotions often driven by anxiety about it all. We did not ask to be assigned a *divine task* of making sense of and finding meaning in this world, while being compelled to operate with mere *human resources.*

The worst of all this is that religious metaphors that we have been given in the dominant report about God's nature and behavior produce unconscious psychological archetypes in human beings, which get acted out unsuspectingly in behavior that is justified by those metaphors. If God solves all his ultimate problems by quick resort to ultimate violence, how is it possible that we can expect humans to do significantly differently? Sick gods make sick people. If God persuades us of his psychotic notion that he is caught in a cosmic conflict, the battleground of which is human history and the human heart, of course it is inevitable that we shall wish, unconsciously or consciously, to help him out, to be on his side in the war, to undertake God's cause against the infidel, to fight the bad guys, to exterminate our enemies, as apparently God tries to do with his.

This is the flag under which ancient Israelite campaigns were fought against the Canaanites, and one often wonders about Israelite campaigns today. This is the flag under which the Christian campaigns of the Crusades were fought, and one often wonders about the right-wing Christian crusades today. This is the flag under which Islam conquered the Mediterranean world in the seventh and eighth centuries, and it is clear that one need not wonder about the al-Qaida ambitions today. A sick God produces sick people. How shall we achieve well-being if God is sick? We shall not, under any circumstances.

There was, of course, another report on God's mental health, though it has been heavily discounted throughout history, often to the point of scoffing disbelief. It is the claim that the dominant report, which has always been everywhere afloat, has nothing to do with God at all, but is instead the sick projection of a lot of untutored human imaginations, by people scared to death of the unknown and the unpredictable in life: a projection of their own terrors on their own idealized mental image of the mentor they thought was God. The other report on God's mental health has had a hard time competing with that dominant report, even though all the evidence is everywhere confirming this alternative report. It has been resisted because it seems so humanly unbelievable, because it claims that God is a God of unconditional grace to all humankind.

Carl Rogers did not think it was an inherently unbelievable idea that humans could exercise unconditional positive regard for each other, even if it often seems very rare and rather unnatural. But even he was most hesitant to believe it true of God. He said he abandoned his Fundamentalist Evangelical roots because the dominant report of God as insane was endemic to any religious thought, as he saw it. Thus he could preach human unconditional grace but could not imagine unconditional grace in God. He just could not wrap his head around Genesis 12 and 17 and Abraham's breakthrough notion that God really is trying to get across to the human race: "I am announcing to you that I will be a God to you and to your children after you, throughout their generations, for an everlasting covenant, no strings attached. You will be my people and I will be your God, and that is all there is to it."

Carl Rogers could not repress the dominant report about the insanity of God ringing in his ears, despite the fact that it was a false report. Thus he could never quite hear the strains of that grace refrain playing all the way through the Old and New Testaments, declaring, as did the prophet Micah (7:18–20), "Who is a God like our God. He pardons iniquity. He passes over transgression. He will not be angry forever. He delights in steadfast love. He will have compassion on us. He is faithful to us when we are unfaithful to him. He tramples our iniquities under his feet, and casts all our sins into the sea of his eternal forgetfulness. Moreover, he guaranteed to us that we are forgiven before we were born and before we could imagine how to be clever sinners." Unfortunately, Carl Rogers is joined by much of the human race throughout history, who cannot imagine any other God than the one I am diagnosing as insane. They cannot imagine that St. Paul knew something essential about God's nature and behavior when he declared doxologically, "I am persuaded that nothing in all God's creation can separate us from the love of God" (Rom. 8:38–39).

Now, that is a fairly healthy God. God, the warrior, the vindictive judge, the impulsive slayer, the genocidal maniac, is a monster, and nobody should honor him. He makes me sick! He makes us all sick. God, the purveyor of unconditional grace, is situation-appropriate, a key gradient of good mental health. We are human; we did not ask to be human, to be born, to be limited in our database, to be creatures of growth and change, to be unfolding persons that inherently need to explore and experiment and imagine, by trial and error. We did not ask for our transcendental task and our mere mundane resources. Any God who does not see that and respond with unconditional positive regard is a very sick monster. That is why John says that the real God is *faithful and just to forgive us!* (1 John 1:9). Did you hear that? It is a matter of justice that for the likes of us, caught in our limited humanness, the only right thing is mercy. "As a father pities his children so God pities us who contemplate him as awesome!" (Ps. 103:9). Now that is a *healthy* God.

WELL-BEING: GOD'S GRACE AND HUMAN HEALTH

We are all interested in human well-being, indeed, in the well-being of the entire cosmos, which, of course, depends very largely on how well we look after human well-being. I have argued so far that our well-being depends directly on God's well-being; that is, we are addressing the problem of God's health and human health, which I have translated into the issue of God's grace and human health. What can we do to insure that the report on God's nature and behavior tells the story of his robust health and inherent good will toward us, thereby insuring that our base of operations and our basic assumptions will enhance human well-being, instead of the lie that he is a monster?

To put the question in a more operationally clinical and scientific form, How can we bring good theology and responsible psychology into that kind of authentic interface that they mutually illumine each other so as to enlighten our interpretation of human nature, what Gerkin called the *living human document*?[1] How can we do that in such a fashion as to indicate what will produce our true well-being in body, mind, and soul, that is, materially and economically, academically and intellectually, aesthetically and spiritually? I am thoroughly persuaded that *psychology* and *spirituality* are two terms for the same domain. Each has its own universe of discourse and therefore its own modus operandi, but the domains of psychology and spirituality are the same: the complex panoply of critical aspects shaping the irrepressible human quest for mundane and transcendental meaning.

Any psychologist who does not take seriously the light that human spirituality can bring to bear on the scientific discipline of psychology is simply not truly serious about his own profession or his own psychology. Any theologian who does not take seriously the light that human psychology can bring to bear on the scientific discipline of theology is simply not truly serious about his own profession or his own spirituality.

The sciences of psychology and theology, done properly and responsibly, inevitably interface at four scientific levels: theory development, research models, data management, and clinical application. At each of these levels, it is the anthropological model that is forming and functioning there, in which psychology and theology interface. Each brings to bear its distinct light for the illumination of the real and comprehensive nature of the living human document, which is the subject of both their scientific work. Moreover, within the anthropological model of human nature, it is the personality theory forming and functioning that is the site of the mutual illumination the two sciences offer each other. Psychology, spirituality, and theology contribute directly to this forming and functioning personality theory.

An illustration of what this means and how this works might be developed on the basis of an ancient biblical story that, in its historic reading, has seemed to report that God is sick, establishing a religious metaphor that has produced really sick human archetypes and sick humans for 3,000 years. That is the story in Genesis 3 about the fall of Adam and Eve, their expulsion from the idyllic world of Eden, and their being cursed by God. There is another way to read this story. As it stands, it is a rewrite in Hebrew parlance of a much more ancient Mesopotamian fertility myth. There is the fruitful tree, the virgin seducing and being seduced, the phallic-symbol snake, and the triple seduction: the snake and Eve mutually seducing each other and Eve's seduction of Adam. Read literally, in terms of long theological traditions, this is a relatively superficial report that our first parents disobeyed a specific arbitrary divine command, God got mad, threw them out of Paradise, and cursed them. That is the monster God.

If one asks why the ancient Hebrews liked this story and adopted it, the answer is obvious: they had a monster God. They experienced the world as profoundly troubled and in trouble. They had the option of accusing God for having created it that way, as they did in their older narrative in Genesis 6, or of letting God off the hook by accusing themselves. The one truth they knew in it all was that anyone reading the story immediately acknowledges that it describes our real-life experience. Life is troubled, we feel inadequate and ashamed about that, we long for love and meaning, we are very anxious about our sexuality and spirituality, we feel cast out of or alienated from our true destiny, and we long for our father but cannot seem to catch hold of his hand. They knew the story somehow rang true to some of our worst perplexities. We are lost souls and at a loss. They did not know that there was another way to read it.

They assumed that the dominant story about a threatening God was the model of reality. However, if we bring the other report to bear on this story and illumine it with a sound psychological perspective, as well, it is readily evident that this is a story about the inevitable adolescence of the human race. It is a story about leaving the womb and the nursery, exploring the possibilities of our own personhood, discovering the knowledge of our potential for good and for evil, and disclosing to ourselves the meaning of our sexuality, spirituality, and individuation. If this is a fall story, Adam and Eve fell up, not down; you might say that they fell out of the crib and got up and walked away, slightly injured but managing, by the grace of God.

With the mutual illumination of sound psychology and good theology, this story becomes the poetic suggestion that Adam and Eve needed to assert their individuality against the constraints of parental authority, even divine authority, to find their true selves. The enigma in the narrative of Genesis 3 is in the realization that the fall was a necessary act of growth and raises the question as to whether that adolescent process for persons and communities is best achieved by evolution or revolution.

Adam and Eve chose revolution. The narrative, properly illumined by good theology and good psychology, is not a story about God cursing them for that. It is a narrative about living with the inevitable consequences of the necessary and unavoidable choices that growth requires: which choices must be made without adequate knowledge of the future, without adequate insight about our options and alternatives, and without sufficient knowledge of the ambiguity of adult responsibility. God's remarks on their escape from infancy are not a curse prescribed, but a destiny described, namely, adult life is hard work and painful in many ways.

An appropriate mutual illumination of our psychospiritual metaphors and the archetypes they produce can afford us a healthy God who forms healthy people. I mean this not as a liturgical litany. I mean it as a clinically operational fact. Human well-being depends on good theology and sound psychology producing whole spirituality. Here I mean spirituality not as a belief in mere transcendental myth. I mean it as the function of the inner person in the quest of that living human document, thoroughly inscribed with the cadences of the poetry and music of truly fulfilling meaning. I mean a kind of well-being that is the wholeness of personhood and community, which derives from a comprehensive and satisfying sense of the meaningfulness of life, individually and in relationship.

This is possible for us all and for all humanity—for you and me, George Bush, al-Qaida, the Democrats, even the French—though, of course, those 15 percent of every human community who suffer from inherited severe borderline psychosis cannot be easily embraced in this because such persons cannot conceptualize and experience this notion of grace, except with appropriate medication. Development of a psychospiritual strategy, and its attendant psychosocial program of behavior, is required. It must reflect a thoroughgoing grace perspective of unconditional positive regard for one another. This stands, then, against the backdrop of the conviction that such an unconditional grace posture is the *real* story about God. Such a perspective has a chance to so shape our assumptions about personality theory and anthropology that a new global model of constructive relationality can be fashioned. This is essential to human well-being, and without it, we will continue down the trajectory of ever-increasing processes of violence as the human mode of coping with life's complexities and perplexities. The grace-way of looking at things must be grounded in a wholesome psychospiritual model. The Islamic Fundamentalists have finally done us a great favor, namely, to pitch to us the clear signal that what shapes human meaning is the issue of whether God is sick or well.

This psychospiritually honest way of reading the God story acknowledges that the problem of human un-well-being—human dysfunction—is not the problem of sin in the modern moralistic construction of that concept, but the problem of sickness, human inadequacy, and incompleteness in the face of the responsibilities of life and the challenges of godliness.

An operational model of this unique kind of personal and global relationality has at least the following 10 practical characteristics. First, the incarnation of *grace* is necessary within the personhood of everyone who cares about this new initiative of unconditional acceptance of the adversary or diverse other. That means unconditional acceptance of the other, just where that person *is* at this moment in his or her health or malignancy of spirit. Second, it requires a profound empathy that places the one who cares within the frame of reference of the diverse or alienated other person or community (e.g., al-Qaida).

This will lead the caring person to discern the sources and nature of the obstructions to grace-filled relationality suffered by the diverse other as well as suggesting possibilities for overcoming alienation. Such unconditional grace affords the alienated person or community the potential for a new sense of self-worth, wholesome meaning, and a healthy God-story. Third, this initiative provides both persons and communities a sense of mutuality in the quest for well-being. Fourth, it implies an acknowledgment that the caring initiator comes to the relationship with human impairments, as well.

Fifth, in this context, there is a chance for it to become evident that the caring person's or community's worldview expresses a comprehensive ambition for the wholeness of the whole world of humans and things, and that the diverse other's well-being is quested for in that setting. Sixth, this should make apparent that the mutual growth of both persons, or communities, is a real and expected possibility. Seventh, both will realize operationally the extent to which human well-being depends on the health of the God each envisions. Islam has long centuries of such a view of Allah as prompted a richly wholesome culture and relationality with Jews and Christians. The grand Spanish Islamic society of the early Middle Ages is an example.

Eighth, it may be anticipated that this strategy will evoke that level of security and trust which sets aside defensive patterns on both sides and defeats the obstructions to mutuality, growth, wholeness, and well-being. Ninth, both persons or communities can then realize that they are being taken seriously and affirmed. Tenth, the effectiveness of this journey in unconditional positive regard can be measured and critiqued psychospiritually at each step along the way, in the light of the expectation that the ultimate achievement of mutual well-being will be realized as psychospiritual maturity, together with all the benefits, materially and economically, academically and intellectually, aesthetically and spiritually, that represent true wholeness.

The diverse others of which I speak may be relatively benign colleagues in a vigorous dialogue in which significant polarity is evident between the views presented, or they may be lethal opponents in military, political, and cultural crises, such as that between al-Qaida and the West today. In the latter case, particularly as it applies to al-Qaida, the diversity and lethality may be driven by one or more of the following dynamics. First, it may be that the adversary is afflicted with borderline psychosis or active psychosis, as diagnosed in the *DSM–IV*. If that is what we are up against in this case, mere dialogue and negotiation will get us nowhere. Only medication of such pathological persons works to produce the constructive management of the symptoms necessary to make mutuality possible. Short of proper medication, the only course of action is the tough love of imposing such boundaries on them as prevents them from perpetrating mayhem on society or themselves.

Or, alternatively, their motive may be a legitimate sociopolitical objective of preserving the Umma—the Islamic domain—from incursions and erosions due to Western military or commercial-industrial interests and the unwelcome, society-opening influences that always accompany such incursions. Third, the adversaries may be motivated by legitimate anguish and fear regarding the trivialization of Islam's spiritual-cultural ideals and values through the offensive, devaluing impact on Islamic culture and spirituality that comes from Western cultural artifacts, such as Hollywood movies or the violent Disney videos, and the values those imply.

The present world conflict, which has taken the form of international violence and terrorism, is the currently most dangerous threat to human well-being. This danger is accompanied by the terrifying advance of AIDS and the waste of resources that might be invested in enhancing advances in medicine, mental health, education, and the creation of a culture of aesthetics in our world. All these terrors continue to violate and erode human well-being because our unconscious and conscious psychospiritual models and archetypes are all formed along the axes of vindictiveness; *quid-pro-quo* strategies of settling scores; setting boundaries on persons and communities by forcing discipline on them; meeting force with force; doing unto others what we would not have them do unto us; and making sure, under the doctrine of preemptive defense, that we do it to them first. These archetypes of fighting fire with fire are products of unconscious metaphors that imply that the world is wired this way, the cosmos is wired this way, and God is wired this way. Got a major problem? Resort to ultimate force. God does. Why should not we? It is how things are wired. God was so ticked off at us that he could not get his head screwed back on straight until he had killed somebody, us or his unique son. That's the familiar way things are set up, we easily unconsciously suppose.

Anton Boisen, Seward Hiltner,[2] and Donald Capps[3] proposed a trajectory of modifying the inner person by reframing the models of external behavior. They hoped that would produce eventual inner change. John Carter, Bruce Narramore,[4] and H. Newton Malony[5] urged a reform of our inner function by restructuring the human moral framework by a combination of rather literal biblical theology and psychodynamic psychology. They thought the *shoulds* of our monster God tradition would do it. Sigmund Freud, Carl Jung, and Eugen Drewermann[6] thought psychoanalytic psychology could rechannel the function of our unconscious archetypes.

The work of all these have their uses, but they do not reach the deep structure challenges where the real work needs to be done. Al-Qaida will continue to find ways to fight for Allah as long as the belief persists that Allah is a God of jihad and fatwa, for exterminating infidels in the Muslim Umma. This is no different than the Christian enterprise of the Crusaders of the twelfth century C.E. and their warrior God who intended for his minions "to deliver the Holy Places from the Infidel Turk." One wonders about present-day crusading spirits. This is no different than the Israelite conviction that they engaged in ethnic cleansing of Canaan in the twelfth century B.C.E. because that was the mandate of God. It startles one to realize that the modern-day Israelites thought up the wicked notion of preemptive defense, deriving it, quite obviously, from their ancient sacred writings.

CONCLUSION

I do not mean to propose here any kind of softheaded trivialization of the problem by seeming to psychologize or spiritualize it in a Sunday school kind of superficiality. Neither do I underestimate the size of the challenge. I intend my proposal to be closer to the hardheaded aggressive rationalism of Ayn Rand than to the manipulative sentimentality of contentious, softheaded American liberalism.

We will not achieve human well-being until we create a world culture of well-being. We shall not achieve that until God gets well. A world culture of well-being implies a world of psychospiritual metaphors that produce healthful unconscious archetypes. To achieve that, we must destroy the sick monster God that reigns unconsciously in all our hearts. The programs of psychological and moral reframing are worth the trouble. Freud and Jung have given us much help. But it is the monster God that must be exorcised and killed if we are to achieve some gains toward the world of well-being we can imagine, instead of the lethal world we continually tend to create.

NOTES

1. Charles V. Gerkin (1984), *The Living Human Document: Re-visioning Pastoral Counseling in a Hermeneutical Mode*, Nashville, TN: Abingdon.

2. LeRoy Aden and J. Harold Ellens, eds. (1990), *Turning Points in Pastoral Care: The Legacy of Anton Boisen and Seward Hiltner*, Grand Rapids, MI: Baker.

3. Donald Capps (1993), *Reframing: A New Method in Pastoral Care*, Minneapolis, MN: Fortress.

4. John D. Carter and Bruce Narramore (1979), *The Integration of Psychology and Theology: An Introduction*, Grand Rapids, MI: Zondervan.

5. Walter H. Clark, H. Newton Malony, James Daane, and Alan R. Tippett (1973), *Religious Experience, Its Nature and Function in the Human Psyche: The First John G. Finch Symposium on Psychology and Religion*, Springfield, MO: Charles C. Thomas; H. Newton Malony, ed. (1977), *Current Perspectives in the Psychology of Religion*, Grand Rapids, MI: Eerdmans; H. Newton Malony, ed. (1980), *A Christian Existential Psychology: The Contributions of John G. Finch*, Lanham, MD: University Press of America; H. Newton Malony, ed. (1988), *Spirit Centered Wholeness: Beyond the Psychology of Self*, Lewiston, NY: Mellen; H. Newton Malony (1983), *Wholeness and Holiness: Readings in the Psychology/Theology of Mental Health*, Grand Rapids, MI: Baker; H. Newton Malony (1995), *Win-Win Relationships: 9 Strategies for Settling Personal Conflicts without Waging War*, Nashville, TN: Broadman.

6. Eugen Drewermann (1993), *Discovering the Royal Child Within: A Spiritual Psychology of "The Little Prince,"* New York: Crossroad.

CHAPTER 2

A Psychotheology of Illness and Health

Popular notions of the meaning of illness and health today tend to grow out of the idea that the ideal for humans is to be alive, healthy, functional, happy, comfortable, wealthy, beautiful, and young. Diversions from that ideal are generally viewed as unfortunate, painful, demeaning, destructive, and wrong. Hidden there is an unwittingly negative view of illness. Humans have a deep need to find meaning, even if it is negative meaning, in all things, especially in illness and pain. The time has come to understand illness theologically. Illness is meaningful, not by the notion that it indicates moral failure or the presence of a potentially deadly disease, nor in its indication that growth to self-actualization is obstructed. It has meaning in terms of the fact that both illness and health are facets of the growth process that makes up life before the face of, and in the presence of, God.

QUEST FOR THE MEANING OF ILLNESS

Professor George Groddeck, a friend of Sigmund Freud, is thought to be the founder of psychosomatic medicine. He was a pioneer in his courageous attempt to relate the results of Freudian research and theory to organic medicine. His struggle to understand the meaning of illness and health is the source of more incisive insight about the matter than his rather low profile and minor fame would suggest. His work warrants renewed attention and is especially helpful with regard to the subject addressed here.

Groddeck argued that sickness and health appear as opposites, but they are not. Just as cold and heat are effects of different wavelengths, so illness and health are effects of life. Illness does not come from the outside, and health from the inside, of an organism. Illness is not necessarily an enemy. It is a creation of the organism that is experiencing it. It is a product of the vital force within the self that affects the organism and about which we know little. We never recognize more than some of its outward manifestations. The organism tries to express something by illness; to be ill has to mean something.

There can be no general universal meaning to illness because the boundary between sickness and health is not definite. We cannot say illness starts here and health ends there, not even theoretically, in the sense that we can point to zero when measuring temperature. We can only determine the meaning that illness has for a specific human being. An ant or an oak tree gives a different meaning to this expression of life than human beings, and Sandi's meaning is not the same as Joan's.

Nonetheless, the question about the meaning of illness is useful to explore, whether one is a physician, faith healer, therapist, shepherd, midwife, or mother. A provisional answer at least should be found or devised for the question of the meaning of illness. Undoubtedly, it would be possible to study a specific illness in a specific person impartially and thereby discover in that life setting what meaning came to that person from the illness, or by means of it.[1]

The general attitudes that people express about illness show a high need in humans to find or create meaningful understanding of the nature, purposes, and role of our suffering. Today, people, in the Western world at least, seem to have some unexamined and probably subconscious assumptions about illness that have a surprisingly negative slant. We do not need to search our own hearts and minds very deeply, or the mind and mood of society, to discover the feeling that sick people are sick because they did not exercise enough, eat properly, take the right vitamins or supplements regularly, diet appropriately, protect themselves thoroughly enough, live wisely enough, stay young long enough, or choose their genes and their parents with adequate selectivity.

One side of every one of us provides meaning to health and illness by assigning moral value to both states and assigning negative moral value to illness, devaluing the person who is suffering or is not perfectly healthy. The corollary of that attitude is the arrogant unconscious assumption that because I am not the one who is ill, I am demonstrably of superior moral character or value. I took my vitamins properly or I jogged far enough and often enough.

There is another set of value judgments that lies just beneath the surface in our personal and communal attitudes toward illness and ill persons. It is more of a philosophical than moral character, but it is related to moralization. It shows up in our temptation to explain the meaning of illness by feeling that the sick are unwell because their misbehaviors, bad genes, destiny, fate, or God have finally caught up with them.

A third set of uncritical attitudes are more social in nature. These are spontaneous feelings that since ill persons are needy, dependent, helpless, unproductive, and imposing on us for their care and attention, rather than being among the caretakers, they are second-class citizens. They are receivers and consumers, not initiators and producers. Something in us arrogantly infers that the ill are getting what they have coming to them, with rare exception, and that they are irresponsible in imposing on us who are well, though we may empathize with them and feel sympathy toward them.

Surely it is this set of thoughtless negative postures, operating at our subconscious or unconscious level, that prompts societies to manage ill persons by warehousing them in impersonal facilities, objectifying them in observation and analysis, and manipulating them with little consideration of patient preference or judgment regarding their treatment and destiny. We are all aware of how frequently this leads to exploitation of suffering persons with exorbitant health care costs, warehousing the poor and indigent as objects rather than persons, and depersonalizing those who most need caring assistance in managing their own affairs.

SETTING THE ISSUE

One of the reasons our attitudes toward illness and sick persons remain thoughtless and subconscious is the difficulty that exists with reaching satisfactory definitions of both illness and health.[2] Health has been defined as the absence of disease; as the state in which the body is able to function without pain; and as the condition in which the body, mind, and spirit operate in unison without dysfunction. It has been defined as the idea of *that* holistic state of health in which total self-actualization is achieved. Likewise, illness has been defined as the presence of disease produced by a foreign agent such as a bacterium or a virus, as the presence of disease resulting from internal malfunction of the bodily organism, as a lack of integration of the physical organism with the psyche and the soul, and as a state of having fallen short of the ideal destiny for which we have the potential as creatures of God.

We should try to devise definitions of health and illness that are formed in a theological perspective. Surely, then, we would describe illness, at the very least, as a lack of wholeness or a state in which wholeness is obstructed. Wholeness ought to mean the vital function of the total person along the lines for which humans, created in God's image, have the built-in potential. One might define wholeness as a state of maximum fulfillment of a person, through growth into God's full-fledged imager and kingdom-building agent. That would be a state in which no disorder or dysfunction of body, mind, or soul would be present in any way to distort or limit the function of the total person. That state would, of course, provide the experience of total self-realization and self-actualization, provided there remained enough other stimuli to promote growth of the self.

Obviously, such a state would be an ideal, never achieved in humans in this earthly life—a heavenly ideal to which we may look forward. Thus the definition of health must be changed into a more modest one. Health is the state of relative wholeness appropriate to that point at which one *is* just now, in the process of growth to self-actualization. Under that definition, *health* is a term that describes certain appropriate conditions of growth, and *illness* describes conditions in which growth is obstructed or distorted.

This is a very important way to think about all this, for under such a definition, one might be physically ill and in pain, but growing significantly in psyche and soul precisely because of that condition. Such a person's bodily illness may enhance his or her health as a total person. Comparably, one may suffer social, psychological, or spiritual pathology and garner significant gains from that in other facets of one's person. A person might be psychologically pathological as a compulsive personality and thus spend excessive time and energy in exercise routines, as a result of which he or she might have great physical health. If illness is seen as the opposite of health, how shall we understand those processes? If we take these examples seriously in our definitions of health and illness, we are led to an enlightened view of illness and a more positive view of suffering persons.

Such an enlightened view will erode away negative attitudes toward sick persons as well as notions that idealize youthfulness, narcissistic preoccupation with the body, the struggle for perpetual vitality, esoteric health regimens, and diet fads. Moreover, such a change in view will surely assist us in seeing ill persons as total persons, rather than as burdensome objects to be merely managed at best and exploited at worst. This view opens us directly to the claims of Christian theology and its illumining outlook on persons and on life.

Present-day attitudes in our world toward ill persons will not square with a Christian way of looking at human beings, nor with a biblical theology of grace. How shall we bring our Judeo-Christian view of God's relationship to us to bear on the quest for an authentic Christian theology of illness? To do that, we must reexamine our theology of evil. Historically, Christianity has viewed evil as an objective reality in our world. This has been seen as a reflection of an objective evil reality in the ethereal world of God and the devil. From this erroneous *faith in evil* has developed the idea that such objective evil shows up in human experience, producing all those things that are undesirable in human life. Thus pain, suffering, illness, and death have been explained as inherently evil, and the result of evil forces.

Such an outlook is, of course, thoroughly ridiculous. At the very least, it completely ignores the biblical claim that Jesus subdued the powers of evil

(1 Peter 3:22). Moreover, it overlooks the Bible as a first-century collection of writings that use the metaphors and colloquial language of their time. The first-century model of reality was that of a three-storied universe that the Jews and Christians borrowed from the way their pagan world looked at things. This they used to speak together in their own language about the problems of life, including the issues of good and evil.

Evil, quite obviously, is not an object or an objective reality that stands out there in our world waiting to afflict us. St. Augustine already saw that in the fourth century C.E. He realized that such an idea as objective evil was both an inadequate and an inappropriate way of looking at things. He described evil as the absence of good. He was trying to express the fact that evil is not an objective force for destruction in God's world or in ours. That would imply that evil has a status somewhat comparable to the status and power of God. We often hear Christians talking about these things in such a way that it sounds like they believe in a good God and an evil God. They seem to suggest that these two divine agents are caught in a cosmic struggle and that it is not yet clear which one will win in the end.

Such an outlook implies that reality is dualistic, rather than the biblical teaching that God is the uncompromised and pristine God of all things. Evil is merely the name we give to the *distance and painful incongruity* we experience between our ideal expectations in life and the real character of life in the worlds we are able to create for ourselves. Similarly, illness is not best understood in terms of a model that defines it as evil and as a consequence of the forces of evil in God's world and ours. Illness is an element or temporary state experienced on the growth continuum of conception—birth, life, maturing, death—and eternal life. Illness is a *distortion* of the comfortable and direct line of growth that we idealize, from birth to self-actualization, but it is not the opposite of growth. Indeed, it is usually a growth inducer.

We grow primarily—perhaps only—from our pain, or at least with pain. God's design for our growth into full-orbed imagers of his nature calls for the maturation and self-realization of the total person of every human. Illness and pain often enhance that growth and speed it by leaps and bounds so that what is unfortunate for the body may enhance the soul or psyche. What is unfortunate for the psyche may enhance the body and mind. Does Dali, for his alleged schizophrenia, not perceive dimensions of insight and creativity that complete him in ways that leave the rest of us apparently deficient and less divinely artistic?

Moreover, when one views the whole order of things, and focuses on what humans usually call evil, it is difficult to discern that there is anything in the world of human experience that might properly be called evil, except the unfortunate things humans do to each other. Is it evil that Mt. Vesuvius erupts and destroys Pompeii and Herculaneum? No. Mt. Vesuvius was an active volcano for thousands of years before those villages were built. The only evil in it, if that term can even be used there, is that human stupidity resulted in the construction of those resort towns at that inappropriate and vulnerable location—that human error resulted in the descendants of those builders being afflicted with pain and death.

Is it evil that a bacterium or virus insinuates itself into a blade of grass that is then eaten by a cow, whose milk is diseased and kills a baby, and perhaps the cow? That is tragic, but not evil. From the point of view of the bacterium, it is a considerable achievement. From the point of view of the cow and the baby, it is painful and grievous. A contest between two forms or orders of life took place, and one lived at the expense of the other, just as humans live at the expense of plant life and lower orders of animal life daily. It is an unfortunate kind of human imperialism to call such processes evil. That accords a moral priority or prerogative to what we call the higher orders of life and an inherent exploitability to the so-called lower orders.

The processes in this illustration of the bacterium and the cow are not evil. This is just the order of things in this created world. The death of the baby is unfortunate and terribly painful to the parents, but it is not an evil event, only a tragic one. It is not the consequence of some evil force in this world. Illness is not evil, but merely the painful corollary of the contest of life forms or the dysfunction of disordered cells and organisms in a world dominated by humans who arrogantly feel that we should be exempt from such inconveniences and discomforts. So we name our private pains and inconveniences evil, even if others of God's organisms are enhanced by the process.

Of course, when humans willfully or ignorantly damage each other or the rest of God's creation when alternative actions were possible, that is evil. It is an immoral thing. That, however, is the only kind of real evil that I can find in the amazing world God has given us. It is therefore in such a context and along such a trajectory that I believe we must seek a Christian theology of illness.

INSIGHTS FROM HISTORY

Ancient Israel

It is easy to notice in the Hebrew Bible that the ancient Israelites saw a close connection between sickness or suffering and the will of Yahweh. Ill persons were seen as suffering from the chastisement of God. This was supposed to produce growth or refinement, as gold is refined in fire. Frequently, suffering was seen as divine punishment for sin, secret or unconfessed, or as an affliction from God, a sign and symbol for the larger community to take note. Such ill persons were assigned special rituals, special places, and special categories in the society. Illness in this model was viewed in terms of the cosmic issues of meaning and purpose, not in terms of the finite issues of cause and effect, such as dominated the Greek perspective in the age of Aristotle's scientific method.

Illness thus was seen as a religious issue, rather than a scientific issue. Deliverance from the illness was understood to be a responsibility of the prophet or priest, rather than of a medical practitioner. The preferred treatment regimen included prayer, magic, and miracle: programs for persuading God to intervene directly. The community's expectations of the ill person were that he or she would confess guilt, beg for healing, engage in the rituals of purification, protect the community by withdrawal from normal human relationships, and accept alienation from God and from the community support system until the illness subsided.

The health–illness continuum was really the simple equation of life and death. Illness was a state of deathness, and healing was a deliverance from deathness. This is an essentially spiritual or religious model. The significance of this ancient Israelite model of health and illness lies in the fact that it is a full-fledged *theology of illness,* albeit an inadequate one rooted in unfortunately limited knowledge. It implies a lack of understanding of the various kinds of dysfunctions that can occur in a person before the face of God and the attendant reasons why they happen. The ancient Israelites did not understand that illness represents a temporary stage in the process of health and growth to self-actualization.

In spite of this limitation, this ancient Israelite theology of illness offers two theological insights that are useful for a sound theology of illness for us today. Those Israelites saw that illness is a dysfunction of the total person and that health is a state involving the whole person. Second, they realized that illness and death, as healing and health, are experiences in which God is obviously active. They knew that these experiences have essentially to do with restoring a person to God's original design for human beings. They saw that sometimes, illness actually contributes to the achievement of that design.

It is not surprising that they tended to see illness or the lack of healing as events or processes in which God was usually acting negatively regarding a person, requiring a moral reason to be found for the illness. Nor is it surprising that they discerned the preferred treatment regimen to be primarily spiritual. An alternative theology of illness would have been one in which illness and health, life and death, were seen as natural elements on the growth continuum in God's world, where grace is the matrix of existence and is also the eternal guaranteed destiny of all life.

Mesopotamia

The view of illness and health among the Assyrians and Babylonians was essentially like that of the Hebrew Bible, indeed, probably the source of the way the Hebrews were thinking about these things. There was, however, one crucial difference: God was not envisioned as a God of grace and covenant in Mesopotamia, but rather as a God of whim and arbitrariness. In consequence, humans were seen as victims of the whims of God when illness struck. Humans had been created to carry out menial tasks in support of God and were made from inferior earthy stuff, while being invested with the calling and imagination of a divinely ordered destiny: human quality with a divine task.

The rituals of healing were spiritual or religious in nature but tended to be halfhearted because the catch-22 existence of humanity bred hopelessness and resignation. The Mesopotamian notion of illness was theological but hardly appointed by God toward some redemptive end. Humans could never expect to satisfy God and achieve a meaningful destiny, either in deliverance from illness or from the deadliness of life.

Egypt

The Ebers Papyrus lists 877 prescriptions for 250 illnesses. The Smith Papyrus is the oldest surgical text in existence and gives 49 case descriptions in a sophisticated, scientific manner. The Egyptians performed brain surgery in 2000–3000 B.C.E. Imhotep, a noted physician among the ancient Egyptians, described healing as an art and a science in very modernistic terms. He practiced a rather careful and astute triage of patients in which he divided those patients who had an illness to treat scientifically from those who had an illness that was intractable. He approached his practice in terms of a rudimentary scientific method, later adopted and elaborated by Aristotle. It was conveyed by his work to Francis Bacon, the father of its modern use. Imhotep used careful records of case histories and analytic evaluations, though his work continued to be shadowed by remnants of religious rituals and popular magic.

The Egyptian approach to illness and health by the 12th Dynasty was not essentially theological, but scientific. The Greeks followed sturdily in this tradition, beginning in the golden age of Pericles and continuing in some degree of integrity well into the Hellenistic era, after Alexander the Great. Asklepios, Hippocrates, and the Roman Galen stand solidly in this line of careful scientific development. The remarkable fact here evident is that in their divorce from a theological perspective on illness and health, the practitioners of Egypt and Greece achieved incredible scientific gains.

Can we take the scientific advance that undergirds the healing arts today and devise a theology of illness that illumines it and makes it more mature, human, and complete? Can we move through present-day preoccupation with scientific cause and effect concerns into the deeper and broader stream of theological issues of meaning and purpose in our quest to understand illness and health? Meaning and purpose seem more central to the matters with which the total human person struggles in the quest for wholeness.

BIBLICAL THEOLOGY

A sound biblical theology of illness takes up its meaning in terms of a cosmic divine context. That context includes the facts of (1) God's presence to us in time and space, (2) God's providence in our unfolding life experience, (3) God's intentional design for us in our unique humanness, and (4) God's passion and compassion for us. Those are the cardinal elements of the truth and consolation of the Gospel. The man Job, and his book in the Hebrew Bible, return ancient Israelite thought to authentic theology about God. They restore the human person to the status of compatriot of God in building the world and the Kingdom of God. The narrative of that ancient patriarch restores humans, in Hebrew thought, to the status of image bearer of God, invested with marvelous potential for reflecting God's nature.

The scripture makes it clear that we are unable to sin ourselves out of God's grace, unable to squirm out of his long embrace. In the most dire of human circumstances, God is not seen as the problem, but as the shepherd of human growth, the source of human survival, the energy behind human thriving and flourishing.

This theological view of illness as a human experience in which God is present, fostering growth and bringing healing of one human facet of illness or another, is obvious in the ministry of Jesus. Even more evident is his objective of bringing persons to total personhood. It is interesting, of course, that Jesus did not heal everyone, but only a paradigmatic few. He healed those largely as a sign and symbol of the presence of the reign of God showing itself in history. When the crowds mistook that intent for mere entertaining magic or mere healing, Jesus determined intentionally not to continue to heal in their region. Moreover, it is of interest that Jesus made some significant attempts to employ the science of the day in his healing, without losing the valuable theological perspective or emphasis.

The theme and pattern that arise from theological roots in the Hebrew Bible and Jesus' ministry depict life as a dynamic line of growth to full personhood in interaction with God. On that growth continuum, illness and health are temporary interactive states, inducing growth and enhancing life as a means toward death, death itself being seen as the step into full and eternal life. On that trajectory, growth is a total person experience. So much is this true that it made complete sense for Jesus to say to the paralyzed man in Capernaum, "Your sins are forgiven," as though that were the thing that was wrong with him. Indeed, it apparently was what was wrong, for thereafter, upon Jesus's invitation, the man was able to stand and walk. The theme and pattern in scripture is one of dynamic growth along a continuum that moves from sin and alienation and illness on one end, to health, wholeness, *shalom*, and salvation on the other. Surely that comprehensive and theologically oriented perspective or model is valuable in constructing a responsible theology of illness and health for today.

St. Paul's manner of viewing human persons is helpful at this point. He spoke of the three states of human life and growth: primordial persons, as in the story of paradise in Genesis 1–3; fallen persons who are alienated from God; and whole persons *in Christ*. It is clear that for Paul, these three states have their meaning against the background of God's unconditional grace as described in Romans 8 and elsewhere. It is also clear that Paul's three states stood on a continuum of growth leading to God's ultimate destiny for us all, namely, our fulfillment as persons. This implied our self-realization and self-actualization as image bearers of God and God's compatriots in bringing in his reign of love and grace on earth.

Paul retained some confusion, throughout his life, about the relationship of the Greek tendencies and the Hebrew roots of his theology. He was never quite sure how unconditional grace made room for the discipline of the id by the ego and superego (the lower passions by the higher passions). However, in the end, the Hebrew theology of grace triumphed in his theology, without erasing the Greek notions that now become very helpful to us in formulating a biblical theology of illness.

Paul used four terms to speak of facets of human personhood. In sound Greek fashion, he spoke of the body *(soma)*, our fleshly nature *(sarx)*, our soul and mind *(nous)*, and our psychospiritual nature *(psyche)*. Our bodies are not the whole of our fleshly nature, but they are the source and center of it. Likewise, our soul is not the whole of our psychospirituality, but it is the source and center of the *psyche*. There is a significant overlap between the *soma/sarx* and *nous/psyche*. This accounts for the important role that endocrine chemistry plays in our psychological states as well as the intricate relationship between our mind-brain processes and the intriguing facets of our mind-soul (see Figure 1.1).

In this Pauline model, the dynamic force animating the fleshly nature is sexuality, and that animating the spiritual nature is spirituality. It is my perception that this model reflects the true nature of humanness in a very helpful manner and that the dynamic force of sexuality and spirituality are not two forces but the same single life force at the center of our selves. In one case, it is somatized as sexuality, and in the other case, it is psychologized as spirituality; that is, when this life force reaches out toward the other human, it is processed through the body as the sexual driver. When it reaches out toward relationship with God, it is processed psychospiritually, and we call it

Figure 1.1 Ellens Person Model I

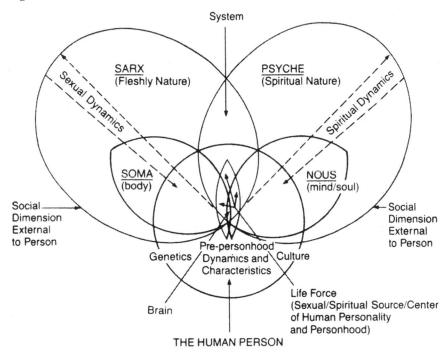

System

SARX
(Fleshly Nature)

PSYCHE
(Spiritual Nature)

Sexual Dynamics

Spiritual Dynamics

SOMA
(body)

NOUS
(mind/soul)

Social
Dimension
External
to Person

Social
Dimension
External
to Person

Pre-personhood
Dynamics and
Characteristics

Genetics

Culture

Brain

Life Force
(Sexual/Spiritual Source/Center
of Human Personality
and Personhood)

THE HUMAN PERSON

spirituality. Sexuality is a proximate quest for relationship and meaning; spirituality is the ultimate quest for relationship and meaning—transcendental meaning. In both cases, the force moves from longings for communication to needs for communion, to urges for union, to ecstasy, and on to eternity (perpetuation of the self).

Such a view of human beings implies that our function is dynamic, growth oriented, and directed to the goal of human self-realization, self-actualization, and self-perpetuation as well as the cherishing of the other (human or divine). In Paul's theology, there is also a strong implication that in human self-actualization, God achieves self-realization and self-actualization, as well. Moreover, the model illustrates in a fine way the Pauline notion that as the two manifestations of the life force in human persons become widely divergent and opposed, illness increases. Conversely, the more integrated our sexuality and spirituality, as central forces of personal development, the more health flourishes in body, mind, and spirit. As the interface or relationship of the two primary facets of a person converge (*sarx* and *psyche*), health can be anticipated, and the model changes from Figure 1.1, which looks like a scared bumble bee, to Figure 1.2, which looks more like a filled balloon soaring aloft and in flight to grand new discoveries.

Figure 1.2 Ellens Person Model II

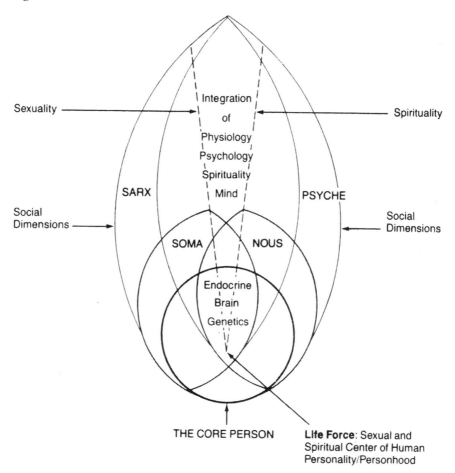

Sexuality ————————→   Integration ←———————— Spirituality
                              of
                          Physiology
                          Psychology
                          Spirituality
                    SARX   Mind   PSYCHE

Social   Social
Dimensions ————————→   ←———————— Dimensions
                    SOMA   NOUS

                         Endocrine
                           Brain
                          Genetics

        THE CORE PERSON   **Life Force**: Sexual and
                                 Spiritual Center of Human
                                 Personality/Personhood

As we learn more about the two-way switching mechanism of the hypothalamus, the intricate interaction of the endocrine system and psychological states, and the apparent relationship of psychological stress with repression of the immune system, we must become more aware of the relevance of this theological model of human nature. We know much, now, about the connection of these things with the prevalence of numerous specific types of disease: the common cold; some forms of deadly cancer, particularly of the gut; and numerous forms of depression, anxiety, and borderline syndrome. The model may be expanded usefully, as in Figure 1.3, to indicate the source, nature, and dynamics of socially pathogenic influences on individual persons, communities, and society in general. In Figure 1.3, the emphasis is

Figure 1.3 Ellens Person Model III

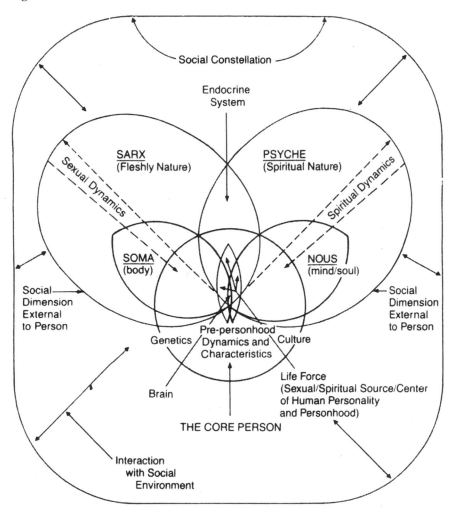

on the interaction of the core person and the total psychosocial person in community.

A PSYCHOTHEOLOGY OF ILLNESS FOR OUR DAY

It is necessary that we craft a sound Judeo-Christian theology of illness for our day. That means a theology of illness based on the Hebrew Bible, the New Testament, and twenty-first-century knowledge about health issues of body, mind, and spirit. This will require an appreciation of previous attempts, a sound esteem for modern science, and an authentic biblical perspective. A sound biblical perspective must be generative, while being neither prescriptive nor restrictive.

We have seen that in their attempt to develop a sensible view of these matters, the Greeks followed the Egyptians in a careful distinction between the scientific and religious descriptions. By the time of Socrates, the Greek approach was appropriately analytic, descriptive, scientific, empirical, and cause and effect oriented. They saw little need to go beyond that to issues of meaning and purpose. Thus they did not line up their philosophical or theological quest with the matters of medicine. They differentiated markedly between the spiritual and psychological issues on one hand, and the physiological matters on the other. This was a corollary of their perception that human physiological nature and drives were essentially animalistic and subhuman. These lower passions were to be subdued and held in check by the higher passions, namely, the intellectual and psychological powers, insofar as possible. Humanness resided, they were sure, essentially in the *psyche* and the *nous.*

The Hebrew outlook was different in some very revealing ways. The Hebrews viewed human nature in a thoroughly unified manner. The whole person was seen as made in the image of God, genitals and all. They discerned no inherent tension between the physiological and the psychological, no conflict between body and soul. They were not really interested in the question of the differentiation of these essential aspects of humanness until after the exile in Babylon (586–500 B.C.E.), when the influences of Persian medicine and Zoroastrian theology impacted the many Judaisms that grew up between then and the time of Christ. There was little compartmentalization of the various facets and functions of persons until the debate between the Pharisees and Sadducees about the resurrection of the soul incited a debate about whether the soul survives death. Prior to that, a human being was discerned to be inherently unitary, rendering absurd the Greek idea of a division between *soma* and *psyche.*

So the Hebrews were focused simultaneously on God and the human being in their model of person, health, illness, life, and death. There was no difference for them between what was theological and anthropological. Their focus was on the meaning and purpose issues implied in the understanding of humanness, an essentially transcendental orientation.

These two traditions are the primary roots of our present Western Judeo-Christian outlook on health and illness. Both contribute important elements to our present way of viewing the question. The scientific method of analytic and descriptive empiricism is central to a sound understanding of health and the management of illness. Thus it is essential to a proper theology of illness. We get that part of our heritage from the Greeks through Aristotle and Bacon. It informs us that the universe is tractable, that both God and his creation are objective, that humans as creatures are related to but objective from the cosmos in general, and that we are persons before the face of God, not extensions of his person or nature. It emphasizes the inherent coherence and clarity of the universe and its inherent laws of function as an objective entity.

The Hebrew side of our heritage urges on us the perception that this tractable and inherently coherent cosmos is an expression of God's imagination, design, spirit, and intentionality regarding humans and history. So the universe is accessible to scientific study because its laws of structure and function are dependable. Such study will predictably lead us to substantial knowledge about the nature of things. These facts are not merely reflections of the clarity of the universe but are revelations of the existence, nature, person, mind, and will of God, in the Hebrew view. We may call this revelation God's general revelation, if we wish to distinguish it from his special revelation of grace in the Bible. Such a view of revelation is in keeping with our Judeo-Christian heritage, provided we do not draw a radical line between the character and content of the two forms of revelation or knowledge. To draw such a line would be a Greek deception and lose the essential unitary perspective in biblical thought, remarkable for its lack of tension between nature and grace.

From a Greek perspective, we must preserve the idea of the empiricist as scientist. From a Hebrew's, we must celebrate the idea of the philosopher-theologian as scientist. In Greek fashion, we must give close attention to matters of cause and effect, while in Hebrew fashion, we must give careful attention to matters of meaning and purpose. Only in this way are we able to develop an authentic and comprehensive contemporary Christian theology of illness.

ULTIMATE MEANING

The Hebrew sense of the ultimate meaning of health and illness is the foundation of the biblical notion that God is working providentially in history and our lives to bring us to the place where there is no weeping, illness, or pain (Rev. 21–22). So God's presence in both health and illness is important to affirm. This not a presence of judgment, but of grace and healing. It is not a matter of guilt and punishment. God does not cause illness, but he is not absent from it. He enters into it in his existential presence, giving meaning to illness and health as parts of the process of our growth to self-actualization. Both health and illness play their parts in our movement to that end. There is a sense in which God, through the growth process which he stimulates and shepherds by his grace and providence, is delivering us from death's domain. However in the process, illness and death as well as life and health are the tools and instruments that implement the deliverance.

WHOLENESS

Popular talk about wholeness and holistic approaches to people care conforms remarkably to biblical perspectives in that it leads us to the useful insights that sickness and sin are radically different categories. They are, nonetheless, corollaries. Likewise, salvation and healing are concepts from different paradigms but corollary names for things with which we deal. Sin does not cause sickness, and salvation does not cause healing, in the sense that we usually use those terms. However, in the biblical outlook, sin has no sensible meaning, except that of failure to achieve the destiny God intends for us in wholesome self-actualization. That is God's ambition for us. To fail in that achievement, to fall short of the mark, willfully or ignorantly, is sin. It is not a failure of duty, but of destiny. Even a failure of duty is sin only in that it is a failure of destiny, an obstruction or sidetrack in the growth process to God's great design for all of us.

However, it is often just those sidetracks, obstructions, and distortions that become the stimuli of remarkable insight and growth. Our sin is precisely the only possible launching pad for the manifestation and experience of God's healing grace. Our pain is the occasion of new insight and growth, as persons. Our neediness becomes the source of the energy for faith, trust, and mature hope. Crucifixion became the moment of truth. Such malfunctions in the growth and unfolding process of life and history probably are better thought of as sickness than as sin. Sickness, in that sense, is a process of divergence from the idealized line of growth, but which often induces various unexpected kinds of growth, in the end enhancing the total process and person—because God is God and grace is grace.

Therefore that growth which constitutes healing in our life experiences may also be called our salvation, and salvation may be called a healing. The value and effect of both is no more or less than the unfolding of the self-realization of a person, as God intended that development to show up, as he originally designed us. Whether the primary effect of growth is physical, spiritual, or psychological does not essentially change the nature or significance of the salutary event or process. It is a pagan Greek notion, not biblical theology, to suppose that physical repair or growth is healing and spiritual growth or repair is salvation. Both are both. God would not recognize that kind of compartmentalization in our model of humans: our concept of the nature of the persons he created for illness and health on our road to growth.

TERMINAL ILLNESS

The outlook suggested here raises interesting implications for the idea of terminal illness. We are all terminal since life is a process of growth along the trajectory of self-actualization that God intended in his design of us. At the same time, we are all growing toward our real life in eternity with God. All health and illness participates in the movement toward being eternally alive. Growth in, through, and over illness marks stages on that process, as does growth in, through, and in spite of health. The meaning of it all is derived from the growth quality of the process for time and eternity. The assurances of providence and grace, as expressions of God's existential presence with us, insure that we will all realize the total fulfillment of the magnificent potentials with which God has invested us as those made in his likeness.

CONCLUSION

So all persons are companions of God in this enterprise of life, building God's reign of grace and love here and now. We are all of infinite value, inviolable worth, God-invested dignity, and eternal significance. Our place at this moment in the growth process may be somewhat different than that of many others, but we are all on the same journey, along the same trajectory. Whether we are ill or well just now is a relative question. We are all terminal, and in an important sense we are all ill, after all. In some major or minor way, we are all ill, for the contest between living organisms is going on within us all continually, and our organs and parts are all functioning with differing degrees of efficiency every day as we live out youth and old age.

The obviously ill have a right to grow healthier and achieve less painful gains in the process of growth toward their destiny, and they have a right to die and thereby achieve the great gains of reaching their final destiny. In any case, they are destined to self-actualization and achievement of God's intended goal for them, as for us all: physically, psychologically, socially, intellectually, and spiritually. The guarantee of that destiny is the universal and unconditional nature of God's healing and saving grace, as described in the Bible. It is particularly certified in Paul's claim that every eye shall see God at death, every knee shall bow, and every tongue shall confess (Rom. 14:11, Phil. 2:11). The outcome of that will be total self-actualization—healing—to the glory of God.

So illness and health may be described in many ways: presence of disease, obstruction of growth, distortion of function. The most authentic way to think of it is as alternate stages in the experience of growing toward our destiny as companions of God. A person may experience himself or herself as idealized self, real self, demeaned self, damaged self, or sick self. We may similarly envision each other. These are all relative terms. If one views oneself as sick while idealizing perfect health, he or she will likely see that sick self as a damaged and demeaned self. If we look at each other similarly, we shall draw similar conclusions. That is what we are always tempted to do. However, if one views oneself, in the light of the above theological outlook on illness, as experiencing an alternative phase of life's growth process, on the God-designed continuum toward self-actualization and self-fulfillment, one is unlikely to feel like a demeaned or damaged self, even when painfully ill.

The self is still a whole self on the pilgrimage of growth to greater completeness. If we viewed the sick and suffering this way, what an improvement of our attitudes would automatically happen. The sick self is a standard self, in a phase that is typical of many stages and phases of life. Healers have options to view ill persons as objects, patients, persons, image bearers of God, or God's companions in the unfolding of life. People are not puppets, but persons with integrity and potential, whom God has engaged as his partners in each of the placid or painful phases of existence. The way we view each other in these regards shapes the way we cherish each other—or fail to do so. That in turn affects the degree to which we heal each other or make each other ill. This is particularly true for psychotherapists to remember in the care of the mentally ill.[3]

A sound and adequate contemporary Judeo-Christian theology of illness, therefore, should be an elaboration of something like the following statement: illness is one of the more distressing of the varied natural conditions experienced by God's creatures, into which God compassionately enters with us, with the gracious ambition of stimulating growth in as many facets of our total persons as possible, confidently expecting in this way to enhance our progressive self-realization and self-actualization as his image bearers and as his companions in the advance of his reign of grace and love in and through us, both in this life and in the fulfilled life into which our deaths welcome us. Because God is God and grace is grace, no one shall fall short of the ultimate total experience of God's rich destiny for us, for "neither death nor life, neither messenger from heaven nor monarch of earth, neither a power from on high nor a power from below, nor anything else in God's whole world has any power to separate us from the love of God" (Rom. 8:37–39).[4]

On that line, any responsible and comprehensive psychotheology of illness—or of health—must begin its development and hold its course.

NOTES

1. G. Groddeck (1977), *The Meaning of Illness: Selected Analytic Writings*, New York: International Universities Press.

2. J. Harold Ellens (1982), *God's Grace and Human Health*, Nashville, TN: Abingdon.

3. See chapter 14, Grace Theology in Psychotherapy.

4. J. B. Phillips, trans. (1958), *The New Testament in Modern English*, London: William Collins.

CHAPTER 3

ANXIETY AND THE RISE OF RELIGIOUS EXPERIENCE

Human religion is universal. Religious experience and expression is evidenced by, and in important ways shapes, all culture. Apparently, to be religious is natural to being human. Humans everywhere worship. To do so seems innate to human personality. Liturgies of worship grow out of psychological and spiritual sources deep within the human personality. Those psychic sources of religion are closely related to the native human anxiety patterns discernible in all normal persons. Some forms of worship and religion meet the deep human psychic needs better than other forms.

Most religious practices in individual life and in communal history reinforce the anxiety of humans through the frustrating dynamics of guilt and the sense of the ultimate helplessness in the face of the problems of morality and the threats attendant on our mortality. Authentic Judeo-Christian religion is unique in its Gospel of grace. That cuts to the center of the human problem with the assurance of both the sustained meaningfulness of life and the promise of immortality. Distinguishing between what is authentic spirituality and what is psychic pathology is therefore crucial.

Already in the ancient world of Greece and Rome, it was strongly suggested that all humans have an inherent need to worship. Despite the Renaissance, modern thought has consistently suspected that ancient suggestion to be true. Since Sir James George Frazer's *The Golden Bough*[1] was first published in 1890, the Western world has affirmed scientifically that humanness and religiosity always and everywhere appear together. The Eastern world seems to have known that consciously and with certainty for a number of millennia.

SYMBOL, RITUAL, AND THEOLOGY

Anthropology, history of religions, and sociology, as scientific disciplines, join archaeology in confirming this quality of our nature, so naively taken for granted throughout all of Western history. Moreover, these disciplines demonstrate the significant religious role played by symbols in ritual and theology. Out of the recognition of this universal religious function of symbols and symbol making arose the awareness of the intricate interrelationship between religion and psychology, between the life of the soul and that of the psyche.[2]

The only remaining potential challenge to this axiom about religion and humanness seems now to lie with the paleontologists such as the scientific community gathered around the work of the Leakey family and that of Stephen Gould and the like. Leakey presumed to uncover the character and culture of the original hominoids who were the progenitors of the hominids. They have demonstrated solid gains in this quest. If this line of investigation makes good on its presumptions, it may turn up a prereligious hominid. However, the current evidence is against it since the earliest tools of the anthropoids so far identified have included ritual and funerary utensils of an apparently religious nature. If such scientists look, one day, into the sunken sockets of an apparently prereligious hominid skull, of course, there will still remain the problem of definition of terms. How will we certify that the primitive character who lost his apparently godless head so long ago was really prereligious in theological tendencies as well as tools? How, moreover, will it be decided which hominoid was hominid and which hominid was *Homo sapiens?*

RELIGIOUS FUNCTION OF ANXIETY

Humanness as we know it, in any case, is apparently essentially religious. Scholars in the field of comparative religion have unveiled a wealth of information in the last century concerning the nature and meaning of the religious character of humanness. The important developments in the science of the psychology of religion in the twentieth century were built on the foundation laid in the pioneering work of William James in his *Varieties of Religious Experience* and were anticipated by the epistemology of Immanuel Kant and the theology of Friedrich Schleiermacher. It was carried forward in the last century by the work of Anton Boisen, Seward Hiltner,[3] Don Capps,[4] David M. Wulff,[5] Wayne E. Oates,[6] H. Newton Malony,[7] and others, who explored human anxiety and its relief in divine grace.

Schleiermacher defined the common ground from which all religious experience grows up. He saw that it was psychological turf. He built his theology on the fact that the feeling of dependence is the universal and constant character of human consciousness that makes us religious. Jung[8] moved us a major step forward in relating the world of the spirit and the world of the psyche. He described human anxiety as the form in which humans realize the experience of dependence. Seward Hiltner[9] carried the idea from anxiety to the relief of grace.

So I am claiming here that religious experience and expression rises from the native and universal human experience of anxiety. Arapura, in his superb little book *Religion as Anxiety and Tranquility*, refers to the "non-accidental but necessary character of religion."[10] He argues that anxiety is a function of self-consciousness, which like *being* is what *necessarily is*,[11] and interplays with the vital human lust for achieving tranquility. So the equation is simple: self-consciousness produces anxiety, which interplays with the vital urges that move the organism to stasis. Thus religious experience and its various expressions are born in this interplay and function as the key factor mediating between the forces of death and life in personality.

Karen Horney illumines this point with her useful definition of anxiety. After describing the kinship of anxiety with fear, she points out that

> when a mother is afraid that her child will die when it has only a pimple or a slight cold we speak of anxiety; but if she is afraid when the child has a serious illness we call her reaction fear. If someone is afraid whenever he stands on a height or when he has to discuss a topic he knows well, we call his reaction anxiety; if someone is afraid when he loses his way high up in the mountains during a heavy thunderstorm we would speak of fear. Thus far we should have a simple and neat distinction: fear is a reaction that is proportionate to the danger one has to face, whereas anxiety is a disproportionate reaction to danger, or even a reaction to imaginary danger.[12]

Horney's contention here is similar to Freud's distinction between objective and neurotic anxiety. Freud called the former an intelligible reaction to danger and the latter an irrational or exaggerated one. Horney is dissatisfied, however, to allow her simple definition to stand untouched. It has one flaw, in her judgment: it does not distinguish between what is proportionate in one culture from what is disproportionate in another. Anxiety about taboos may be appropriate in the value setting of a primitive culture. Anxiety about the same thing in twentieth-century American culture would be disproportionate and neurotic. Horney, therefore, helpfully amplifies her definition:

> All these considerations suggest a change in the definition. Fear and anxiety are both proportionate reactions to danger, but in the case of fear the danger is a transparent, objective one, and in the case of anxiety it is hidden and subjective. That is, the intensity of the anxiety is proportionate to the meaning the situation has for the person concerned, and the reasons why he is thus anxious are essentially unknown to him.

The practical implication of the distinction between fear and anxiety is that the attempt to argue a neurotic out of his anxiety—a method of persuasion—is useless. His anxiety concerns not the situation as it stands actually in reality, but the situation as it appears to him.[13]

The perception to which Horney refers at this juncture is often a subconscious perception of an anxiety-affording situation. Humans often have anxiety, therefore, without being clearly aware of it. Nonetheless, that anxiety calls for resolution. The natural forces of the human physical and psychic organism that press for tranquility function as vigorously on the subconscious as on the conscious level: "In fact, we seem to go to any lengths to escape anxiety or to avoid feeling it."[14]

The fact that anxiety, whether disproportionate on proportionate, conscious or subconscious, is frequently irrational and manifests itself in irrational pressures toward resolution does not discount the problem, but rather merely complicates it. Irrational anxiety or expression of anxiety "presents an implicit admonition that something within us is out of gear, and therefore, it is a challenge to overhaul something within us."[15] The human organism employs four strategies to effect that change. Humans rationalize, deny, or narcotize anxiety or "avoid thoughts, feeling impulses and situations which might arouse it."[16]

Albert C. Outler assessed this accurately and constructively when he wrote,

> Religious anxiety is both neurotic and ontological at one and the same time. It is neurotic to the extent that it misconstrues the symbols of "groundlessness" and so reacts *in*appropriately. From this follows the kaleidoscope of religiosity—with its superstitions and stultifying effects that the psychiatrist knows all too well. At the same time, our sense of alienation from God turns into a dread of God's alienation from us. The Deity is, quite literally, dreadful, and the guilt-ridden soul is anxious lest the offended Creator will jerk the rug out from under the offending creature, leaving him suspended over nothing! Augustine speaks of his dread of *abyssus*. The literal meaning of this term is "ocean-depth." Augustine had an anxiety-affect about the ocean: It reminded him—as neurotic anxiety feelings may remind anyone—of life's unsteadiness. Neurotic or no, the symbols of disequilibrium are reminders of the profoundest threat we ever recognize—life's lapsing into meaninglessness.
>
> ...Anxiety is the inner dread of this unsteady support. Yet the truth is that there is no such thing as a firm footing in the created world itself. Those creaturely values on which we depend do not pretend to be a firm and final ground. Our feeling of groundlessness (and the dread of it) is meant to prod us toward the truth—that God alone is our true Ground and End.[17]

Out of the physical-psychological ferment between anxiety and tranquility come forth human religious experience and expression. Religion is part of the machinery of mediation between the forces of death and life in the inner person. How and why anxiety is born in humans and gives rise to religion is, of course, a further question. Another matter still is the question of the efficiency with which religions of various kinds succeed in managing or responding to the native human *angst*.

In reflecting on the religious quest of the Egyptians, in *Red Land, Black Land*, Barbara Mertz signified the commonality of their predicament with our own four millennia later and expressed the insight poetically. She described the native need and genius for religion in her closing paragraph:

> Whether they feared their demons or not, the Egyptians did fear death—the first physical death and that second death from which there is no resurrection. They spent a good part of their lives fighting annihilation, and in doing so they built up the most complicated structure of mortuary ritual any people ever produced. We are the beneficiaries of it, in terms of museum collections and scholarly books; and perhaps we will not find the painted mummy cases and weird amulets so bizarre if we see beneath their extravagance, a *common human terror and a common hope*.[18]

That common human terror and that common hope is the springboard of all religious experience and expression. The Egyptian system may not have been as effective or as true as contemporary Christianity, but the crucial point here is that both spring from the same native humanness, and both endeavor to meet the same need and resolve it.

What, then, is that need? How and why is our common terror and common hope the springboard for our spiritual quest, and how well do our various religious systems satisfy that quest? It seems apparent that we are all born with an inherent quandary about where we came from, where we are going, how we ought then to carry ourselves, and what it all means after all. Questions of origins, nature, destiny, ethics, and aesthetics are already at play in the formative minds of young children, and those same questions carry us to our grave. Moreover, to be human seems invariably to mean that we have an unquenchable thirst to know what is the good, the true, and the beautiful, and this puts us all on the spiritual quest for the proximate and the ultimate meaning of things. That is the definition of spirituality, it seems to me. We escape the warm womb to find ourselves in this quandary, and nearly as soon as we get something of a grip on it, we are imposed on by a new and even more pressing ambiguity: death,

Nobody gets out of life alive. The quest of life takes on the contours of tragic adventure from the moment we come bumping and splashing down the birth canal. We find ourselves on the long, psychologically arduous

adventure of accommodation to the massive and mostly uncontrollable—and
hence threatening—unknown of life. In this anxious destiny is born the perpetual tension between the paradise of tranquility we can envision and long
for and the possibilities of terror that we really experience. The once and future paradise becomes a permanent part of our psychic symbology and character. It is then a short step to fashioning some notion of God, largely created
in our own image, as the reason for our *angst* or the source of its relief.

Why is it, however, that we seem compelled to struggle so gravely and
seriously with these major questions of meaning, rather than merely enjoying
life as it passes by? Undoubtedly, it is because we perceive the *angst* as evil and
perpetually fear it will eclipse the meaningfulness of things altogether; that
is, humans have conjured up a conundrum called the problem of evil, and we
see it in contest with our best interests and our ideal imaginations. Nearly
as soon as we realize self-consciousness, we discern that we are capable of
both majestic and malignant roles and possibilities. We see ourselves and each
other as both majestically magnificent and malignantly malicious. We learn
early, I think, that there is in the universe itself a comparable potential for
magnificence and malignancy. In that reinforcement of our natural anxiety, we
are driven to pursue meaning. Undoubtedly, this reflects the genius of God's
image in us and in our need to see things wholesome, whole, and holy.

It was this impasse regarding the incongruity of evil that shaped Kierkegaard's definition of *angst* and religion.[19] Rudolph Otto grounded his outlook
on these matters in the intuitive mystical aspect of our consciousness of the
human predicament. He was sure he found the definitive stuff of religion in
the *numinose Gefuhl* and believed it afforded revelation of the certainty and
nature of God's existence.[20] Eliade seems to be closer to the realities of experience and fact when he asserts that the human quest for meaning arises out
of the "terror of history":

> How shall we resolve the paradoxical situation created by the two-fold
> fact that man, on the one hand, finds himself in *time*, given over to history,
> and on the other he knows that he will be "damned" if he allows himself
> to be exhausted by temporality and historicity; that consequently, he must
> at all costs find *in this world* a road that issues upon a trans-historical and
> a-temporal plane.[21]

For Eliade, our common human terror is in our existing awareness of the terminal character of finitude, and Tillich seems to agree when he says that finitude in awareness is anxiety.[22] Our common hope is *that* paradise is an ideal
world that comes from transcending finitude, a state of affairs we can envision as God's image bearers, but one which, in our humanness, we can never
create. For Eliade, to achieve meaning is to gain the certainty that historical
tragedies have a trans-historical meaning.[23] This is to achieve freedom from
finitude and anxiety. This is the achievement of sound religion.

Arapura endorses this idea by his note that "the sense of the wrongness of existence is common...to all mankind's consciousness."[24] Religious experience and expression is a dynamic process by which we attempt to give structured response to the fact that we are dying persons dealing with the unacceptable unknown of our own *mortality* and therefore that we perceive ourselves as inadequate when faced with the irresolvable unknown of our own *morality*, namely, the loss of a sense of worthwhileness.[25] Religion is the operative psychological machinery and tools we produce or experience for managing the insecurity that this state of affairs generates. Practicing religion or cultivating spiritual experience is that dimension of human operations that reduces our anxiety about the deadliness of life, translating it into the tranquility of salvation: eternal life.

In this process of reducing anxiety to certainty about eternal life, religion often takes an unfortunate and self-defeating turn. It is a relatively short step from our common human terror, Kierkegaard's angst, our sense of the wrongness of things internalized as personal guilt, to the projection on the cosmos of a concept of a threatening God. We seem, by nature, inclined to internalize threat as pain and pain as guilt. As children do, so do all human beings internalize threat and pain as guilt. If we are guilty, it must be before the face of someone who is in a position to exercise the power and authority to hold us accountable and does. We are tempted automatically to reason that this must be God, so our theology is psychologically, and even psychopathologically, structured from the outset. So we move from the threat of the unknown within and without, to anxiety, thence to guilt and a sense of the wrongness of life, and from guilt to a projection of God as a dangerous deity.

This predictable process is self-defeating because it produces a reinforcement of our anxiety about a dangerous God, rather than a resolution of it in a sense God's grace. The whole of human history seems fraught with this impasse; what humans have endeavored to achieve by religion we have seldom been able to accomplish, namely, transcendence above our finitude, morality, mortality, and divine threat. Too often, what we achieve in our reach from anxiety, to guilt, to God is a psychotheology fashioned in our own image as creatures under threat. So we project our inner dilemma on the cosmos as a God who threatens us. We create God in our psychospiritual likeness. That god then reigns as a superego, imposing constrictions and constraints, rather than affording freedom. He reinforces anxiety, rather than relief. He urges us to legalistic rituals for worship and ethics, rather than to a life of healthy wholeness with freedom of spirit.

GRACE AND ANXIETY

The only exception or alternative to this impasse and its psychoreligious pathology that history presents to us is the concept of divine grace, which makes its appearance uniquely in Judaism. Here and nowhere else in the history of religion there bursts forth, in the faith vision of Abraham, the notion that God arbitrarily transcends the wrongness of the universe and of our humanness; that God unconditionally accepts us as we are, where we are; and that God assures us that we are inherently worthwhile, in spite of ourselves. This assurance is designed by God to make plain to us that we do get out of life alive and well, no matter what. It is that faith vision that the Christian faith inherited and finds epitomized in Jesus of Nazareth as the Christ of God.

That is the reason that, despite the prevalent popular notion to the contrary, there are two, and only two, kinds of religion in the history of humankind: those that operate on the assumption that God is for us, and those that operate on the assumption that God is against us, or at least a dangerous threat to us. Religions which assume that God is a threat build elaborate strategies in ethics and worship rituals designed to provide techniques for self-justification. These are beset by the psychological bondage of mad dashes down blind alleys. Those which assume that God is for us express themselves in authentic celebrations of grace and gratitude. Such healthy religion provides the freedom of life as an open-ended creative quest, in which every risk—theological exploration, moral experimentation, and spiritual playfulness—is ultimately safe, for grace is greater than all our sin.

Only Judeo-Christian faith forms are formed and informed by such a theology of God as a God of radical, unconditional, and universal grace. God's grace is radical in that we cannot hide from it or defend against it or sin ourselves out of it. It is unconditional in that it is an arbitrary gift of God to us because of our value to God and not because of our goodness. It is universal in that no one can fall from God's grace or squirm out of God's long embrace. No other faiths have achieved that perspective. Unfortunately, much of the history of both Judaism and Christianity has been a serious departure from this unique heritage and a regression into pagan preoccupation with *angst*-driven legalisms and the destructively evil heresy of orthodoxy. This is witness to the degree to which our common human terror is the endemic producer and shaper of our natural religion and spirituality.

"Life is a tragic adventure," said John F. Kennedy. That is surely true of the history of religions, including Judaism and Christianity. The faith vision of God as a God of grace sprang forth in Abraham's sense of a covenanting God in Genesis 12 and 17. It took Judaism 1,500 years after Abraham for Israelite religion to develop into a legalistic program for maintaining order and discipline in David's kingdom, leading to a relatively chaotic and anxiety-laden history for the next 500 years and the exile in Babylon. Then Israelite religion attempted to reconstitute itself.

If one were to epitomize Jesus's presence and purposes as the reason for the rise of Christianity, it would be his appeal for the restoration of a spirituality of radical, unconditional, and universal grace. This was plainly evident in Jesus's way of handling people. It took the Christian movement only 500–1,000 years before the strains and structures of scholasticism and legalism were rampant at the rise of the high Middle Ages. Christianity had lost its clean vision of the radical and unconditional character of grace and become a full-blown caricature of its true self, conceiving of God as a threatening deity to be propitiated by legalistic rituals and strategies for self-justification. Its deterioration produced the reaction of the Reformation of the sixteenth century. Luther and Calvin specifically set on the course of restoring the grace orientation to the center of the Christian faith. The Reformed movements needed only 200 years to erode the keen charism of grace theology and reduce it to oppressive scholastic and legalistic orthodoxies.

Unfortunately, Buddhism and Hinduism, which are so often compared with Christianity, are in point of fact escapist programs designed to enact a pattern of psychological denial of divine threat and the pain of the human enigma. Their spiritualities of withdrawal into the inner self, into the transcending self, and thence into Nirvana, are spiritualities of escapist denial. The theology of karma to achieve Nirvana is often touted as comparable to God's grace. It is, in fact, the opposite or converse of the true understanding of radical, unconditional, and universal grace in God for us.

Grace is so unbelievable that it leaves us a little uneasy about having no leverage and not being in control because we are at the mercy of God and his grace. If we cannot or will not cast ourselves into the arms of God, assured that he knows that the only justice for the likes of us is mercy, then even grace is an anxiety inducer, and religion and spirituality are psychologically defeated by deterioration into the psychopathology of tentativeness and doubt. These in turn prompt us to create rigid worship rituals and stultifying theological orthodoxies, designed to manipulate a threatening God into decency he would otherwise have spurned.

It is clear that the dynamics of religious experience are intricately interwoven with the psychology and psychopathology of anxiety. In understanding religious or spiritual experience and expression, these psychodynamics must be taken into account as seriously as, or more seriously than, more ethereal factors at work in our psyche and souls. For example, only if we evaluate Judeo-Christian ritual, theology, and ethics in terms of the way anxiety shapes them can we clear the decks for addressing such issues as their role as divine revelation in the scriptures. This is necessary to equip ourselves to separate the cultural and psychological garbage from the good news of the grace in those scriptures.

Much religious ritual in Judaism and Christianity, such as prayer and worship litanies, is crafted with the apparent design of motivating God to do something benevolent for us, which he would not have the good sense or presence of mind to do if left to his own recognizance. Prayer and worship as celebration of gratitude for God's grace is a profoundly different thing, psychologically and spiritually, than liturgies to persuade or please or manipulate God. The difference between the two is the difference between anxiety-driven religion and grace-shaped faith and worship. In his letter to the church at Rome, Paul expresses this rhetorical question, for which the answer is implied: "Since God is for us, what can be against us?"

The sole recommendation for the Judeo-Christian perspective of grace is that it is the definitive resolution of our native psychological predicament and its spiritual consequences. We are faced with the sense of the wrongness of existence and the fragile inadequacy of humanness before the face of the responsibilities of life and the challenges of godliness. Jesus is there in history, and one cannot get around him or around the fact of his way of handling people. His style affirms our worthwhileness as humans and resolves our anxiety into tranquility, through the psychodynamics of cherishing acceptance of us as we are. He affirms us as we are, thus affording us the psychic freedom to become what we are potentially, in body, mind, and spirit, as those created in the likeness of God. That is the only chance for the likes of us humans.

CONCLUSION

Much of what represents itself as Judeo-Christian religion is psychologically distorted and pathological. Pastors and counselors must be willing and able to differentiate radically between health and sickness in the life of the psyche and the soul. Much of what represents itself today as theological and ethical truth is, in point of fact, not the result of the insights of grace, but of the pathology of the psyche. Rather than being the imperatives of a proper reading of sacred scripture or the applications of Christian perspective, these are really the dogma of distorted spirits, unformed by grace. The recent resurgence of many of the charismatic, mystical, intuitive, and subjective forms of spirituality manifest characteristics which suggest that these religious programs often tend to be merely reheated expressions of previous escapist and legalist programs for manipulating God into goodwill toward the religious practitioner. These always cut the taproot of grace.

It is crucial that authentic religious experience and psychic pathology or its consequence be differentiated. Then worship can be real and redemptively healing. Then spirituality can be freedom, not bondage. Then life can be the relief and reflection of grace.

Though the human anxiety syndrome does not account for the grace insight and the Christian faith, the human need for acceptance, forgiveness, and affirmation, to which divine grace addresses itself, is as wholly the product of our common human terror and our common hope as is the characteristic driving force behind any spiritual quest in any religion. We were created to celebrate life in the security of walking hand in hand with God as our father, so to speak, and we experience life as the alienation of those who have lost the touch of his hand. That may just be what the terror of history really amounts to. That may be the real nature of our mystification with reality and our confusion of face in the unfolding of the universe. The ancient Hebrew myth of the garden tragedy may be closer to the truth than is history. Then our common human terror and our common hope is what St. Augustine suggested it was in his poignant prayer: "O Lord, you have made us for yourself and our souls are restless until they rest, O God, in you."

NOTES

1. James G. Frazer (1959), *The Golden Bough*, ed. Theodore Gaster, New York: Criterion.

2. Carl G. Jung (1964), *Man and His Symbols*, Garden City, NJ: Doubleday. See also Jung (1958), *Undiscovered Self*, trans. R.F.C. Hull, Boston: Little, Brown.

3. LeRoy Aden and J. Harold Ellens, eds. (1990), *Turning Points in Pastoral Care: The Legacy of Anton Boisen and Seward Hiltner*, Grand Rapids, MI: Baker. See also Seward Hiltner (1972), *Theological Dynamics*, Nashville, TN: Abingdon; and Seward Hiltner and Karl Menninger, eds. (1963), *Constructive Aspects of Anxiety*, Nashville, TN: Abingdon.

4. Donald Capps and Janet Jacobs, eds. (1995), *The Struggle for Life: A Companion to William James' Varieties of Religious Experience*, Society for the Scientific Study of Religion Monograph Series 9, Newton, KS: Mennonite Press.

5. David M. Wulff (1991), *Psychology of Religion: Classic and Contemporary Views*, New York: John Wiley.

6. Wayne E. Oates (1973), *The Psychology of Religion*, Waco, TX: Word.

7. Walter H. Clark, H. Newton Malony, James Daane, and Alan R. Tippett (1973), *Religious Experience, Its Nature and Function in the Human Psyche: The First John G. Finch Symposium on Psychology and Religion*, Springfield, MO: Charles C. Thomas.

8. Jung, *Undiscovered Self*.

9. Hiltner and Menninger, *Constructive Aspects*.

10. J. G. Arapura (1973), *Religion as Anxiety and Tranquility*, Paris: Mouton, 7.

11. Ibid.

12. Karen Horney (1937), *The Neurotic Personality of Our Time*, New York: W. W. Norton, 41–42.

13. Ibid., 43–44.

14. Ibid., 46.

15. Ibid., 47.

16. Ibid., 48.

17. Albert C. Outler (1963), "Anxiety and Grace: An Augustinian Perspective," in Hiltner and Menninger, *Constructive Aspects*, 89, 104.

18. Barbara Mertz (1966), *Red Land, Black Land*, New York: Coward, McCann, Geoghegan, 367 (emphasis added).

19. See Edward J. Carnell (1965), *The Burden of Soren Kierkegaard*, Grand Rapids, MI: Eerdmans.

20. Rudolph Otto (1958), *The Idea of the Holy*, trans. John W. Harvey, New York: Oxford University Press.

21. Marcea Eliade (1958), *Yoga: Immortality and Freedom*, New York: Pantheon, xix.

22. Paul Tillich (1957), *The Meaning of Persons*, trans. Edwin Hudson, New York: Harper. See also Tillich (1951), *Systematic Theology*, 2 vols., Chicago: University of Chicago Press; and Tillich (1948), *The Protestant Era*, trans. James Luther Adams, Chicago: University of Chicago Press.

23. Eliade, *Yoga*.

24. Arapura, *Religion*, 80.

25. Horney, *Neurotic*, 47.

CHAPTER 4

THE BIBLE AND HUMAN HEALTH

In his admirable book *The Yahwist: The Bible's First Theologian*, Peter Ellis demonstrated that the undergirding stratum of Judeo-Christian biblical theology is the sturdy tradition of unconditional and universal divine grace.[1] Ellis's argument assumes the accuracy of the general claims of the form-critical school of biblical criticism and its notions regarding multiple, distinct, and to some degree disparate sources for the first five or six books of the Hebrew Bible.

With a trained analytic eye, one can trace readily and with considerable precision the theological strains of the Yahwist and priestly traditions in those books of the Bible and, to a somewhat lesser extent, an Elohist strain as well. The first of those is made up of the passages that call God Yahweh in the ancient Hebrew language. The second is composed of those that give us the laws formulated by the priests during the Babylonian exile. The third contains those chapters that call God by the name El or Elohim.

The great theologians of the New Testament had little difficulty demonstrating that the life and ministry of Jesus Christ incarnated precisely the thrust of the Yahwist theologian, who tells us about God's surprising grace toward humankind. The Christian scriptures, in consequence, became a towering theological and pastoral expression of God's radical grace, spelled out especially in those early chapters of Genesis (12 and 17), for example.

Brevard S. Childs has done the world of biblical study something of a favor with his book *Introduction to the Old Testament as Scripture*.[2] He argues for a decreasing emphasis on form-critical principles of interpretation of the Pentateuch, in terms of the notion that it is based on numerous separate sources of literary tradition. He is less interested in how those ancient sources were edited to form the present text of the first five books of the Bible. He is more concerned about how we should understand the ancient scriptures in terms of the way the ancient believing community and early Christianity employed those scriptures as authoritative canonical revelations of God's word. Childs's work represents a watershed in biblical scholarship. However, though Childs finds the tension between the biblical theology of unconditional grace and the conditional judgment passages in the Pentateuch to be more troublesome than does Ellis or Rolf P. Knierim,[3] the consummate scholar of form-critical method, the overriding clarity of radical grace as the substructure of the entire Bible is confirmed by Childs's canonical assessment.

The Bible sounds a clear and singular trumpet, whose notes convey singularly good news. It is the good news that first uniquely exploded in the Judaic theological tradition and was captured pristinely by Abraham's faith vision. It is the good news that God accepts us as and where we are for the sake of what we can, therefore, become. It is the good news about healing and wholeness for the pathological, inadequate, distorted, and lost persons of this world. It is the word about the only chance for the likes of us.

In sum, the theology of grace asserts that God is in the enterprise of healing. That grace, which is character-rooted in God, is radical in its incisive thrust to the center of human pathology: the anxiety-driven self-preoccupation that is both the cause and result of human alienation and of the world of sickness and sin that devolves from that alienation. That grace is unconditional because it is not merely something God does, but is, and hence it is an attribute and disposition inherent and inevitable to God. The Yahwist would have us apprehend, furthermore, that grace is universal in its scope and intent. The import is that humans are drawn by the word of God to notice that the historical and empirical evidence available about the nature of God leads to a worldview in which God's *raison d'etre*, as humanly perceived, is the overt cultivation of the wholeness and wholesomeness of humans and of all creation.

That is the essential reason I wish in this volume to explore the psychological consequences of a thoroughgoing biblical theology of divine grace. A proper assessment of the theological idea and its psychological import requires some exploration of the problematic and pathological nature of the human setting to which grace speaks, an indication of how grace speaks to the human predicament, and a consolidation of the conceptual base for drawing out the psychological consequences.

THE HUMAN PREDICAMENT

Since humans first sensed the complexity and ambiguity of our spiritual and psychological natures, with their capacity for malignancy and magnificence, the most essential and universal human experience has been anxiety. As I noted in chapter 3, Barbara Mertz expressed it as "our common human terror and our common hope." Generic human anxiety is both systemic and situational in all persons. It is so radical in nature, that is, so close to the essence of human nature and identity, that everything human is in some degree shaped by it. Eric Fromm adequately described the tragic side of its impact in human affairs in his book *The Anatomy of Human Destructiveness*.[4] Others have argued for the ways in which generic human anxiety is also a potentially constructive force in our growth.[5] Seward Hiltner has effectively related human anxiety and divine grace.[6] Mertz seems accurate, therefore, in relating generic human anxiety to both our terror and our hope.

Our Terror

The terror dimension of anxiety is readily identified by and in all humans. It ranges broadly from our struggle to come to terms with death and our omnipresent mortality, to such forms of exaggerated anxiety as those that are usually identified as, or that produce the plethora of pathologies we clinically call, neuroses. From the moment the uterine contractions begin, signaling impending birth, until the last gasp of life's breath in enfeebled old age, life offers an overarching set of anxiety-inducing threats. These take the form of threats to stasis, to goal achievement, to personal fulfillment, to self-actualization, and to vital existence itself. The entire spectrum of life's experience process may be comprehensively and definitely described as a conscious and subconscious endeavor at gaining control of our individual destiny.

The native sense of psychological and spiritual fracturedness that all humans feel is surely rooted in that initial loss of the paradise-like world of the womb, in which security is normally the overriding quality of experience. That loss is not experienced benignly when we are born, but ingrains in our earliest and most essential precognitive psychospiritual experience a sense of the essential violent and tragic character of life. That humans ever achieve any genuine stasis and functionality after the birth trauma is really quite surprising and is evidence of the divine gift of the resilient force of life and will.[7]

The beginning of terrors is really the experience of being torn violently and painfully from that womb-setting to which we were adjusted, in that sense committed, and which we love systemically, in the sense of being identified with, attached to, and dependent on it. Birth therefore means the loss experience: not merely loss from separation, but from separation perceived as alienation. That alienation is experienced in conjunction with an overwhelming sense of fragileness, vulnerability, and disenfranchisement. In terms of the classic dynamics of grief, that vulnerability is probably interpreted by the precognitive neonate as unworthiness. Children internalize pain as inherent wrongness in themselves, later given the cognitively crafted names of guilt and shame. Our alienation from God and the godly, personally and as a community, reinforces all this sense of our own wrongness—alienation from paradise, from God, from the godly, and from our own best expectations for ourselves.

It is of little surprise, therefore, that our sense of the authenticity of the biblical story of the Fall is so spontaneous. Genesis 3 accounts for, illumines, and interprets our most fundamental awareness: we are creatures of loss, a loss we experience and ultimately perceive as alienation and that feels like a state of powerlessness and unworthiness. Moreover, those experiences and perceptions lie chronologically, logically, and psychologically so close to our origins and our essence that we sense them as definitive of our identity. We are not just sick and lonely. We sense that we are alienated and lost souls.

For Adam and Eve, created at full bloom and ensconced in the garden of paradise in the creation myth, the story of the Fall describes a psychospiritual experience akin to the general human trauma of birth. Here we see combined their birth trauma and their postpubertal, oedipal-entrenched process of adolescent disengagement from parents, authority, and home. The story informs us about all the attendant and inherent separation anxiety, ambivalence, and endangered certification and self-esteem.

In short, our common human terror is that of being wrenched from our mothers' wombs and being unable to catch hold of our fathers' hands. The essential psychological and spiritual experience is that of being orphaned, and as is always the case with children who experience pain and grief loss, we internalize that sense of lostness, personally and communally, as guilt and shame. That guilt and shame ultimately produce anger because the rationality of those experiences is almost impossible to identify. Moreover, anger reinforces our sense of alienation, producing our psychological and spiritual depression; distortions; pathologies; and hostile, inappropriate behavior. Here lies the threat of the loss of hope and of the meaningfulness and worthwhileness of things. This is the engine driving our sin or psychospiritual sickness.

Our Hope

On the other hand, the separation experience of birth as well as that of adolescent disengagement brings with it the promise of hope. Both are pregnant with new possibilities. Birth brings a new breath of fresh air, as does the adolescent–young adult adjustment process and growth. In this the ontogeny of the person, so to speak, recapitulates the phylogeny of all created life.

In the biblical story, both the Creation and the Fall are oriented toward the future, both are driven by the dynamics of expectation, and both are filled with the potential of new life and a new world. The first is a kind of paradise experience, the second, tragic; but in a certain fundamental sense, both are part of the birth process of the universe and of human life. Both reach for the denouement of salvation: the completion and resolution of all things. The biblical story of creation, fall, and redemption is a mythic paradigm, stretched on the canvas of history, depicting the story of the universal human psychodynamic process of womb tranquility, birth trauma, adolescent disengagement, and maturation.[8] As in the paradigm, so in the psychology of the development of persons, the trauma of our genesis and the pain and risks of adolescence are drawn together into a comprehensive birth process from which the person comes, reaching consciously and subconsciously for the denouement of health and maturity. This process stretches itself toward healing resolution of things and closure.

Now health and maturation, which I shall from this point allude to in such terms as *healing* and *wholeness*, are achieved by stages, in fits and starts, with distortions, regressions, and pathologies, hopeful surges and dead-end streets. This is not unlike the biblical paradigm in which God at various times in bits and pieces invested the fathers and mothers with saving insights through the prophets, and finally illumined and healed us through his son (Heb. 1). The whole process in the human person, as in the paradigmatic salvation history myth in the Bible, reaches hopefully forward, expecting fulfillment of the total potential of wholeness inherent in humans as God's image bearers and in God's entire cosmic experiment.

The whole of life and history, therefore, can be described as the process of trauma moving toward hope, tragedy driving to denouement, pained and distorted life reaching for wholeness, anxiety wanting reduction, and dissonance longing for resolution and tranquility.

ANXIETY REDUCTION AND HUMAN HEALTH

Since the whole process of personal and cosmic function moves from incompleteness and pathology (lostness, distortion, and palpable illness) to maturity and wholeness (health, fulfillment, and palpable salvation), the efficiency with which this is accomplished depends directly on the effectiveness of the reduction of distorting obstructions. In the biblical paradigm for the created world and the human community, the reduction of obstructions has to do with the removal of the bonds of chaos in Genesis 1:1, of primitivity and naïveté in Genesis 2 and 3, and of idolatry in the rest of scripture. In the individualized psychodynamic odyssey of each person, the reduction of obstructions to wholeness involves anxiety reduction and thus transcendence over the pathology and distortions anxiety brings. Idolatry is the practice of holding to false anxiety reducers such as substance abuse, legalistic or constrictive religious traditions, obsessive sexual behavior, or other forms of escape from reality, health, and growth.

Incidentally, in both the historical cosmic quest and the individual odyssey, wholeness is achieved ultimately *sola gratia* but not *soli Deo gloria*, that is, it is achieved by grace alone but not only for the glory of God, as Fundamentalist and Evangelical theology claims. Because grace is grace, the wholeness that it brings is, through incarnation, namely, its infusion into our humanness, for the sake of the Creation. God is oriented toward his creation, not toward a narcissistic divine self. God's grace is oriented toward his entire creation, but particularly toward humans. History, the Bible, and sound psychotherapy are in that sense human centered. God, theology, and Christian psychology, when authentically perceived and expressed, are for and preoccupied with suffering persons and a suffering world (worlds).

Anxiety reduction processes in the odyssey of personal growth may, of course, be constructive or destructive. I am convinced that all distortions, pathologies, and dead-end streets (self-destructive courses) in human psycho-spiritual development are the result of destructive anxiety reduction mecha-nisms at the level of the psyche or at the level of social function, or both. Conversely, wholesome growth, health, and maturation are achieved to the degree that constructive anxiety reduction mechanisms are introduced and utilized. One might say that, viewed psychologically, the Fall was Adam's con-structive anxiety reduction mechanism. Surely he was anxiety laden in the hopeful quandary with which he struggled, regarding his potential to be like God, knowing good and evil. He resolved his initial anxiety as healthy adoles-cents usually do, by asserting his decision-making independence, thus setting in motion his individuation, responsibility, self-actualization, and maturity.

Destructive anxiety reduction mechanisms are those that produce inhi-bitory defense processes in human growth. Constructive anxiety reduction mechanisms are those that enhance one's openness for assertive risk-taking processes in human growth. The former obstruct, delay, distort, limit, or sicken and thus prevent the efficient move toward total self-actualization as an image bearer of God whose destiny it is to realize palpable fulfillment of one's God-given psychospiritual potential. Constructive anxiety reduc-tion mechanisms support, direct, reinforce, equip, embellish, and expand the human person and thus promote the efficient move toward total self-actualization.

That realization of human destiny as the fulfillment of the full range of the psychospiritual potential with which God has invested us is the very defini-tion of health and wholeness. Every function or behavior designed to bring that about is a healing act and the very definition of healing. All our sinful-ness and our sickness is thus a falling short of the glory of God because it is an obstruction of his glorious ambition for us: a falling short of the glory of real humanness. Functionality and dysfunction have their meaning against that backdrop.

THE ROLE OF RELIGION

The history of religion is the history of the human endeavor to devise func-tional anxiety reduction mechanisms or tools that are capable of managing situational and systemic anxiety, which I have referred to previously with the German word *angst*. That long religious history divides easily into two radically opposite camps, shaped by differing strategies for anxiety reduction. The most prominent camp, historically, is the one shaped by the anxiety reduction strategy of human merit, achievement, measuring up to prescribed psychosocial standards of belief and behavior that then authorize self-justification. This is essentially a program for self-esteem and self-justification based on satisfying some divine demands or communal doctrines, thus achieving the position of ethical or psychosocial power.

This posture is self-centered and self-directed, tending to be legalistic, mechanistic, and orthodox. It is not growth oriented, but status and stasis oriented, since it manages only the symptoms of the inner anxiety. The generic human angst is never effectively reduced. It is, in the end, self-defeating. It cannot cut through to the heart of the central sense of lostness and the orphaned nature of human persons. It may provide a pseudo-womb-return experience, such as some forms of institutionalized religion provide, but it never puts the grasping human hand back into the hand of the consoling Father. In this strategy, God remains the adversary who must be placated, outflanked, or intimidated. God becomes a mere projection of the anxiety-ridden and guilt-laden psyche of the religionist, whose unworthiness and lostness drives him or her to worship or work righteousness. This religious strategy for anxiety reduction produces and enhances psychopathology.

With one exception, religions throughout human history fall into this first camp: anxiety reduction by prescribed human achievement and self-justification. They constitute a psychoreligious power play scheme with all the potential pathology inherent in that set of defense mechanisms.

GOD'S GRACE

The only exception to this general psychospiritual tragedy of human history is the unique Judeo-Christian theology of grace. It is precisely the mainstream theology of the Old Testament, coming to flower in the ministry of Jesus of Nazareth and the Pauline theology of the New Testament. This constitutes our only healing option. Only here is religion a *constructive* anxiety reduction instrument.

This biblical theology is a healing option because it cuts through to the heart of our essential lostness and orphaned nature. It is not a theology of personal achievement or self-justification, but of unconditional divine acceptance. It is not a strategy for an ethical or psychosocial power play, but a way of self acceptance. It is not self-centered, but goal directed toward the psychospiritual completion of the whole person. It is not mechanistic or legalistic, but dynamic: growth oriented, not status oriented. It mollifies some of the pain of our symptoms of psychospiritual unwholesomeness, but it treats the disease and the dis-ease of our alienation from God and from what is potentially good in us. It does not lead us back to the womb, but puts our hand in the hand of our Father, not back to paradise, but ahead to "a holy city." When properly mediated, this divine grace perspective, set forth in the Bible, heals human pathology in mind and spirit. It is, in fact, the most comprehensive and relevant psychotherapeutic theory and practice ever conceived.

As revealed in Judeo-Christian biblical narrative, God is not a threat, but our consolation, whose name is Yahweh, the faithful one, who guarantees by his name and nature that he will always be for us what he has always been for humanity. That name is therefore a strong tower (security). "The righteous run into it and are safe" (Prov. 18:10b). Moreover, *the righteous* means, according to Micah (7:18–20) and St. Paul (Rom. 8), those persons whom God has unconditionally accepted and to whom he has therefore *imputed* total righteousness: all humankind.

Unfortunately, superficial reading of the history of Judaism and Christianity will not confirm the radical uniqueness of that tradition of constructive anxiety reduction strategy. By the golden age of David's kingdom, a pagan legalism and mechanistic atonement theology had already begun to grow up in Israelite religion and became rampant by the time of the Babylonian exile. It is clear from the Gospel narratives that the ministry of Jesus had to do with an attempt to cut through formalistic religion to get to the spiritual essence of a sound grace theology. However, by the fifth century of the Christian era, the seeds of a pagan legalism were again sown; by the eighth century, a sturdy growth was evident; and by the eleventh century, this scholastic formalism had fruited, eclipsing the vision of God's grace.

Luther grasped the essence of grace once again, but scholasticism had demeaned Protestant grace theology, both Lutheran and Reformed, by two centuries later. At the personal level, even in the best times, popular religion has usually remained extensively threat-motivated paganism, despite the quality of the church's theology and ministry. Furthermore, in each generation, there seems to arise a new form of Christian paganism that manifests itself in popular church movements that are anxiety inducing and essentially pathogenic in their strategies for anxiety reduction. The fastest-growing churches tend consistently to be those that appeal to theologically untutored communities with notions that foster simplistic constructs of formulaic propositional theology and legalistic codes and ethics. These are essentially strategies of self-righteousness, self-justification, and salvation by personal rigors and discipline.

That stands against the Gospel of grace and the mainstream of biblical theology. The substance of the story of creation, fall, disharmony in human affairs, the covenant with Abraham for the healing of the nations, the Exodus, and the prospect of a Davidic *shalom* is a story of the unfolding of divine grace to Israel and humankind. The grace theology in the mythic narrative, of course, hinges on creation, fall, and covenant. Adam appears on the scene as a special bearer of the divine nature and image in a divinely ordered world. The God-imaging quality of Adam, in the creation story, describes the essential nature and character of humans. David J. A. Clines urges us to take this seriously enough to recognize that this doctrine elevates all humankind to the highest status conceivable, "short of complete divinization."[9]

In that divinely ordered world, Adam was assigned the stature and status of compatriot of God. That status describes, not his essential nature as imager, but his role and relationship with God. He keeps the garden, names the animals, seeks a mate, receives Eve as God's gift for appropriate companionship, and walks with God in the cool of the evening. His status is imputed to him by God, arbitrarily. The story never refers to Adam as a son of God or child of God or servant of God. He is portrayed consistently as companion and compatriot. Moreover, that status is a covenant status, not negotiated by Adam, but—in the style of the ancient Mesopotamian regents—imputed and guaranteed.

Part of Adam's wholesome character as compatriot of God is the quality of his imagination. He can imagine alternative worlds, alternative models of relationship, alternative perceptions of the good for which to quest, even evil perceptions of the good, and other anxiety-inducing possibilities, options, and challenges. When Adam selected the alternative option of independence, the childlike harmony of his universe metamorphosed into a dissonance and discordance that, but for grace, would have been deadly to the extent that it increasingly amplified Adam's alienation from the garden, the God-walks, his wife-talks, his own tranquility, and his true destiny as a person in whom all the rich potential for wholeness could be actualized.

The deadly dynamic in that independent course was the potential for an overwhelming anxiety increase, to the point at which Adam would have been consumed by coping with his lostness, his inability to grasp again his Father's hand. Adam's status of God-compatriot seemed hopelessly forfeited and his course of behavior at fundamental odds with his own essential nature as an imager of God. It was almost as though his God-imaging nature as independent creator was in tension with his God-compatriot nature as cokeeper of the garden. That dissonance was the potential for sickness and death in the Fall story of Genesis 3. The other side of that same story, of course, is the option for Adam and Eve of freedom from the cradle and maturity into adolescent independence and adult agency.

The crucial issue in this remarkable psychospiritual myth is this: when Adam fell, God, despite his prior declaration, "You shall surely die," refused to change Adam's essential status as a God-compatriot in the building of God's world. It was an arbitrarily imputed status in the first place, and now it is an arbitrarily maintained status. God does not negotiate it with Adam in the story. Adam's life now has about it the deadly pathological possibilities of overwhelming alienation, lostness, distortion, dissonance, sin, and sickness. However, God came to Adam in the story, sat where he sat, adopted the new circumstances of Adam's life as the new arena for the relationship, made clear immediately the unconditional nature of the compatriot status (Gen. 3:15), and proceeded with the original business of Adam's move toward wholeness, completeness, growth, and healing. The ground rules seem somewhat modified, but only in terms of the new requirements for constructive anxiety reduction: the *protoevangelium* of Genesis 3:15 and the reach toward Genesis 12:1–4 and 17:1–8: "I will bless you . . . you will be a blessing . . . and by you all the families of the earth shall bless themselves."

The critical element of the theology of grace, throughout scripture, in consequence, is the essential inviolability of that status for human beings, arbitrarily imputed by God to Adam and the whole human race. This is the ingenious insight of ancient Israelite religion, inherited by Christianity, to some extent inherited by Rabbinic Judaism, and it needs to be highlighted these days in Islam if it is again to be a healing force in the world. In the tragedy of our anxiety, we perceive lostness and alienation. Out of that dissonance comes our sin and our sickness, psychologically and spiritually. From God's perspective, however, our status is unchanged, no matter what. We are unconditionally affirmed, just where we are in our life pilgrimage, wherever we are at the moment in the growth journey—unconditionally affirmed as those destined for communion with God, the divine design of the most healing infrastructure for real life. The Gospel asserts that unconditionally certified status for all humankind.

HUMAN HEALTH

The predicament of human existence, thus, is not our lostness, but our perceived lostness. Our destiny is not that of needing to achieve a successful power play to get right with God or to get the right leverage with God. Our destiny is to accept and realize the benefits of our status: divine compatriots in building God's kind of world in human society and culture, no matter how whole or holy we may or may not be. The benefits of this realization are the relief of grace, the affirmation of our real selves, the unconditional acceptance of God's unconditional acceptance of us, and the celebration of our generic freedom from the need for generic anxiety: systemic ("Fear not, I am thy God") and situational ("Be anxious in nothing. . . . Take no thought for the morrow").

It is not surprising, then, that St. Paul, in developing the rudiments of a Christian view of human nature, should speak of "primordial man," "fallen man," and "the man in Christ." It is interesting that there is an apparent tension, in Paul's writings in the New Testament, between his Greek humanist roots and his Hebrew spirituality, as we noted previously. He worries about the role of divine law in human religious life, the need to suppress the lower passions (animal instincts) by the higher passions (rationality), the need for the "fleshly human nature" to be held in check by the psychospiritual qualities of our selfhood. Yet he is radical in his "free and unconditional grace theology" and the doctrine of imputed righteousness to all humans, no matter how "wicked" or sick they may be (Rom. 8).

J. Christiaan Beker has resolved this paradox in Paul in a delightful manner in his book *Paul the Apostle* by demonstrating conclusively that Paul never intends to write a systematic theology, not even in Romans.[10] Beker points out that Paul is always hammering out his theology, his notions of the nature of the church and of the nature of human beings, in terms of a very specific parish situation. He points out that Paul's thrust is always to demonstrate and celebrate the triumph of God in his grace in human life: triumph over and cancellation of any and all deficits and dysfunctions in humans that would separate us from God and from our true selves, thus greatly increasing our anxiety.

So Paul can speak *against* the requirements of the law and *for* radical grace in Galatians, where he is opposing the Jerusalem Judaizers, and *for* the law, as certifier of Jewish priority, though not superiority, in God's work in the world in his epistle to the Roman church. In the Roman church, he was trying to settle a Gentile prejudice against the Jews, who had been thrown out of Rome. The Gentiles were preventing the Jews from returning. Beker points out that Paul is wishing to catch the eye of the Jerusalem church to demonstrate that he is not separatist in his ambition to evangelize the Gentiles. He fears that they might get this impression from his remarks to the Galatians that they do not need to keep the Jewish religious laws to be true believers.

Paul's theology is clearly that mainstream of the whole Bible, namely, our imputed and guaranteed status in God's grace, no matter what. That is the supremely relevant constructive anxiety reduction mechanism of all history and the best psychotherapeutic model ever fashioned for humans. It addresses the essential *angst* behind all psychopathology and spiritual disorder. It is the essential insight for healing and wholeness for humans.

Many attempts have been made to articulate the crucial nature and relevance of God's grace for human health. Most have been grounded and mired in issues of free will and divine election. It is a tragedy of near cosmic proportions that Calvinism and the Arminian tradition, after the breakthrough to grace theology in the Reformation, perpetuated the relatively superficial dialogue of the old Roman Catholic medieval scholasticism, while Anglicanism, the Anabaptists, and Methodism settled for a rather neurotic form of private pietism. These supplanted radical grace theology with a philosophically pragmatic or psychologically pragmatic form of muted grace; but muted grace is no grace at all. Compromised grace is pagan conditional self-righteousness. Conditional grace is no grace at all.

Bonhoeffer's notion that grace which does not produce a radically changed life is "cheap grace" is a betrayal of the biblical truth about grace.[11] Of course, everyone would wish for God's grace in any human life to bear the fruit of a whole and holy life, but the case is that even when it does not do so, God's grace is still unconditional and totally forgiving and accepting of that flawed person. Bonhoeffer replaces grace with old-fashioned and incorrect medieval moralism and mechanistic religion. His "cheap grace" idea implies that he longs again for a kind of legalism and conditionalism that will shape us up. Grace is free, radical, unconditional, and universal, or it is not grace, no good news at all, since if it is not, it fails to get to the center of the pathology we are otherwise hopelessly locked into forever. It fails to free us from the destructive and distracting anxiety that produces all our sickness and sin.

Some exciting studies of the biblical theology of grace require sturdy attention by psychologists today. Karl Barth, of course, broke the theology of grace out of the medieval prison of scholastic categories with his stimulating existentialist theology of election. James Daane's book *The Freedom of God* is a lucid step beyond Barth, in the tradition of Paul.[12] It is a theology of the triumph of God, hammered out on the situational anvil of parish preaching. Daane defeats scholasticism with its time-bound God by rooting election, as does Barth, in Christ and his historical function. Daane asserts persuasively that God's election of us all to salvation is grounded in the free decree of God that is historical as well as eternal, and that has its culmination in Jesus Christ. Neil Punt has argued for decades that in authentic biblical theology, particularly in Paul's emphasis, it is clear that in Jesus Christ, humanity is elected by God, and that the redemptive consequences of that belong to all humankind, unless overtly or consciously rejected.[13] Even here, unfortunately, Punt is playing around the edges of an ultimate conditionalism that cuts the taproot of biblical grace. More recently, Philip Yancey wrote *What's So Amazing about Grace?*, in which he attempts to popularize the Pauline theology of grace.[14]

These, though they still do not go far enough in understanding grace, constitute great strides toward a thoroughgoing theology of grace that can illumine the essential nature of humans as God-compatriots. As the radical nature of that status becomes clearer to the theologians, their service to the psychologists, and vice versa, will substantially increase. Psychologists need to take with increasing seriousness (1) human fracturedness or fallenness as the source of human psychopathology; (2) the healing dynamic of grace incarnated in humans for each other, described by Carl Rogers as unconditional positive regard; (3) the relationship between that clinical function and the divine grace paradigm behind it; and (4) the manner in which this essentially theological view of human nature must shape theoretical and applied psychology.

This definitive perspective is necessary if we are to handle humans healingly, to produce more than mere restoration of minimal function and to produce, instead, authentic wholeness. When we have achieved this consciousness in psychologists, their service to the theologians and pastors will be greatly enhanced regarding this very practical matter of defining and explicating grace at the operational level. That is, after all, the only level on which all of this counts for anything anyway. Perhaps Aquinas was right in his notion that what we perceive by faith in divine revelation, we would have come to as well, if we had been able to track only the empirical evidence of human nature to its center.

One might object that my emphasis applies only to psychological illness not associated with chemistry disorders. This would be a telling criticism since psychologists are increasingly agreed that as much as 80% of all psychopathology we see in the clinic is rooted in some kind of biochemical disturbance. However, the hypothalamus is a two-switching instrument, so biological disorder produces psychological dysfunction, and psychological disorder, such as sustained anxiety, even low grade, produces biochemical disturbances. The universal human sense of lostness and the anxiety attendant on it may be a significant factor in the high degree of pathogenic biochemical disorder in the human population worldwide.

CONCLUSION

Secular and humanist psychology has provided valuable insight regarding symptomology, dynamics, and central disorders of the human psyche and soul. Secular descriptions of character and personality disorders have achieved profound depth and precision. Strategies generally in use for management of pathologies have great value. Christian perspective, however, is indispensable in illumining the root cause and cure for our common human terror and our common hope. We seek, after all, not just the restoration of psychosocial function in our patients and parishioners, but we seek wholeness: self-actualization, self-affirmation, and health, rooted and grounded in the security of unconditional divine affirmation.

NOTES

1. Peter Ellis (1968), *The Yahwist: The Bible's First Theologian*, Notre Dame, IN: Fides.

2. Brevard S. Childs (1979), *Introduction to the Old Testament as Scripture*, Philadelphia: Fortress.

3. Rolf P. Knierim (1995), *The Task of Old Testament Theology: Method and Cases*, Grand Rapids, MI: Eerdmans. See also Wonil Kim, Deborah Ellens, Michael Floyd,

and Marvin A. Sweeney (2000), *Reading the Hebrew Bible for a New Millennium: Form, Concept, and Theological Perspective*, 2 vols., Harrisburg, PA: Trinity International.

4. Eric Fromm (1973), *The Anatomy of Human Destructiveness*, New York: Holt, Rinehart, Winston. See also J. Harold Ellens, ed. (2004), *The Destructive Power of Religion: Violence in Judaism, Christianity, and Islam*, 4 vols., Westport, CT: Praeger.

5. John G. Finch (1976), *The Message of Anxiety*, taped lecture, CAPS-WACPS Convention, Santa Barbara, CA.

6. Seward Hiltner and Karl Menninger, eds. (1963), *Constructive Aspects of Anxiety*, Nashville, TN: Abingdon.

7. Rollo May (1969), *Love and Will*, New York: W. W. Norton.

8. C. Markham Berry (1980), "Entering Canaan: Adolescence as a Stage of Spiritual Growth," *Bulletin of CAPS* 6(4), 8–13.

9. David J. A. Clines (1968), "The Image of God in Man," *Tyndale Bulletin* 19, 53. See also 60, 87–90, 97–99.

10. J. Christiaan Beker (1980), *Paul the Apostle: The Triumph of God in Life and Thought*, Philadelphia: Fortress.

11. Dietrich Bonhoeffer (1965), *The Cost of Discipleship*, New York: Macmillan.

12. James Daane (1973), *The Freedom of God*, Grand Rapids, MI: Eerdmans.

13. Neil Punt (1980), *Unconditional Good News: Toward an Understanding of Biblical Universalism*, Grand Rapids, MI: Eerdmans.

14. Philip Yancey (1986), *What's So Amazing about Grace?*, Grand Rapids, MI: Zondervan.

CHAPTER 5

MODERN NOTIONS ABOUT
HUMAN NATURE

It seems increasingly crucial to our self-understanding as humans, and to the work in the helping professions, to clarify the concepts of humanness prevalent in our culture and in our psychological theory and practice. Every day, in our clients, in our cultural value system, and in ourselves, we encounter numerous bizarre and destructive models of who and what humans are and are thought to be. In that regard, it seems quite useful to recall that the development of the Western world was influenced by numerous traditions about the nature of humans. Perhaps the most influential, for better or worse, is that of Paul, the Apostle, as hinted at in chapter 4.

Though Paul's notion is not always self-evident or easily ferreted out from the New Testament, he is the only theologian in those Christian scriptures who developed anything approaching a science of human nature. Paul himself was influenced by three ancient traditions: the Mesopotamian, to which he is a contrast, as well as the Greek and Hebrew, both which he absorbed, integrating them into his Christian anthropology. It is worthwhile to note here, at some length, the nature of those sources of Western thought mediated through Paul and attempt to suggest how we encounter them in our time and can deal with them.

MESOPOTAMIAN ANTHROPOLOGY

The Mesopotamian concept of human nature was essentially demeaning and dehumanizing. The ancient civilizations from what is now Iraq, Iran, and eastern Syria had a peculiar record of having developed a worldview basically rooted in a monotheism and proliferated in a secondary polytheism.

The Sumerians, Chaldeans, Babylonians, and Assyrians were not remarkably different from one another in this regard. Marduk was the Babylonian progenitor of all things and functioned in terms of a subordinate hierarchy of gods, who enhanced and/or complicated his enterprises.

In any case, all these civilizations derived from this theology a concept of humans as creatures who were demeaned and dehumanized by being trapped in an arbitrary, unfriendly, divine order of things. The gods had made humans from the inferior earthly substance of clay and then had given them the divine destiny of being servants of the gods to supply their needs and deliver them from menial survival tasks. Humans were of earthly substance with heavenly achievement demands. Man was trapped by the very constituent nature of the gods as gods. Humans as humans were trapped by the constituent nature of the universe.

In this worldview, humans could never escape the predicament of their inferiority because they were seen as *innately* inferior. In the face of that, the gods unreasonably demanded transcendent divine levels of achievement by humans. It was in terms of this enigma that the Mesopotamians tended to explain the problem of evil: the problem of suffering, sickness, and human dysfunction. They held that the problem of psychological maladies was the consequence of this impasse in which humans found themselves, and the more stoic and optimistic of them suggested that the only way to salvation was by a combination of three things: vigorous hard work, a good streak of luck, and the endeavor to outsmart or outflank the gods.

That notion of pseudo-optimism, of course, worked only for poets and philosophers. As in Christian faith in a secular world, apologetics is impressive only for apologists; so also in Mesopotamia, that poetic notion of an outside chance of human survival by outsmarting the gods was consoling only to poets. In the end, there reigned a sinister kind of pessimism like that in Hegel's world, where his optimistic notion of the progressive upward evolution of history reigned. Schopenhauer and Nietzsche saw the determinism in Hegel's system and concluded that it boxed humans into a painful ordeal of existence. Of Hegel's model, in which both the good and bad of history contribute to onward and upward progress, they would have declared, in effect, "The rub is that humans are trapped in that magnificent evolution, and that is demeaning and pessimistic. Such progress may seem wonderful to the professor in his study in Berlin. It may work well in the German lecture hall. It will not do much for the poor devils maimed by war in Alsace-Loraine, Vietnam, or Iraq." Similarly, the Mesopotamian notion of the nature of humanness was essentially demeaning.

GREEK ANTHROPOLOGY

In contrast, the Greek idea of human nature was infinitely more secular and extremely optimistic: humans were seen as magnificent. The Greeks evolved in their anthropology from a posture similar to that of Mesopotamia to the grandeur of a sophisticated humanism. In Greece in pre-Homeric times, one would have been inclined on occasion to seek out the oracle at Delphi and inquire of the gods about one's destiny. We remember that Oedipus, the unwitting aspirant to the throne of Thebes, went to Delphi. The epic and dramatic literature of Homer, Hesiod, Aeschylus, Sophocles, and Euripides repeatedly refers to the ancient Greeks traveling to Delphi for religious purposes. Plato's dialogues and Socrates's reported discourses imply that it was a natural and good thing to inquire of Apollo at the oracle at Delphi.

When visiting the oracle, one entered the temple portals under the inscription "Know thyself!" Hans Dieter Betz points out that in pre-Homeric times, that meant, "Remember, you are just a man!" When one went through those gates, it was crucial to confess one's status to Apollo. A dialogue with God is implied in the superscription. The pilgrim said, "O Apollo, Thou art!" and Apollo replied, "Know thyself. Remember thou art merely human." Betz points out that merely human meant the same thing as to err is human. That was a confronting experience for the Greek, but as is true of all honest confrontation, it had in it the seeds of health.

The Greek who confronted himself in terms of the primitive meaning of Delphi was already coming to grips with his mere humanness, coming to grips with the fact that he was indeed the kind of creature in which it was native to err. That sounds demeaning, but the implication is magnificent. As psychological healers and informed Christians, we should understand that better than anyone, knowing that if we come honestly to grips with our realities, we are already a long way down the road to managing them constructively. Fortunately, that is what happened for the Greeks. It was the universal education impact of that primitive anthropology, mediated into the Greek cultural and psychological process by the oracle at Delphi, that produced the magnificent humanist experiment that the Greeks achieved in the fifth century B.C.E.

From that point on, through the epic Homeric eon to the Ionian scientific age of the sixth century B.C.E., and the golden age of Pericles 500 years before Christ, when Socrates held forth with his creative humanist thought, there developed a progressive metamorphosis in which the second stage of Greek notions about human nature was born. That second stage took shape in the Greek idea that to go to Delphi and read the superscription *"gnothi auton"* (know thyself) meant not only "remember your mere humanness," but "accept your real humanness compassionately and joyfully, not despairingly."

To be human was one thing. To be compassionately human was quite a new thing. It was a transcendent step magnificently beyond the primitive insight of honest self-acceptance. The Greeks discovered that the more they thought about that, the more significant humans seemed, and the less significant the gods seemed to be. That was a breakthrough of ingenious wisdom and self-affirmation.

Greek theology began with a kind of animistic notion of the gods infesting every facet of nature. It was a primitive attempt to explain the mysterious powers present in the created world. That metamorphosed to the point at which gods were given names, personalities, and domains. Poseidon was the god of the sea, for example. The problem of gods and power and threats in nature was then raised from animism to polytheism. So it was not just a matter of encountering an indefinable spiritual power when a mysterious wave suddenly sprang up out of the sea and overcame you, destroying your goods and family. Now you could deal with Poseidon. Once you gave him a name, a biography, a personality, and a domain, you could start to manage him. You could sacrifice to him before you left the Athenian harbor of Piraeus for the Peloponnesus. You could placate him. You could develop liturgies and rituals to manipulate him.

While Hebrew and Greek anthropology are remarkably different from their Mesopotamian precursors, they are also remarkably different from each other. The Greek notion seems to have evolved from primitive, demeaning anxiety about fragile humanness to the magnificent confidence of Socratic humanism. Apparently, as the Dorian migrants in what became the great Greek peninsula pulled themselves upward from the status of victims of the vagaries of nature to the status of masters of land and sea, their dynamic struggle replaced their fear of the mysterious spirit-filled unknown of nature with a panoply of identifiable gods. They moved from nomadic hunters to domesticated farmers and on to civilized urbanites. The gods they named and described had personalities that could be analyzed, and their behavior could therefore be predicted to some extent, depended on, and even managed.

From that point, the Greeks struggled to replace these increasingly manageable, and therefore rather laughable, gods with heroic, demigodlike men, and finally, with real humans. They were at last in charge of their own destiny, secure in their unmystified rationality. The roles of a Christ-like Prometheus, of a Herakles who civilizes with brute force, and of a Jason who civilizes by humane means are intriguing and wonderful, as one endeavors to understand the evolution of Greek anthropology. Tracing the moments in Greek cultural history when the awesome gods became humorous, the humorous gods became laughable, and the laughable gods became scandalous and irrelevant is itself a surprising and hilarious enterprise. Equally awesome and profoundly sobering is the visualization of how *fragile* and *demeaned* humans became vigorous, clever, and durable characters; how those characters became honorable, estimable, and heroic persons; and how heroic human persons became more moral than the gods, more humane than their supposed creators, more masterful than the incredible, preoccupied, and irrelevant population of Olympus. That magnificent metamorphosis was the miracle of Greece.

Zeus, for example, was repeatedly pictured in venal pursuits, unbecoming to the heroic and virtuous. He was perpetually chasing young human females around the countryside, while his wife Hera was perpetually scolding, maligning, and berating him. The gods first became identifiable, then manageable, then laughable, and finally irrelevant. As the gods became irrelevant, humans became increasingly significant. The significance lay in the fact that humans began to see themselves, not as merely human, but as compassionately and *transcendentally* human. The Greeks came to the conclusion that it is not only true that to err is human, but that to forgive is equally human. There is about human beings that potential for compassion that is ultimately redeeming in their view.

Finally, the golden age of Greek humanism arrived, with the achievement of the notion that humans were not just compassionately and transcendentally human. So magnificently human was humanity, they concluded, that the whole of human destiny was in human hands. The slogan of the golden age was "Man is the measure of all things." In that process, of course, the Greeks had to deal also with the problem of evil. They dealt with the problem in nature and the universe by saying that the problems of pain and suffering and evil were only apparent: "What we used to think were the whims of the gods afflicting us out of avarice, insensitivity, or ignorance, are really only the normal, natural processes of nature. The only real evil is in man's inhumanity to man."

The Greeks endeavored to manage that in the humanistic age by identifying the two sides of human nature: magnificent human rationality and unfortunate human animality. These constituted the magnificent and the malignant in humanity, as the Greeks came to see things. These represented the contest between the mind and the body, the *psyche* and the *sarx*, the spirit and the flesh. The destiny of rational humans was therefore seen as the responsibility to subject the *sarx* to the dominion of the *psyche*, to place the flesh under the control of the mind or spirit, human rationality. This primacy of the intellect and the implied triumph of the spirit over the flesh, the higher passions over the lower, was thus conceived by the Greeks as the road to salvation.

The centuries that follow the golden age, of course, tell an interesting story of despair and disillusion. Man as god proved unable to manage his god-ness, or even his goodness. Existentialist loss of meaning set in and brought on a wholesale lunge into primitive mystery religions, then bizarre supernaturalism followed. That unfortunate course is similar to the pattern of history from the humanism of nineteenth-century Western rationalism to the existentialist despair of Camus, Sartre, Nietzsche, and Kierkegaard. It has withered Western philosophy and culture, as may be seen in the romantic insanity of the 1960s and 1970s or the current preoccupation with New Age esoteric thought, astrology, karma, and strange theories of reincarnation.

HEBREW ANTHROPOLOGY

The third significant anthropological tradition in the ancient world that fed the New Testament concept of human nature is the Hebrew model in which Jesus and Paul were raised. It is a subtle, simple, majestic tradition. It is essentially the story of mankind in the Old Testament. As we noted in the introduction to this volume, it is the story of Yahweh, the covenanting God, embracing unconditionally his sons and daughters of the human community.

The story of humans in Hebrew thought may be looked at from various directions. First, it is a unitary notion throughout. The Hebrew concept of humanness knows nothing of the division of the body, mind, and spirit. It knows nothing of the tension or contrast the Greeks saw between flesh and spirit, *sarx* and *psyche*. For the Hebrews, a human being is one and whole. It is not so much the body that requires redirection or suppression; it is not so much a matter of dominance of *soma* (physical body) or *sarx* (fleshly nature) by *psyche*. It is out of the heart that the issues of life flow, namely, out of the center of one's self. Humans are persons to the Hebrews, persons and personalities, and must be dealt with as totalities. This was so true for the Hebrews that they had a great deal of difficulty conceptualizing life after death. There is no reference in the Old Testament to a specific experience of a soul going to heaven at death, or going to hell. The Hebrews continued to talk about life after death and Sheol as an undifferentiated and undefined matter. One died and entered into a different kind of existence, but the concept of differentiation was not complete. One reason was that they had difficulty dealing with any notion that a person could be split—that when the body is dead, there is something else that goes somewhere and continues in existence. They thought of persons as one. The unitary concept of the person is the first essential principle in the Hebrew notion of human nature.

The second element in Hebrew ideas about the nature of humanness is that humans are coregents and coworkers with God in God's world, as mentioned in previous chapters. That is a majestic notion of human nature, and it stands in contrast with the human predicament in this world of dissonance and pain. St. Paul picked up the Hebrew notion of humanness and dealt with it in three terms. He speaks, as indicated earlier, of primordial humans: in the pristine state of conformity to God's primeval design. He speaks, secondly, of fallen humanity, as depicted in Romans 1–5, where the contrast is boldly focused between God's design for humans and what we have made of it. Finally, Paul speaks of the human as a whole person "in Christ."

It seems clear that when Paul said he was a Hebrew of the Hebrews, one of the things definitely implied is his heavy dependence on this Semitic Hebrew anthropological model and tradition. Fortunately, or perhaps unfortunately, for Paul and his own peace of mind, and his personal psychointellectual integration, he was caught up in a world where he found himself dealing with a strong tension between the humanist notion of the Greek mainstream of thought and the God-centered, or theistic, perspective about humans in the Hebrew tradition.

Paul was not toying with humanism, although from a certain perspective, his anthropology might be described as a Christian humanism. He was trying to integrate the unitary Hebrew notion of man and the compartmentalized Greek concept. These two seemed to be at war within him: *soma/sarx* versus *psyche*, the lower versus higher passions. Ridderbos deals with the problem of *soma, sarx*, and *psyche* in Paul and points out that the apostle ends up with a Christian model of humanness in which the Hebrew and Greek traditions are reasonably and adequately integrated. There remains, however, a tension, which comes out in the following manner, as regards our concerns as Christian counselors and therapists.

Paul consistently wishes to say that primordial humans, in the face of the predicament of fallen mankind, always exist as a kind of ideal. Salvation comes for Paul, nevertheless, only when we transcend both the pristine state of Eden and the state of our brokenness, alienation, fallenness, and pathology and become whole persons in Christ. What does that mean for Paul? It means for persons, always in the context of the community, the church, to experience the relief of Christ: to be in the way of Christ and, in that certain sense, to incarnate Christ, to be the "Body of Christ," as Paul terms it. It means for a human to be one in whom Christ can be seen to function.

However, while trying to hold firmly to that on one hand, Paul deals with the problem of the disorder in human nature in terms of the Greek categories: flesh and spirit. "There is a war within me," he declares. It is a tension between *psyche* and *soma/sarx*. That tension Paul sometimes tends to resolve as the Greeks did: the management and suppression of the flesh by the dominance of the mind, rationality, or spirit. Clearly it was a problem for Paul to work out. In the end, Paul is really sure that the only salvation is in Christ. It is a gift. It is unconditional. It is free and unmerited and it is given to every human, whether he or she is aware of it or not. At the same time, there is a discipline implied in that gift of grace. The discipline implied is the management of the lower passions by the higher, a strictly Greek idea, of which Paul is never quite cured, despite his declarations of God's radical grace (Rom. 8).

MODERN VIEWS OF HUMANNESS

We are dealing in our world with essentially four models of humanness today. These function in our cultural, social, and psychological processes in such a way as to shape our sense of self, of others, and of the legitimate expectations we should have regarding our possibilities as humans. In our own minds, in the minds of our colleagues, both Christian and secular, and in the minds of our clients, undoubtedly an even more crucial fact, the four models shape life.

One of these anthropological models prominent at this time is the Mesopotamian: that devastating demeaning notion of humans as trapped. It seems to me that Schopenhauer can be thanked for that. Hegel conceived of the whole of the human experiment in a very optimistic way, claiming that history is the interplay of the thesis, antithesis, and a synthesis; and as a consequence of that dynamic, history is moving progressively both forward and upward to the kingdom of God. As noted previously, this perspective incited in Schopenhauer the insight that humans are victimized by the determinism of Hegel's optimism. Out of that came the despair of Nietzsche.

Humans are trapped. The existentialism of Camus and Sartre, the general philosophical tone and temper of the twentieth century, the attitude of many of our patients and companions, is really the Mesopotamian anthropology reawakened: the personally demeaning despair of the trapped human.

The second prevalent model of humanness is the notion of the Greeks. That is the incredible optimism of the secular human who styles "himself as the measure of all things," whose destiny is in his own hands. All he needs to do is get sufficient education, gain sufficient insight, develop sufficient rationality, or receive sufficient psychoanalysis or psychotherapy, and he is saved for himself and for his creative destiny.

The third model of humanity is a secularized Hebrew notion, the idea of humans as unitary beings, who have all the prerogatives and possibilities of our meaning and destiny genetically and biochemically written into the structure of our individuality. This is a hybrid of the idea of humans as magnificently preprogrammed by genetic design, on one hand, and the radical notion of the virtue of selfishness, on the other. To be healthy and human in this model means to be more totally and authentically individual and thus be more wholesome for everybody.

Ayn Rand was a champion of this latter notion, especially in her book *Virtue of Selfishness*. She suggested that the whole notion of Christianity is really a subterfuge. If you really want to be wholesome for the world, you must cultivate creative selfishness. If you are really good for yourself, you are really best for everybody else, as well. The idea of genetically preprogrammed humans is reinforced by the influence on our view of humanness that is caused by the remarkable advances in interpretation of the DNA chain. This further complicates our concept of humanness, as we move closer to the possibilities of genetic management or manipulation. There is something so close to the truth about both facets of this third modern model that it really is a subtle and tempting possibility. Both aspects of this third model have a significant dimension of truth in them.

The fourth anthropology prominently afloat in the Western world today is the Christian model. Ridderbos probably goes too far in his conclusion that

Paul successfully integrates the Greek and Hebrew ideas, formulating a thoroughgoing Christian anthropology. It is probably closer to the truth to contend that Paul might profitably have stayed closer to the Hebrew model of human nature. The Christian concept of human nature has at least these dimensions: It requires that we take our human predicament seriously, namely, that we acknowledge that the problem of human beings is a radical problem. The problem of our disorder, of our disorientation, of our brokenness, alienation, and proclivity to lose the sense of the meaningfulness of things cuts right through to the very center of our existence.

In the final analysis, our problem is not how many sins we have committed, but who we know ourselves to be. It is a problem of identity so that a Christian concept of humans is the concept of persons fundamentally disordered but possessing two crucial redemptive potentials. The first one, prominent in the Hebrew notion, is the native, healthy, integrating urge of life itself to health, to wholesomeness, and to what we are designed by God to be. The second is the possibility in Christ to become not only a compatriot of God, but a healer of his world through the experience of God's gracious acceptance of us; that is, we can become the incarnation of the spirit that was incarnated in Christ. We can achieve this quality, identity, and status now, in the present moment. We can be the Body of Christ in the world in our time. In that sense, we can be Christ for others, not just compatriots of God, but God in Christ, present through us for a needy world of fractured humans.

CONCLUSION

We encounter all these models and their consequences continually in our interaction with clients. If we fail to clarify the model of man in these terms, we tend to lose efficiency in achieving healing. One of the great disorders we constantly encounter and should recognize is the disorder of identity. Some of the worst human suffering is observed in the person who cannot conceive of himself or herself as one beloved, a potential object of graciousness. Yet that is the fundamental element in the Christian concept of human nature.

For Jesus, grace meant unconditionally accepting the adulterous woman in John 8, ordaining the denying Peter in spite of himself, embracing Judas at the betrayal in the garden and calling him friend. So when Jesus said, "As the father sent me into the world, so send I you," he must have meant that we should deal in the Christian notion of humans, namely, as the purveyors and potential receivers of that experience of unconditional and radically invasive grace that outflanks all our pathologies and defenses and settles our wrongness at its source and center.

CHAPTER 6

PSYCHOLOGY AND SPIRITUAL CONVERSION

There is a clear correlation between the present-day models of psychological development such as those of Piaget,[1] Kohlberg,[2] Erikson,[3] and Fowler.[4] This is particularly true in the light of Massey's[5] claim that adults grow or change mainly under the impact of a "significant emotional event." Spiritual conversion is such an event, and its characteristics can be described and accounted for in identifiable psychodynamic terms. Some types of Christian conversion are pathogenic in the sense that they create mental illness or aggravate it when it exists in a person. Other kinds of Christian conversion are not pathological and offer life-enhancing influences for our psychological and social health.

The difference between the two is easy to identify. Spiritual conversion that causes a person to experience a greater sense of freedom, forgiveness, security, and joy is healthy conversion. Spiritual conversion that produces legalism in ideas or ethics, or constrains a person with a structure of threat, anxiety, fear of God, and the like, is sick and causes spiritual sickness. Sick spiritual change often indicates prior personality pathology, mental illness, which becomes exaggerated or aggravated by the conversion experience. Healthy spiritual conversion, in any religion, produces an experience of God's unconditional and radical grace for humans and is accompanied by the kind of faith posture that is marked by trust, relief, and joy.

TRANSFORMING MOMENTS

James Loder attempted to illumine our understanding of convictional experiences by his book *The Transforming Moment*.[6] From his own personal experience and numerous case histories, he derived a deep appreciation for human life events that produce a remarkable change of direction: real conversion of one's life. These epitomes of human life transitions illustrate his work. He expresses a serious appreciation of parapsychological moments of knowing such as intuition, extrasensory perception, prescience, and intimations of the divine spirit. His various publications contribute in important ways to our understanding of these aspects of human spirituality. He is interested in decreasing our excessive confidence in empirical science as the exclusive or even primary channel to truth. He is confident that spiritual insight is as certain a kind of truth as the results of laboratory experiments.

In his attempt to avoid reducing our experiences of spiritual conversion to mere psychological events, devoid of any relationship to the presence of the divine spirit, Loder often runs the risk of landing in a kind of nineteenth-century subjective pietism. He launches the argument of his book from a traumatic personal experience of temporary paralysis he endured following an auto accident. He interprets this event as a distinctive spiritual conversion because the paralysis was completely removed after intense prayer and supplication to God. Unfortunately, Loder seems to interpret as a spiritual event what seems quite clearly to have been a spontaneous remission of classic hysterical paralysis.

However, in the process of this rather gratuitous error in diagnosis, Loder raises the central question about the interface of psychology and spirituality in the relatively common instances of the psychospiritual renovation of human lives. He tries hard to describe the watershed that distinguishes subjective psychological process from true spirituality and personalized divine illumination in human life.

Consequently, Loder's book makes one useful contribution. It illustrates both the legitimate quest for understanding psychospiritual dynamics in human development, while occasionally demonstrating the excesses into which some serious conservative religionists are tempted in their fear of exploring the psychological sides of spirituality and the spiritual sides of psychology. This error is all too common among Fundamentalist Evangelical Christians. This position tends to denigrate the legitimate domains and contributions of the discreet sciences. They seem to fear that the natural and social sciences will eclipse theology and spiritual authenticity.

Responsible people of faith, particularly informed Christians, understand that the principle of Occam's razor applies as much today as in the Middle Ages, when Occam lived. His principle advised us that when data or experience can be managed or explained by a simple hypothesis, a more complex hypothesis may not honestly be devised to account for it. When human experience or information can be accounted for satisfactorily by psychology, physics, chemistry, sociology, geology, or the like, it ought not to be spiritualized. Theological and spiritual experiences or data, where they are authentic, can, no doubt, stand on their own feet as well as these other disciplines.

STRUCTURALIST MODELS

For that reason, the structuralist thinkers have devised models of personality development that offer more than the ethereal theories of Loder. Fowler,[7] for example, offers a thoroughgoing description of the structuralist view of psychosocial development applied to growth in faith and spiritual maturity. It explains such experiences as Loder's personal crisis and other life-transforming moments, without downplaying or demeaning sound psychological interpretations. Fowler grounds his work on human spirituality in Piaget's model of cognitive development, Kohlberg's model of moral development, and Erikson's model of psychosocial development. He correctly perceives that these three models are not in tension, but mutually illumine and elaborate each other.

Piaget demonstrated that human development can be described in terms of six stages: infancy, early childhood, childhood, adolescence, young adulthood, and adulthood or maturity. Piaget emphasized that there are distinctive developmental characteristics evident in each stage. His empirical research indicated that these stages can be described concretely as a pattern of movement from mere primal sensory experience and reaction in infancy, to preoperational and intuitive responses to environment in childhood, and then to formal operations, in which the adolescent tends to think in dogmatic patterns of right and wrong. Young adults become more dialogical and open to others' opinions, and finally, mature adults tend to receive many different ideas from various sources and synthesize them into their own sense of truth and right.

Kohlberg's model of human moral development correlates precisely with Piaget's notions of cognitive development. He emphasized that in infancy, we respond to positive and negative rewards. As we move into childhood, we are capable of self-control in terms of a greater variety of principles of good and bad things or conduct. Adolescence and young adulthood move us to self-assertion and then greater mutuality, concord, and a law-and-order mentality. As we progress morally into adulthood and maturity, we operate increasingly on the basis of concern for others and personal conscientiousness. Full maturity normally brings with it a sense of appreciation of the perspectives of others and their claims on us as well as an outlook of universal ethical principles and loyalty to all humankind.

Erikson's distinctive contribution focused on the social development humans experience. We move, according to Erikson, from the trust-mistrust of infancy to hope and autonomy in childhood, during which we exercise our own will and sense of purpose, at the risk of experiences of shame and doubt as well as fear and guilt. In adolescence, we struggle with the tensions of accomplishment versus inferiority, as we reach for competence, and with establishing our own identity versus role confusion, as we reach for fidelity or authenticity: learning what it means to be true to self. Adulthood brings intimacy and love, generativity and creativity, and integrity, unless we fail and fall into isolation, stagnation, and despair.

FOWLER'S STRUCTURALIST MODEL OF SPIRITUALITY

Fowler presents a framework for understanding faith development based on the structuralist models. His work moves to one point: the way in which humans come to a focused sense of spiritual meaning, faith, and self-sacrificial love. This experience leads to an inner freedom, peace, and hope and a palpable sense of the presence of God. Fowler notes that for the human infant, the world is limited to primary family relationships, and its sense of reality is intuitive and magical or numinous. Childhood brings a wider social experience and a literal and mystical sense of reality. Santa Claus never comes down the chimney, and it is not clear he could ever make it through that small pipe, but he is real and does come and brings fine objects of delight. God and Santa Claus are undifferentiated. Parents versus Santa Claus as the source of Christmas presents is not a tolerable question. It violates the necessary mysticism.

Fowler continues by pointing out that in adolescence, we begin to analyze such myths and move comfortably into a humorous revaluing of Santa Claus, and we begin our symbolic thinking about issues of meaning and commitment. We are able to make this transition by becoming very dogmatic about our new perceptions of reality, in which things are usually rather starkly true or false, right or wrong, black or white. Dogmatic, literalistic and legalistic adult religionists seem never to have moved beyond this adolescent stage. Adulthood should bring with it that spiritual growth that moves us to see that our perception of the world of divine transcendence, and the essential meanings attendant on that, are always experienced in terms of symbols and their meanings. Maturity brings us to the appreciation of the variety of symbolic meanings humans have contrived for capturing their understanding of their own spirituality and the presence of God in it.

Westerhof thought that we are socialized into our religious convictions and growth in faith.[8] The influences of the community and its training programs are dominant in his model of faith development. Joy claimed that faith development was a direct influence of the divine spirit on an individual human spirit and that the structuralists were not only on the wrong track, but had rendered spirituality godless by failing to emphasize the power and role of the Holy Spirit.[9] Fowler disagreed with both Westerhof and Joy, claiming that faith development depends more on the built-in structures of human personality development demonstrated by Piaget, Kohlberg, and Erikson than on mere socialization. Moreover, it was the central point of Fowler's model that in faith development, as in all other aspects of this world, God works, by means of the Holy Spirit, through the functional structures and natural laws inherent to the created world. God works in us according to and by means of the laws that he has laid down in the very structure of the universe—and hence the structures of our unfolding lives.

STRUCTURALISM AND SPIRIT EXPERIENCE

Humans are inherently spiritual; that is, we irrepressibly seek meaning in everything from the moment we are born until we die. Our quest for meaning deals with everything we experience around us and everything we can imagine. As we progress in life, we reach increasingly toward transcendental meanings that deal with the major matters of the meaning of our morality and our morality: life and death issues. We grow through the natural patterns the structuralists outlined. As we move from one stage to the next, each gain opens us to the needs and potential patterns characteristic of that new stage. The content of the spiritual growth at each stage will depend in important ways on the information, attitudes, values, and faith commitments of the community in which we live our genetic inheritance, and the personal experiences and events that befall us.

Whether our experiences in life are painful or pleasurable, they may prove to be destructive or constructive, depending on how they are integrated into our selves. That integration process depends on the characteristic pattern inherent in the particular stage in which the experience is received, the outlook of the community on the kind of experience we have had, our genetics, and the information we have about such an experience and what it might mean. Christian conversion is an integration process or event that sets our individual experience in a context that allows and prompts faith and a sense of God's grace to function as the center and ground of meaning, purpose, hope, and relationships. It is crucial, therefore, in keeping with the point made in chapter 1, that if we are to have healthy conversions, we must have a healthy God. A sick notion of God will produce a sick conversion into a sick faith perspective.

If Christian conversion takes place as a dramatic integration event, rather than a developmental process over time, the manner in which it recapitulates or reprocesses all the previous stages of the person's growth is usually intensely obvious. This recapitulation gives a new grounding for our orientation to life, our values, and our sense of virtue, in the "light of faith's new center of value, images of power and decisive master story.... When the recapitulative process has done its work, the person has a new foundation of inner integration from which to move decisively toward the next stage."[10]

Morris Massey observed, in keeping with our analysis thus far, that humans continue to grow largely as a result of significant emotional events, which stimulate movement to the next stage of built-in development.[11]

Sometimes persons may experience arrested growth at one of the childhood, adolescent, or early adult stages. Massey may have discovered the trigger mechanism that usually moves us from one stage of growth to the next. Significant emotional events may be generated by deep inner needs or by profound outer stimuli.

Robert Fuller believes that it is our capacity to trust the unknown that lies beyond each stage, that empowers us to reach out to and embrace the next stage of our growth.[12] He argues that at each stage of growth from infancy to mature adulthood, we develop a paradigm that explains our current experience to us and manages it without undue anxiety. As we grow to the point that we are taking in a lot of experience data that are no longer managed well by our current paradigm, we need a new framework for understanding our expanded world of experience. We are not automatically handed a larger paradigm or a new way of thinking about things.

We must be able to trust God and the universe that if we transform our set of principles for understanding our world, we will be able to find a new paradigm in terms of which to manage it without excessive anxiety. Fuller declares that such trust in the unknown is a religious act and experience, and only such religious acts of faith or belief that the universe or God can be trusted to afford us a new paradigm or framework empower us to take on the unknown experience of growth into the next natural stage of our development. Only by such an act of trust can we go from infancy to childhood, from childhood to adolescence, and from there to the stages of maturity.

The inner pressure to reach out for a new framework, rather than stagnate in an immature stage of growth, comes from new interior insights and new exterior stimuli. In any case, what usually forces us across the boundary into a new thought structure for handling experience and reality is a new set of insights or information, a new relationship, or a new trauma. These are experiences that take place in our minds and in our hearts, affecting our cognitive psychosocial and our moral-spiritual levels of knowing. Such events are significant in size or value when they are life changing, providing a new or renewed sense of meaning, outlook, and being.

ROBERT C. FULLER'S THESIS

Fuller provides a well-developed and persuasive heuristic argument, backed by a wealth of convincing evidence and rational analysis. He demonstrates that religious insights and ideas function crucially to mediate the healthy movement of human personalities through the transitions we make from one developmental stage to the next, and through the life-shaping trauma that often confronts us. Indeed, he contends that the religious ideas and experiences facilitate these growth transitions better than any other forces shaping our sense of meaning and our worldviews.

Fuller makes it plain that human maturation, fulfillment, and self-actualization depend on values and experiences that are religious in character. Using psychological theory and clinical research, he creates a model of the structure and development of the human life cycle, giving particular attention to Erikson's eight states of psychosocial process. Fuller places great emphasis on the way religion emerges in the lives of individuals and the role it plays in our unfolding lives. He has a rich appreciation of the religious dynamics that are necessary for our growth to achieve wholeness and completeness as persons. Translated into biblical language, Fuller's thesis is that faith in God and in the providence and grace of God to which the Bible testifies is the key concept that incites our health and growth in the adaptive process of achieving a mature and creatively fulfilling adult life.

Fuller applies his model to religion and childhood development, belief and identity formation, values and midlife transitions, integrity formation, aging, dying, and religion and self-transcendence. His concern is to locate the place of religion within the overall structure of mature personality and to reexamine modern attitudes toward human nature by investigating the religious aspects of personal development. So we are here concerned with the way psychological understandings of human fulfillment enable us to understand the role faith and spirituality play in our lives.

Science and technology have devalued the role given to religious considerations in Western thought in the last two centuries, largely because spiritual function is less easily quantified in cause and effect equations than are the more tangible things we study or experience. In the effort to use the empirical model of physics, the social sciences have sometimes overlooked their significant linkage with theology or philosophy. The structuralists have given us a great advantage in providing a framework within which psychology and the other social sciences can study the issues of cause and effect in human development, while at the same time affording substantive address to matters of meaning and purpose. In the end, it is the resolution of meaning and purpose issues that people seek and hunger for, in terms of which we fashion life's satisfying psychological solutions, and which provide the force that moves us from one structural stage to the next in our growth process.

The original aims of the empirical method that the natural and social sciences employ are "shaped by the desire to derive public and definitive information" by selecting out those data from life's total range of experience that can be objectively discerned.[13] Structuralism, particularly as articulated by Fowler and Fuller, provides a mechanism for reenlisting those sciences in the task of giving us a well-rounded vision of human nature and its complex functions, including those of faith and religious desire.

Fuller notes that four kinds of causality need to be addressed to understand honestly and comprehensively humanity's interaction with the universe and life: material (physiology, instincts, and genetics), environmental, mental/

attitudinal, and spiritual or ultimate. General psychology addresses the first two. Speculative philosophy and religious research address all four and make a special contribution regarding the last two. Clinical and other research evidence indicates that a comprehensive appreciation of how humans function and how religious factors influence the course of human development requires us to focus on the "extent to which humanity's pursuit of happiness and fulfillment is contingent upon 'adapting' to a spiritual environment beyond the limits of our physical and social worlds."[14] The evidence currently available demonstrates an inherently and inescapably religious dimension of human experience that is accessible to and consistent with the methods and spirit of comprehensive scientific inquiry.

David Tracy, in *Blessed Rage for Order*, makes a point of special usefulness at this juncture in our discussion.[15] He raises the notion that in our process of growth and development, we frequently arrive at locations in the unfolding of ourselves at which we confront what he engagingly calls *limit experiences*. Such experiences arise in us when we reach the point in any stage of our growth at which our rational or doctrinal framework, our worldview, will no longer adequately accommodate or account for the actual data of our experience or learning. Fuller expands on this idea as follows:

> The limit dimension of human experience refers to those situations in which persons find themselves confronted with an ultimate limit or horizon to their experience. A "limit experience" is any moment of life that forces us to acknowledge the limits or limitations of a strictly rational or empirical approach to life. They impart an awareness that many of life's most profound challenges prompt us to look beyond the resources and perspectives of the finite personality . . . What distinguishes a limit experience from other types of experience is that it forces the individual to the recognition that reason, logic, and worldly resources are . . . incapable of adjusting us to some of the most recurring themes in human experience.[16]

Positive limit experiences, as in rewarding worship, conversion, or significant bursts of illumination, have a revelatory character insofar as they afford persons "a direct experience of a More or Beyond. . . . Negative limit experiences emerge amidst feelings of grief, confusion or meaninglessness." Positive "limit experiences impart sensations of bliss, ecstasy, euphoria, and contentment. They impart to the conscious personality a firm conviction in the existence and even availability of a supersensible reality,"[17] such as God and the divine providence and grace insinuated into our lives and experience as we grow. In this regard, William James declared that the "heart of religion . . . is the conviction that (1) the visible world is part of an unseen spiritual universe from which it draws its ultimate meaning or purpose, and (2) that union or harmonious relation with that higher universe is our true end as well as the key to achieving personal wholeness and well-being."[18]

Limit experiences confront us with the awareness that there is some power, some dimension of reality, some potential experience, or some higher level of consciousness, namely, our hunger for and perception of God's grace and providence in life. This and this alone can resolve those disharmonies and feelings of incompleteness which occur in us when we are at the *limits* of our human comprehension and condition.[19]

Such moments persuade us that life's full richness and psychospiritual fulfillment lie beyond the limit of the material world, accessible by the natural and social sciences. They lie, therefore, beyond the limits known to the psychological sciences.

Fuller's conceptualization of religion, as he acknowledges, will not satisfy those who think of it only as a formal process of ritual behavior or as a functional process of dogma, with its role in instruction and illumination. Fuller's perspective, as that of James, anchors religion "not in God but rather in a certain dimension of experiences common to individuals as they pursue their various courses of life."[20] He is quite correct in this approach since notions about God are the content of second-level abstraction in our religious experience, derivative from religious experiences, whether they are learning the biblical story in Sunday school, reading theology, worshipping, or having personal conversation; that is, concepts about God are the human experiences by which we name and structure our deeper, primary-level spiritual hunger and revelatory perceptions.

The primary-level structure and content of religious perception is that afforded by our direct experiences of faith, trust, assurance of the More and Beyond, and projections of God-concepts on our limit events. These primary religious experiences develop their *structure* in our infancy and childhood out of our ingrained hunger for God, for ultimacy, and for meaning. This hunger is invested in all of us by our being created in the image of God. We develop the *content* that fills this hunger out of experiences of faith, trust, and assurance, in relationship with such significant others as parents, teachers, mentors, and friends. St. Augustine was psychologically as well as spiritually accurate in his doxological confession, "You have made us for yourself and our souls are restless until they rest, O God, in you!"

THE THESIS APPLIED

True faith always exists only in the context of honest and profound doubt. Fuller helps us focus the fact that the personal empirical approach to religious conceptualization "permits us to view religious faith not as a set of unproven beliefs that we either do or do not hold but rather as a style of living influenced by the kinds of insights that occur just beyond the limits of either reason or sensory experience."[21] Thus the pragmatic application of Fuller's thesis is persuasive.

At many critical times in life, our sense of well-being depends on our capacity for adaptation to that world that lies beyond our five senses: the transcendent or spiritual world that we can intuit but can neither see nor define. Embracing the transitions of midlife and aging, and continually re-defining our moral sense of things are such times. These phases of life are important parts of our development, and all lead us to the need for larger paradigms than have served us before these times in life. They call for new dimensions and new intensities of that faith which makes it possible for us to step across old thresholds into new ways of thinking.[22]

Fuller recognizes Erikson's structuralist framework as a model of the way humans gain skills to cope with the expanding experience, opportunity, and responsibility that life affords. Erikson rejects Freud's pathology-oriented view of human personality, placing the primary emphasis not on the role of instinctual drives, but on conscious ego formation. He credits the ego with the capacity to regulate a person's relationship with the environment in ways that "not only achieve personal wholeness but make positive contributions to the fulfillment of others as well."[23] This gives attitudinal influences a greater role in shaping our well-being, adaptation, growth, and faith.

Each of the structural stages describes how a person is presented with a new developmental challenge, requiring a new developmental method for relating with the internal and external environment for the purpose of suc-cessfully resolving and integrating the perplexities and growth possibilities of new experiences. In our progress from one stage to the next, we discover dimensions of reality that do not integrate well in terms of our previous framework of understanding. We arrive at the horizon of our understanding and perception: a limit experience. This crisis requires a rethinking and a refeeling of our framework of understanding and meaning: our worldview.

At the first level, the human infant must resolve the crisis of trust versus mistrust and so acquire hope: "the belief that our wishes can be obtained in spite of difficulties. Hope is the virtue that makes faith possible, and adult faith in turn nourishes hope and inspires us to care for others."[24] At the sec-ond stage, we must process a crisis of will: "the unbroken determination to exercise free choice as well as self-restraint, in spite of unavoidable moments of shame and doubt."[25] The third stage deals with personal initiative and with rising above a sense of guilt. It resolves the crisis of purpose: "the cour-age to envisage and pursue valued goals without being inhibited by fear of punishment or guilt."[26] These three initial stages are the crises of infancy and early childhood that we negotiate during the ages of birth to two years, two to four years, and four to five years, respectively.[27]

The fourth structuralist stage confronts us at 6–11 years with the cri-sis of inferiority versus industry and challenges us to acquire the virtue of competence: "the free exercise of intelligence and physical skills to complete tasks unimpaired by feelings of inferiority."[28] This completes the childhood

process. The progress from stage 1 to 4 is a progression from coping with
primal physiological to more advanced psychological and spiritual maturation—"and importantly, as the life cycle progresses the triggering experience
of human development and transformation is increasingly likely to come in
the form of a limit experience."[29]

Early human development is shaped largely by imitation and identification
with others, who model the way to manage the transition required by a limit
experience. Other significant personalities impact us. The notion of God is
a cultural symbol concept mediated to us by the imitation and identification
process as well as by an irrepressible inner hunger and the quest it drives.
We acquire such symbol concepts because of an inherent appetite for the
meaning that the symbols afford us. "As childhood gives way to adolescence
and young adulthood, pressures come to bear upon a religious faith acquired
from without on the basis of parental authority. The late teens and twenties
afford individuals their first opportunities to make the somewhat turbulent
transition from a secondhand to a firsthand religious faith."[30]

Thus stage 5, ages 12–22 or so, leads humans to deal with the crisis of
identity and acquisition of the virtue of fidelity: the ability to sustain loyalty
to an important commitment over time and under the duress of life's tempo-
ral and eternal challenges, to take a stand for ones own faith perspective, for
its own personal reasons.

Fidelity is the rock on which identity, character, and maturity depend. In-
fants disengage from parental intimacy and progress to individual identity by
choosing transitional objects and spaces that empower this change. So also
adolescents must use nonrational notions to establish the new worldview
that will take in the increasing acquisition of knowledge and more mature
insight. In this way, the child and the budding adult preserve a sense that
life continues to be safe and trustworthy, despite remarkable change. This
persistence of trust as they transition to their new paradigms is an act of
faith, faith that the world will not disintegrate if they take leave of their
earlier views of the world and of themselves, and reach for a new framework
of thought.

How much more truly urgent is such religious confidence in God or the
universe for those of us whose need for certainty carries us to the boundary
questions about the very meaning of human existence. This happens when,
in midlife, we begin to think earnestly about death. Up from the deep places
of our natures and spirits arise the religious longings that drive us to align
our lives with the resources of spirit that are central to existence itself. These
longings speak the language of that which symbolizes "what feels profoundly
true even though it is not demonstrable. From a psychological perspective,
religious faith can thus be viewed as an ongoing expression of those psychological processes that make it possible for humans to venture forth into life
on the basis of trust."[31] Erikson remarked in this regard that religious faith

"translates into significant words, images, and codes the exceeding darkness which surrounds man's existence, and the light which pervades it beyond all desert or comprehension."[32] Fuller continues,

> Religious faith operates within the emerging identity as an adaptive and integrating force. Because religion roots the meaning and purpose of life in the transcendental reality of God, it makes it possible for individuals to locate themselves and their actions within a larger frame of reference . . . about who they are, what they stand for, and what they stand against. Religious faith also frees individuals from being at the total mercy of events in the outer world . . . to bring their own set of values and goals to bear upon the interpretation of everyday life . . . the kind of mature and self-controlled behavior that the psychologist Gordon Allport calls "propriate striving"—conduct motivated by self-chosen values rather than by environmental or instinctual forces. . . . Religious faith reinforces a positive sense of self-worth by aligning our personal identity and moral outlook with an understanding of God's creative activity in the world.[33]

Serious doubt is the essential matrix of great faith, as noted previously. The human personality that is encouraged and stimulated to full maturation ultimately experiences faith resurging and reasserting itself over doubt under the suasion of pragmatic, mystical, or intellectual-contemplative-reflective experience. Personalities that do not come to this fulfillment are, in effect, arrested at one of the stages prior to full self-actualization. Conscious religious belief and intentional cultivation of spirituality provide zest or meaning to our lives so that these vital experiences must be recognized as realities (1) that may not be discounted, (2) that must be seen as having utility for personal wholeness, and (3) that demonstrate that faith corresponds to the nature and structure of the way thing are wired in this world of human life.

It should be noted as well how often, ordinary human experiences verify the practical truth of faith; therefore we should "act faithfully upon [religious beliefs] even without logical proof. . . . The mystical validation of faith refers to those limit experiences in which individuals somewhat ineluctably"[34] find ourselves facing and are helped across the boundaries of life that reach beyond our senses. That is the location at which we can experience, as do many persons, a direct sense of transcendent presence and power. This constitutes "empirical evidence for considering the nonphysical reality as a clue to the nature and meaning of life." It is self-evident why religions emphasize the importance of "prayer, meditation, ritual and altered states of consciousness."[35] These are the experiences which afford us firsthand experience of the spiritual "More" that we sense when we have crossed the boundaries of conscious thought.

Intellectual or contemplative validation of religious experience is made up of the rational insights that the properties of reality, which are empirically perceivable, are not self-explanatory. Reason then contradicts its own limits when it confronts itself with the question as to why there is a universe at all: "although reason can ask the question of its own origin, it is inherently incapable of deriving the answer." Realizing that reason is an inadequate tool for explaining our connection to the "intrinsic meaning and purpose of life" compels the acknowledgment of the "validity of concepts that do not confine themselves to the limits of logical reason."[36]

Allport said that mature faith must be well differentiated, dynamic, productive of a consistent morality, comprehensive, integral, and heuristic.[37] That means that religious experience must provide us with a firsthand faith—not be eroded by the ossification of dogmatism or traditionalism—imply coherent ethical principles, afford an integrated meaning for the whole of life, and possess the suasive quality of an appealing belief system and worldview. If it is to provide the foundation for mature identity, it must afford us ideological direction for continuing personality development at each stage.

At stage 6, ages 20–35, we face the crisis of intimacy and our quest for the virtue of true love. There follows the 35–60 stage, which contains the crisis of generativity versus self-absorption and the quest for the realization of care for what we have created and for the world context of that creation. The final stage of old age, from 60 or 65 to death, is the universalizing phase, in which we expand our capacity for understanding and caring enough to embrace all truth and all reality. If we mature to this degree, we are mellowed with the assurance that all the productivity of mature human quest is of the spirit and leads to a universal embrace of all truth and all persons. Stages 6–8 (ages 20 to death) are dominated by the quest for a profound, warrantable, and durable sense of the meaning of all life and existence; for an ethical-moral maturity, in which we take responsibility for ourselves, our world; and for communicating that caring perspective to those who follow us.

This capacity for a strenuous moral and spiritual life of authentic and transcendent quality, that is, supratraditional mode and style, is a developmental achievement, and not an inherited disposition. It implies a type of ultimate individuation in which our socially defined ego gradually gives way to a wider and more universal and transcendent range of potentials, constituting the core of authentic selfhood. This process postulates and reaches out toward the reality and existence that transcend our selves, our time, and our place in space. If we possess a notion or theology of ultimate reality that is formatively a part of our ego structure, and so is authentic to our real inner self—a genuine firsthand religious spirituality—our moral consciousness postulates and reaches out to a "God through whom we can come to feel intimately identified with our fellow living creatures and in terms of whose demands we are prompted to take seriously the requirements of the remote future,"[38] indeed, of eternity.

In the words of William James,

> When . . . we believe that a God is there, and that he is one of the claimants, the infinite perspective opens out. The scale of the symphony is incalculably prolonged. The more imperative ideals now begin to speak with an altogether new objectivity and significance, and to utter the penetrating, shattering, tragically challenging note of appeal.[39]

James believed that if the only reason for believing in God were its ethical necessity, the emergence of "religious faith in the fully rational adult is yet justified by its own evolutionary-adaptive functions," that is, by the manner in which it empowers us to negotiate successfully our way through our limit experiences into the next stage of our development and growth and into that broadening of our doctrinal or philosophical framework that makes it possible for us to integrate healthily our ever-expanding world of understanding, truth, and experience, thus achieving the resources to be a wholly ethical personality. "Every sort of energy and endurance, of courage and capacity for handling life's evil, is set free in those who have religious faith [and thus for] this reason the strenuous type of character will on the battle-field of human history always outwear the easy-going type, and religion will drive irreligion to the wall."[40]

Whitehead's reinforcement of this notion is expressed in the claim that religion emerges out of the "longing of the spirit that the facts of existence should find their justification in the nature of existence."[41] Fuller connects Viktor E. Frankl's *will to meaning* to this ethical-moral proclivity of the human spirit, with its inherent religious dynamics, and demonstrates how this process is the vital driver of Fowler's universalizing quality of the mature adult.[42] Fuller concludes cogently with a set of summary observations. Humans encounter limit experiences regularly throughout life. When we do, the dynamics of ego psychology are inadequate to center our personalities. We are driven to seek our genuine selfhood in a world that is above or beyond the material and historical. That implies an intimation of a world of reality out there, beyond those two boundaries. In old age, when we face impending death, the import of this becomes increasingly urgent.

Throughout life, we are challenged to trust our paradigm transitions by trusting God and the universe. As we begin to consider our demise, our scope of thought and trust must expand to take in the wholeness of life and eternity. If we are to feel that our lives have integrity, we must be able to believe that the entire matrix of time and eternity has coherence and integrity; that is, it is meaningful and real, or genuine. What we have accomplished with our lives is important, but whether it has any intrinsic meaning in the face of eternity is the useful question to which we seek the answer as we age.

That is not so much a scientific or ethical issue as a religious or spiritual one. Science cannot tell us much about the intrinsic character and integrity of existence.[43]

> The religiosity of this stage must go well beyond the beliefs and doctrines of the churches because it must accept the doubts and frailties humans have when they so starkly face life's greatest trauma. Wisdom emerges as these doubts have been fully admitted and accepted even while continuing to affirm the intrinsic meaningfulness of life in all of its human ambiguities.[44]

True maturity can finally arrive in the stage from 60 to death, and transcendent religious insight and formative worldview ideas are the crucial maturing dynamic of this old age. This ultimate maturity and self-actualization means the achievement of (1) *detachment,* "the refusal to confuse the quality of our being with the quantity of our having"; (2) *hope,* emotional strength and desire to look forward continually, despite the adversities of life and the certainty of death, with the confidence "that there is a will or power central to the universe that is receptive toward our efforts, and will in the end, bestow wholeness upon our lives"; (3) *humor,* the ability to preserve integrity amid incalculable loss of loved ones and of life; and (4) *vision,* the ability to see "beyond the limit or boundary of the finite self and disclose a supersensible reality that envelops or surrounds the physical." This is a vision that shifts the focus of our selfhood from the material to the spiritual, from the physical to the metaphysical, and "from the finite to the infinite; . . . this vision gradually 'invites us to a total, selfless surrender in which the distinction between life and death slowly loses its pain.'"[45]

Elizabeth Kubler-Ross emphasized that the person with intrinsic faith has relative ease in accepting death. In her interviews of aging people, she found acceptance of death long before those persons faced serious illness. Their firsthand faith had long since brought them to the point of identifying their intrinsic self with their spiritual dimension. They conceived of themselves as a soul that had a body, rather than a body that had a soul. Their acceptance of death was a function of their vision of light beyond the end of the tunnel, so to speak. Death did not look to them like a final barrier, but like a kind of healing release from a body of decreasing use and value. Death confronts us in a way that discloses a limit dimension of life that can be handled best by learning to identify ourselves with a supersensible reality beyond the limits of our finite personalities.[46]

In the light of all this, it is obviously not possible for us to consider the full scope of our life span authentically without noting how central is the religious character of life's most crucial and profound developmental challenges and the spiritual understandings that empower us to meet them. The hunger of our hearts is for God. Moreover, it is the significant emotional events of life that occur at the limits or boundaries of our growth stages or paradigms that are crucial in making the spiritual forces needed and effective.

THE CENTRAL CLAIM

The unfolding of the Christian self is a precarious and enchanting thing to see in others and to experience in ourselves. It is a mystifying, though not particularly mysterious, process of growth and development, as we have begun to see. It includes the entire person, body, mind, and spirit. It always drives toward perfection in the sense of wholeness or completeness of personhood. It has mainly to do, however, with the spirit, that is, with those aspects of our persons to which we usually refer with such terms as *spirituality* and *psychology* because things of the spirit have always to do with our sense of meaning and understanding.

Undoubtedly, we should learn more and more to see the psychology and spirituality of human persons as involving the same domain or operation of the human spirit. The two terms should likely be interchangeable, each encompassing all of what we have historically meant by both. Surely this is the biblical way of referring to and dealing with the functions of the psyche.

The development of the psyche, in all of its aspects, is mystifying in the sense that it is so wonderfully distinctive in each individual human that it is never possible to predict just how the world of the inner person will take its shape for each of us. On the other hand, the process is hardly mysterious. We know a very great deal about it, particularly in terms of the history of psychological research. We can, in fact, predict a great deal about the patterns our development will take and the behavior individual persons will manifest at various ages and stages of the unfolding. These predictable patterns are present in the growth we customarily call spiritual as well as that which is referred to generally as psychological.

Therefore it is the claim of this chapter that the dynamics at work in our spiritual transitions and in our significant emotional events are approximately as follows: when a person experiences a significant new life-shaping insight, relationship, trauma, or meaning challenge, that event experience cuts down through all the structures and defense processes of our personality structure or developmental formation and reaches all the way down to the characterological level. There, at that level, the cognitive, psychosocial, and moral-spiritual content of the significant emotional event or the challenging limit experience produces a paradigm shift in the values and belief system we have previously formed. The assumptions, commitments, loves, values, and beliefs that have prevailed until then are changed by the new insight, relationship, or trauma. These structures, which heretofore functioned as the ground of our being and our integrating perspective, are now all illumined in a new way with the new light of the new significant event of the psyche.

As in the shift of the visual pattern in a kaleidoscope, as one turns the barrel a few degrees, so also at the value and belief level of the psyche, the shift in experience produces an alteration in the paradigm and a significantly modified system of valuing and believing. The change does not alter the inherent nature of the crystals in the kaleidoscope nor the inherent nature of personality dynamics. The person, gender, and mood may remain essentially the same in a person. But while everything is essentially the same, everything, nevertheless, is wholly different—seen in a different light, from a different perspective, forming a different sense of truth and reality. The person has experienced a conversion.

RELIGIOUS CONVERSION

Authentic religious conversion is a life-changing significant emotional event, provoked by arriving at a paradigm boundary and its limit experience. It is produced by the impact of a new insight, relationship, or trauma. It involves a new personal *relationship* with God, as the God of unconditional, radical, and universal grace. For Christians, this experience usually includes a new sense of the meaning of the person and work of Jesus Christ in the world. The converting forces include a new *insight* regarding the truth about God and oneself. It often includes the trauma of facing a new world of moral claim and vocational destiny.

Sometimes conversion starts in trauma—moral, physical, or psychological—and then moves through new insight to a new relationship. At other times, it starts with a new sense of relationship with God, often mediated through a new quality of relationship with another human, and then moves on to new insight and the trauma of a revision of one's personality. At still other times, it starts in new insights and grows to include the other two factors. Sometimes it takes place mainly on only one of the three levels.

In any case, Christian conversion is psychodynamically and sociodynamically like any other conversion and can be accounted for wholly as a significant emotional event of the psyche in terms of standard psychosocial models, such as those we have discussed. Humans are converted from other faiths and from the lack of any faith at all. People are likewise converted from Christian faith to other faiths or to atheism and agnosticism. Humans are sometimes converted from hope to hopelessness, cynicism, or existential despair, and vice versa. During the last half century, conversions in all these directions, and many others, have been a common event.

The crucial insight here is that all these shifts are the same kind of psychodynamic and spiritual event. The key differences are differences in the content of the insight, relationship, or trauma—the content of the conversion. Sometimes the conversion experience is of such a sort that the paradigm shift constitutes a new integration of the person's nature in terms of God and his grace, particularly revealed in Jesus Christ. That is Christian conversion, and we correctly speak of it as redemptive since it can be demonstrated empirically that such conversion, when it is not distorted by psychopathology, frees, heals, motivates, renews, and embellishes human life.

If, on the other hand, it is Christian conversion that is so poorly worked out in a personality fraught with psychological illness, as we sometimes see, the so-called conversion experience may well enlarge neurotic guilt and compulsivity, exaggerating anxiety and social dysfunction and deepening narcissism, with its manipulative egotism. That is hardly a Christian conversion, and surely not redemptive, even if the person's confession is profusely about God and Jesus Christ. Spiritual crisis may worsen mental illness, rather than improve it.

Other conversions can also be redemptive: from fascism to humanitarianism, for example. Or other conversions can be sick: from benign American civil religion to obsessive addiction to a cult, with its arbitrary authority figure and enslaving structure. The content of the conversion and the direction of the psychological and spiritual reintegration of the personality of the converted person makes all the difference regarding its health and usefulness. Any given conversion may be Christian, non-Christian, anti-Christian, or have nothing whatsoever to do with Christianity. Each of us experiences a conversion every time we reach a limiting boundary in the life paradigm in which we are working and need to expand our world of insight and experience to make room for our expanding values and beliefs. Each time we move from one stage in the life cycle to the next, we are converted and reintegrated, with more or less efficiency.

Fundamentalist conversions, in any religion, tend to lead the convert to a more structured system of legalist ethics, a rigid belief system, and a value system emphasizing worthiness and affirmation based on achievement, obedience, conformity, dogma, and self-justifying strategies. Such conversions are self-defeating and psychologically sick, and they frequently make people mentally ill. Conversions may take place suddenly or in a growth process over considerable time. What distinguishes one conversion from another is its content, not its dynamic. The process of all true conversions is a psychosocial process, accountable wholly in psychological and sociological terms.

This is a critical point for numerous reasons. First, it compels all humans to recognize that we take the position, perspective, or commitment we hold in life because of the initial faith assumptions that underlie our worldview and hence our behavior. Second, it compels us to recognize that such a perspective is held for psychodynamic reasons, not merely for rational, supernatural, theological, or cultural reasons. Third, it compels us all to acknowledge that the psychodynamics that impel us spiritually as well as in every other way form a growth continuum that we can condition in important ways by the insights we seek, the relationships to which we give ourselves, and the trauma to which we are willing to open ourselves without denial or repression. Fourth, it compels us to recognize that the growth continuum runs through a structured matrix of psychosocial growth stages, no matter what we do, which shape our destiny by the providence of God. Fifth, it compels us to insure that the content and conditions of that growth continuum, matrix, and process in the lives of those for whom we have responsibility in home or clinic are profoundly fraught with the good news and personal manifestation of God's healing grace.

Sixth, it compels us to remember that when pathology appears in Christian life, we must look for its sources in psychosocial factors. Seventh, it compels us to reject the supernaturalizing of conversion, typical of some literalist Christians, self-defeating as it is in its three main implications: (1) that spirituality is somewhat apart from and different than ordinary life, (2) that the spiritual world is antipathetic to the natural world, and (3) that being God's people means being a little strange, culturally, socially, and spiritually. Eighth, it compels us to remember that God's world is one world and comprehends all processes together as a unity and not schizophrenically, that the whole process is natural and not supernatural, and that God's preferred modus operandi throughout history, in nature and in grace, has always been to use the established forces of his natural processes for all things. Thus the taste of salt and its chemical reasons, the falling leaf and its gravitational guide, the physics of snowflake crystals or the formation of coal are all as supernatural as the work of the Holy Spirit is supernatural. To put it the other way around, the work of the Holy Spirit, the processes of Christian conversion, and the forces operative in our transforming moments are no more supernatural than the formation of coal under the physiochemical laws of hydrocarbons under pressure. All are natural, moved by forces natural to the experience of humans. Only on that view will we have the motivation and creativity to fashion the models for understanding what happens to persons in conversion and therefore how to enhance that process for healing growth, an undertaking to which religious institutions continue to give so much time and treasure in such apparently naive ways, and about which psychologists continue to be so ignorant and ambivalent. Ninth, it compels us to eradicate all remnants of suspicion about the authenticity or quality of each other's conversions because they differ from our own in event or process.

Benedict J. Groeschel has provided an interesting model of spirituality conceived from the perspective of the contemplative monastic ideal.[47] He appreciates appropriately the essential psychodynamic drivers of spiritual growth. He notes that we move under the urges of anxiety on one hand, and the lust for peace and freedom, on the other. We move through three phases, purgative, illuminative, and unitive; and on two levels, faith and practical life experience. He notes that the further we move toward the unitive phase of maturity, namely, unity with self and God in contemplation, the more we achieve a reintegration of personality and personhood through a progressive conversion process with the same essential dynamics as were indicated previously for the significant emotional event.

This is, I sense, also the primary manner in which Fowler sees conversion functioning within the structuralist paradigm. However, conversion to a new style of faith and life is experienced in all manner and forms imaginable. They range from the process of a general structuralist psychosocial growth over a lifetime within a believing community, on one hand, to sudden life-altering events, on the other.[48] All forms function in essentially the same psychodynamic way, with essentially the same psychosocial and spiritual outcomes.

Fowler and Fuller, particularly, help us to appreciate the ideal ultimate outcome of the growth event or process of Christian conversion. True conversion leads to the universalizing stage when we are able to embrace all in the joy and freedom of realizing that all are embraced by God in his universal grace and redemptive love.

CONCLUSION

As we have seen, there is a broad stream of literature in pastoral psychology and Christian education as well as in transcendental and structuralist psychology that relates directly and deeply with the thesis and argument of this chapter. Fuller's understanding of the crucial role of spirituality in human psychological growth and Fowler's perspective on the nature of faith are among the most important insights available regarding the function of our perception of God in the unfolding of our Christian self.

Fowler's concept of faith is wider and deeper than just religious content or context. It exceeds the bounds of theological commitment or belief:

Faith is a person's or group's way of moving into the force field of life. It is our way of finding coherence in and giving meaning to the multiple forces and relations that make up our lives. Faith is a person's way of seeing himself or herself in relation to others against a background of shared meaning and purpose. . . . Prior to our being religious or irreligious, before we come to think of ourselves as Catholics, Protestants, Jews or Muslims, we are already engaged with issues of faith. Whether we become nonbelievers, agnostics or atheists, we are concerned with how to put our lives together and with what will make life worth living. Moreover, we look for something to love that loves us, something to value that gives us value, something to honor and respect that has the power to sustain our being.[49]

With Wilfred Cantwell Smith, Fowler insists that words such as *religious* or *belief* refer to the cumulative traditions societies collect from the faith of people of the past.[50] If *religious* and *belief* refer to those cumulative traditions, then perhaps *spiritual* and *spirituality* might more correctly be used to refer to Fowler's definition of faith or the capacity and experience in humans from which faith springs. Faith is the inner human dynamic that reaches for meaning. Religion is the cumulative fruit of the history of past expressions of that inner dynamic as it was experienced, formulated, and testified to by our antecedents, and which history we recapitulate in traditions of doctrine, liturgy, perspective, and practice.

Without question, the faith perspective of Smith and Fowler can be clearly seen as the backdrop to Fuller's understanding of faith as the meaning insights that modify our worldview and make successful coping and growth possible, especially at those crisis points when we stand before the affective and conceptual limits of our experience and need a personal inner vision that leads us beyond ourselves and our world of understanding to the More, to the Beyond: to God. In this view, faith and religion are reciprocal. Each grows and is dynamically vitalized by interaction with the other. Each generation makes its contribution to shaping the cumulative tradition, as it in turn focuses and sharpens the faith experience of the new generation. The tradition awakens faith in a person, and that person's unique expression of it extends and modifies the tradition.

Fuller agrees and thinks that what marks religion off as different from philosophy, psychology, or sociology as an inspiration and pathway to human maturation is its outlook on the sacred as "the principle sphere to which humans ought to adapt themselves. . . . Human fulfillment cannot be understood totally in terms of our ability to adapt successfully to the social and economic spheres of life."[51] The life cycle develops in a context of moral and metaphysical considerations, so living life must take seriously the religious "hypothesis that, in the final analysis, wholeness is dependent upon the degree to which we can locate our lives within a wider spiritual environment."[52] Religious symbology, in the form of doctrinal systems, confessional documents, or personal formulations of belief, can be empirically demonstrated to enhance human negotiation of the limit experiences of life. Effectiveness in that process is clearly essential to maturation and wholeness.

The communities of believers, throughout history, have called humanity to face the crises of our limit experiences at each stage of life with the faith response of conversion.[53] The Bible itself poses the challenge of metanoia, conversion, a change of mind. *Conversion* is a good term for the remarkable moments, events, or processes we encounter, those significant changes of mind and worldview that occur when we are at the boundary of our growth in any given state and must enlarge our framework of insight and understanding to take in and integrate the expanding volumes of truth that are bearing in on us as we grow. To mature from one stage to the next, we must be converted; that is, we must be awakened to a new dimension of faith in or experience of a transcendent vision that enlarges our paradigm, revises and expands our worldview, and reintegrates our selves and our experience within a new framework of conviction and perspective. When we reach the limit experiences that challenge us to this conversion, and then resist the demands of the new and expanded vision of truth, faith, or perspective, we regress and entrench ourselves in the immature worldview of the previous stage of our development. Usually, we then proceed to idealize that retarded outlook or formulation with dogmatism.

It seems clear, then, that what really happens in conversion is this: at a crucial and formative moment in a transition through the psychological stages of structural development, a person experiences the impact of a profound new insight, relationship, or trauma. This impact cuts down through the defensive structures of our personality, through the conceptual framework of our worldview, through the formative coping patterns that have shaped our nature and function, and disturbs, reorders, and reintegrates our values and belief systems at our characterological level. This reintegration takes its shape around the new insight, relationship, or traumatic force we have experienced at that boundary or limit event.

As we are cracked open by new insights of truth or relationships with others and with God, particularly in those times that we are at our wit's end, at the boundaries of our prevailing stage of development, we are available for the leaps of growth that faith affords and that bring us into our next stage of development. Those are the moments when we know beyond proof the truth beyond the data, that our souls are restless until they rest in God and in his incomparable grace—and that we cannot sin ourselves out of his grace nor squirm out of his long embrace.

NOTES

1. J. Piaget (1967), *Six Psychological Studies*, New York: Random House; J. Piaget (1969), *The Psychology of the Child*, New York: Random House; J. Piaget (1977), *The Development of Thought: Equilibration of Cognitive Structures*, trans. A. Rosin, New York: Viking. See also Mary Stewart van Leeuwen (1983), *The Sorcerer's Apprentice*, Grand Rapids, MI: Baker; Van Leeuwen (1985), *The Person in Psychology: A Contemporary Christian Appraisal*, Grand Rapids, MI: Eerdmans.

2. L. Kohlberg (1963), "Development of Children's Orientation toward a Moral Order," *Vita Humana* 6, 11–16; Kohlberg (1973), "Continuities in Childhood and Adult Moral Development Revisited," in *Lifespan Developmental Psychology: Personality and Socialization*, ed. P. Baltes and K. Shaic, New York: Academic Press, 202; Kohlberg (1974), "Education, Moral Development and Faith," *Journal of Moral Education* 4(1), 5–16; Kohlberg (1976), "Moral Stages and Moralization," in *Moral Development and Behavior: Theory, Research, and Social Issues*, ed. T. Likona, New York: Holt, Rinehart Winston.

3. Erik H. Erikson (1980), *Identity and the Life Cycle*, New York: W. W. Norton; Erikson (1963), *Childhood and Society*, 2nd ed., New York: W. W. Norton; Erikson (1982), *The Life Cycle Completed: A Review*, New York: W. W. Norton.

4. James W. Fowler (1976), "Faith Development Theory and the Aims of Religious Socialization," in *Emerging Issues in Religious Education*, ed. G. Durka and J. Smith, New York: Paulist; Fowler (1980), "Moral Stages and the Development of Faith," in *Moral Development, Moral Education, and Kohlberg: Basic Issues in Philosophy, Psychology, Religion, and Education*, ed. B. Munsey, Birmingham, AL: Religious Education Press; Fowler (1981), *Stages of Faith: The Psychology of Human Development and the Quest for Meaning*, San Francisco: Harper and Row; Fowler (1984), *Becoming Adult, Becoming Christian: Adult Development and Christian Faith*, San Francisco: Harper and Row.

5. Morris Massey (1972), *What You Are Is Where You Were When*, Series on Life Cycle Development, videotape, Boulder: University of Colorado.

6. James E. Loder (1981), *The Transforming Moment*, New York: Harper.

7. Fowler, *Stages of Faith*.

8. John Westerhof (1976), *Will Our Children Have Faith?*, New York: Seabury.

9. D. M. Joy (1983), *Moral Development Foundations: Judeo-Christian Alternatives to Piaget/Kohlberg*, Nashville, TN: Abingdon.

10. Fowler, *Stages of Faith*, 290–91.

11. Massey, *What You Are*.

12. Robert C. Fuller (1988), *Religion and the Life Cycle*, Philadelphia: Fortress.

13. Ibid., 5.

14. Ibid., 7.

15. David Tracy (1975), *Blessed Rage for Order: The New Pluralism in Theology*, New York: Seabury.

16. Fuller, *Religion*, 10.

17. Ibid., 11.

18. William James (1956), *The Will to Believe*, New York: Dove; James (1958), *Varieties of Religious Experience*, New York: Morrow. See also Fuller, *Religion*, 11.

19. Fuller, *Religion*, 11.

20. Ibid., 12.

21. Ibid.

22. Ibid., 12–13.

23. Ibid., 17.

24. Ibid.

25. Ibid.

26. Ibid.

27. Ibid., 19–23.

28. Ibid., 23–24.

29. Ibid., 25.

30. Ibid., 33.

31. Ibid., 38.

32. As quoted ibid., 38–39.

33. Ibid.

34. Ibid., 45.

35. Ibid., 46.

36. Ibid.

37. Gordon W. Allport (1937), *Personality: A Psychological Interpretation*, New York: Henry Holt; Allport (1950), *The Individual and His Religion: A Psychological Interpretation*, New York: Macmillan; Allport (1960), *Personality and Social Encounter:*

Selected Essays, Boston: Beacon; Allport (1961), *Pattern and Growth in Personality*, New York: Holt, Rinehart, Winston.

38. Fuller, *Religion*, 66.

39. James, *Will to Believe*, 212.

40. Ibid., 13.

41. As quoted in Fuller, *Religion*, 67. E. E. Whitehead and J. D. Whitehead (1984), *Seasons of Strength: New Visions of Adult Christian Maturing*, Garden City, NJ: Doubleday Image. See also D. J. Levenson (1978), "The Anatomy of the Life Cycle," *Psychiatric Opinion* 15, 29–48, and Levenson (1978), *The Seasons of a Man's Life*, New York: Knopf. See also Gail Sheehy (1976), *Passages: Predictable Crises of Adult Life*, New York: Dutton.

42. Victor E. Frankl (1962), *Man's Search for Meaning: An Introduction to Logotherapy*, Boston: Beacon; Frankl (1975), *The Unconscious God: Psychotherapy and Theology*, New York: Simon and Schuster.

43. Fuller, *Religion*, 72–73.

44. Ibid., 78.

45. Henri Nouwen and Walter Gaffney (1976), *Aging: The Fulfillment of Life*, Garden City, NJ: Image, 36. See also Fuller, *Religion*, 81–82.

46. Elizabeth Kubler-Ross (1969), *On Death and Dying*, New York: Macmillan.

47. B. J. Groeschel (1984), *Spiritual Passages: The Psychology of Spiritual Development "for Those Who Seek,"* New York: Crossroad.

48. Hugh T. Kerr and John M. Mulder (1983), *Conversions: The Christian Experience*, Grand Rapids, MI: Eerdmans.

49. Fowler, *Stages of Faith*, 4, 5.

50. Wilfred C. Smith (1963), *The Meaning and End of Religion: A New Approach to the Religious Traditions of Mankind*, New York: Macmillan.

51. Fuller, *Religion*, 117.

52. Ibid., 149.

53. J. Harold Ellens (1988), "The Psychodynamics of Christian Conversion," in *The Church and Pastoral Care*, ed. L. Aden and J. H. Ellens, Grand Rapids, MI: Baker.

CHAPTER 7

COMMUNICATION AS PSYCHOLOGICAL HEALING

A lady entered my clinic one day and said to me, "I want to divorce my husband." I asked her, "Do you have grounds?" "Oh, yes," she replied, "we have 40 acres, but it is held in both our names, so we each automatically get half of it." "That is not exactly what I meant to ask," I carefully parried. "I mean, do you have a grudge?" Confidently, she responded, "We have a two-car garage, large enough for both of our vehicles, and we have never really had any misunderstanding about that." I tried again: "Madam, what I am trying to get at is this: does he beat you up, or anything like that?" "No," she said, "I get up an hour before him every morning. I serve him a nice warm breakfast, pack his lunch, and send him off to work with plenty of time to spare. He has always really appreciated that." Desperately holding myself together, I asked her evenly, "Well, then, for heaven's sake, why do you want to get a divorce?" "Because we have this terrible communication problem," she declared. "You simply cannot carry on a sensible conversation with that man!"

Language is likely the loveliest likeness of humans to God. Our ability to communicate is certainly the most glorious expression of our human nature and of God's image in us. But as we discover early in life, it is also complex and problematic. Three of its crucial elements in communal relations are its psychological dynamics, its theoretical complexities, and the inefficiency of its process in daily life, psychotherapy, and caring relationships. One of the surest ways of making certain that communication fails, and its failure obstructs human growth, is to assume that it is happening and give no thought, energy, or conscious intentionality to causing it to happen well.

A SIMPLE COMMUNICATION MODEL

A simple model describes the complexity of the psychological process of communication and learning. When a person wishes to express something in words to another person, that process begins deep in the unconscious of the sending person. The message begins as an emotional sensation in the sender's psyche, and it must be raised to the conscious cognitive level before even the sender knows what message he or she wishes to communicate. If the sender is able to raise that emotion to the cognitive thought level, the sensation can be turned into a concept. That transition is crucial and precarious because it is possible for the communication process to fail right at that point. Sometimes we just cannot think out clearly what we are feeling and would like the other person to feel, as well.

If the sender succeeds in turning the original emotion into a thought, it becomes possible to cross the next transition point, namely, changing the thought into words. Sometimes we think things out in words immediately on feeling the feelings. However, there are moments when we think in graphic pictures instead of words. Then we must not only change the feeling into concepts and sentences, but we must turn the pictures in our mind into verbal expressions. It is easy to see how the communication we originally intended can get watered down or changed or decreased at this stage of moving from concepts to words in sentences.

The next step in communication is verbalizing the sentences we have created in our minds. We may do that by writing them or speaking them. If we are very shy or dyslexic, unaccustomed to speaking in public, or fearful of intimate relationships, we may find ourselves having difficulty expressing our own thoughts and sentences. Usually, people need to learn how to do that well. It is important to recognize how easily communication between two people, even if they are close friends, can break down before the receiver has heard the message of the sender. Each transition from feeling to thought, from thought to words, and from sentences in the mind to sentences expressed verbally is a point in the communication process at which the entire thing can fail completely or get very distorted from what the sender really wants to get across.

The next issue in communication is the choice of language. I was a soldier for many years. Having been born in Michigan, I was surprised when assigned to Ft. Smith, Arkansas, that I could not understand the language of the fine educated Americans I met there in restaurants and on the street. Their way of expressing the vowels of the English language, and the interesting synonyms in their local dialect for words that are standard in the upper Midwest, was so strange to my ear that I just could not understand their conversation. The choice and nature of the language used as the channel over which to send the message the sender wants the receiver to experience is crucial. If the two persons in conversation only know completely different languages, such as my English and Petrov's Russian, communication is sure to break down completely at the point at which we begin to put our thoughts into words and those words' sentences into the language communication channel. We are going to be using two different language channels that do not connect. We must have a mutually understood language channel to communicate well.

Communication begins with a felt need on the affective or gut level, making the sender aware of the sensation the sender desires to share with the receiver. Raised to the thought level and embellished with feedback from one's memory bank of past ideas and experiences, it is ready for broadcasting in words. The verbal channel will then make all the difference in the world. Turning thoughts into words is a little like loading freight onto train cars. We use words as freight cars. They have their own form, shape, sound, and appearance in print, but we decide together what freight they can appropriately carry. What we decide to load on any given word is quite arbitrarily determined, and the word succeeds in carrying that particular freight only because we have agreed on the meaning freight any given verbal symbol is to carry. There is nothing inherent to the sound or structure of a word that has to do with its meaning, except in rare cases, when the sound of a word suggests the sense of it, as in words like *thump, splash,* or *sizzle.*

So we load meaning on words, and they are connected in a train of thought and verbal expression that we can then express in sentences and paragraphs. Then they are sent down the way to another person, whom we hope will unload the meaning freight as we loaded it. If he or she speaks German and I am speaking Russian, the trains are on two different tracks, the communication is going down two different channels, and the communication will not connect. The relationship will fail. This receiver will be unable to unload the meaning freight.

If, however, the train we load with meaning freight is operating in the same channel or on the same track as that of the receiver, it will arrive at his or her cognitive station, so to speak, at which that receiving person must unload the freight from the train of words we have expressed. Only then can the receiver experience a communication from us and have the treasury of thought and feeling the sender wished to convey. If we have a congenial receiver, our hearer will likely unload our meaning and internalize it as a thought, comparable to the cognitive concept that we, as sender, formulated in the first place. The more collegial, that is, the more of an intellectual and spiritual peer the receiver is to the sender, the more likely the meaning freight unloaded will be quite the same as that which the sender loaded on the sentence train initially. The cognitive concept in the mind and psyche of the receiver will be very much the same as that in the mind and psyche of the sender. It is easy to see how important this process is to the effect we have on each other, particularly on those persons whose growth we influence in the movement from one stage of the life cycle to the next.

As the receiving person unloads the meaning freight from the sender's train of thought and word, and then internalizes that thought or cognitive concept as a feeling sensation at the affective or emotional level, the receiver will have the chance to share the original feeling that prompted the sender to communication at the outset. This internalization will, of course, be embellished in turn by the past learning, experience, and memory of the receiver. As the internalization process succeeds, the thought may be reflected on in terms of the hearer's memory, learning, and experience, and then referred to his or her feeling world. The internal feedback loop within the mind and psyche, within the memory and thought system, of both the sender and receiver is obviously actively involved in this entire process of communication and mutual understanding.

How important is communication to psychological health, growth, life change, learning, and real relationship! How precarious are all the points of transition, on the side of both the sender and the receiver, at which the communication may break down and the relationship fail! The meaning freight unloaded may be incomplete or damaged in comparison with that which was loaded. The intent of the sender may thus be different than the perception of the receiver. If either has a biased intent, uncongenial or offensive to the other, the meaning freight will be damaged because it is being fitted into a framework that does not fit its original shape. If both have a good spirit and good will toward each other and toward the ideas shared, there is a high likelihood of effective communication and psychological as well as intellectual connection.

At this point in the relationship, the receiver is likely to become the sender, replying to the initial message. The entire precarious process begins all over again. In the exchange, both persons are busy testing the environment for signs and signals that might add to the meaning of the communication. Both are looking for body language and facial expressions or gestures that confirm or contradict the verbal messages exchanged. Moreover, both also note other environmental factors that affect relationship, making communication more difficult for one or the other; for example, if there is a great amount of noise or distraction in the setting in which the two are communicating, the receiver in each case will unconsciously tend to compensate for the disturbance in the way he or she discerns the meaning of the sender's expressions. A mother holding a squirming and bawling child may be trying to tell you that she loves you deeply, but her communication is going to be severely strained and distracted. You will need to take the distraction into consideration to discern her real affective and verbal intent in expressing herself to you. We usually make those accommodations without needing to really think about it consciously.

At each transition point from the initial feeling to thought, thought to verbalization, verbalization to expression, expression to decoding, decoding to coherent perception of the intended thought, and internalization of the concept received to affective sensation, there is an enormous potential for breakdown. Sometimes we simply cannot get our feelings precisely into words, and sometimes we do not even understand our feelings precisely. So, too, it is similarly true inversely, in receiving another person's thoughts and feelings. Moreover, when we increase the pressure of authority, threat, time constraint, or anxiety, we inversely affect, that is, we decrease, efficient communication.

CONTEXT COUNTS

Effective communication depends very much on a common ground of experience, a common universe of discourse, and a mutuality of orientation between communicating persons. It is important in relationship building and in life conversion transitions that persons involved have as broad a breadth of personality as possible. In each of us is what might be called a pre-self. It is made up of all those components that are inherent in us before we become relating persons. These factors include our genetics, our memory, our cultural setting, and our mother tongue as well as our emotional and biophysical predispositions. We acquire a specific sense of our selfhood through using these inherent components as the basis of our growth, socialization, psychological formation, and life cycle transitions. Thereby we achieve a conscious and intentional emotional and intellectual formation and function.

It is clear, in this model, that our personal history, from conception to cognitive awareness at about age six or seven, is remarkably important and formative. Together with our ongoing formal education, it determines the breadth of our personality. When we encounter another person, our potential for effective communication with him or her is determined by the scope of our communication potential encounter front. The scope of the front is determined by how broadly developed is each of our personalities. The greater the breadth in the growth and development of each of us, the wider the scope of overlap between our understandings, interests, and perceptions. The broader each of our scopes in emotional and intellectual maturity, the more we have to share, and the wider the front of our real encounter, that is, the wider the degree of history and experience overlapping in our potential for effectively communicating and really connecting.[1]

The broader the scope of each person's knowledge, skills, native abilities, maturity, congeniality, and outlook, the greater the range of overlap they share. As persons share in dialogue, they expand each other's resource base and hence expand the scope of the communication front they share. Psychological analysis of human communication reveals that one of the intriguing things that endangers interpersonal communication efficiency and complicates relationship is the difference between the two human brain hemispheres. Some of us are mainly left brain–dominant, others primarily right brain–dominant.

Left brain–dominant persons process the meaning that they derive from life experience primarily through their left brain. That side of the brain functions largely in terms of linear logic, mathematical conceptualization of insight, computer-like thought processes, structured intellectual precision, attention to detail, problem solving, and movement always toward the bottom line of any situation. Right brain–dominant persons process the meaning life offers them through the right brain, primarily. Right brain function has to do more prominently with emotional ways of experiencing life and knowing meaning, emphasizing the perceptive value of color, texture, form, gestalts of experience or insight, and the pleasure of a process, rather than the achievement of a solution.

Women are 70 percent right brain–dominant, and men are 70 percent left brain–dominant. The rest of us have approximately equal function in both hemispheres. Those with fairly high function in both hemispheres negotiate more effectively the precarious points at which human communication can potentially break down and so tend to contribute in a highly efficient way to high-quality relationships. The corollary of this proficiency is that these persons also negotiate the life cycle transitions much more effectively, expanding their paradigms more readily than others, as they come to the limit experiences of life. Such folk, consequently, are less likely to be psychologically retarded or find themselves inclined to arrest their development in a premature state of life cycle progress. For example, left brain–dominant persons may arrest their psychological and spiritual development at the adolescent stage because they are rigid and not readily able to embrace a broader and more universalizing paradigm of thought or worldview. They remain dogmatic and self-assured in a fundamentalistic outlook, without enough imagination to perceive that truth, particularly God's truth, requires a wider worldview. Fear constricts them to familiar bottom-line solutions or propositions that pass for truth with them.

Comparably, right brain–dominant persons may have difficulty in stepping outside of their emotional world of perception to get an objective view of things. Consequently, they may tend to wallow in emotional, sentimental, familiar, antique, and childhood memories, feeling secure and cozy in that undisturbed psychological matrix. They may therefore resist crossing boundaries and moving into challenging new experiences, avoiding exploration of new ideas or courses of action. Thus they may achieve the independence of young adulthood but remain in the group-think of their clan or community, and when pressed about it or challenged by some new need to adapt to change, they may regress to adolescent dogmatism and entrench themselves in what is traditional and apparently safe, even when it proves to be dysfunctional in their life situation.

The likelihood is very small that a right brain–dominant person will be able to internalize precisely the same affective sensation from a verbal concept as the left brain–dominant person who sent the message and felt the feeling that prompted it. Marrying an opposite may not be impossible, but it creates a lifelong challenge. Two such people simply experience life and reality in quite different manners. Neither is better than the other; they are merely different. In meeting some of the challenges of life and responsibility for growth in the life cycle, one may work better; in meeting other challenges in life, the other may be more effective. They are simply different. Right-brained nurturing and emotion is much more effective in keeping an infant alive and healthy than in fixing the faucet, though both are important. Left-brained planning to find the money to send that child to college as a late adolescent or young adult is more important than making sure the kid is always comfortable and cozy. Both are necessary. They are, nonetheless, remarkably different. If I ask a left-brain patient to look at the wall of my study, covered with books, and tell me what he sees, he will likely reply, "I see shelves of books, seven shelves high and three sections wide, that contain books of various sizes arranged alphabetically by author within the subject categories running alphabetically from political science through psychology and on to natural science and theology." If, however, I ask a right-brain patient the same question, he will probably respond, "I see a colorful array of objects, obviously books, arranged in interesting patterns of sizes, shapes, and colors, forming a lovely wall and exuding a feeling of warm coziness, pleasant security, and reassuring homeyness." The former patient will want the church to provide worship services that predominate in heady theological thought and logical argument. The latter will want worship that fits together in rewarding and reassuring patterns of celebration: feelings and progressions of praise, prayerful reflection, and consolation—the expressions that feed and cathart the deep needs of the psyche.

THE NOETIC CONTINUUM OF MATURATION

It is important to point out here that for both right- and left-brain persons, the issue is psychological. For the left-brain person, logic affords security and satisfaction, while for the right-brain person, relationships and emotional events afford that security. It is possible to illustrate graphically the progression through which human psychological forces drive our felt needs, insights, concepts, expressions, style, and achievement of meaning in life's experiences and growth. We start out life with enormous psychological needs. Born scared, we all begin with deep psychological needs to come to terms with the meaning of our early experience of coming down the birth canal and landing in a wholly alien world over which we have no control and in which we are completely helpless. All humans begin, thus, with considerable primal anxiety, sensations of loss of the security of the womb, and a sense of being alienated from everything that could insure our safety, security, and comfort.

The rest of our 80–90 years of life is devoted completely to the endeavor of reducing our anxiety by increasing our control over our environment. An apparently natural process develops out of this early reach for security in the form of projected notions about a superior person who has the power to make us secure. Perhaps this starts with the image of the all knowing, all powerful, and all caring parent who is looking after us. However, this notion of security in relationship with a superior person readily translates into projections of a God concept, into which we integrate the perceptions about God that life brings to us or that we are taught. These projections may be shaped by the sense that we live before the face of a cosmic threat or that we stand on secure ground with God in the relief of his kind unconditional grace and acceptance. This psychological quest for God has the capacity to provide us a sense of profound trust, security, and, in crisis, the ease of forgiveness and reconciliation. The quality of this sense of security or dis-ease depends on the quality of parenting we experience and the security of our life setting.

As we mature, those theological projections and insights expand to create a complete worldview, and we have landed in philosophy. Philosophy is also a psychological enterprise. Its core has to do with finding ways to universalize the sense of meaning we derive from our specific experiences of threat or security, anxiety or tranquility. We construct our worldview, that is, our sense of how things are in the world of human life, in terms of our sense of security or anxiety. The reason philosophy always seems like a thing of the head (intellect) rather than of the heart (psyche) is because its methods for achieving anxiety reduction and a sense of security involve a resort to rationality and logic. Philosophers pursue the psychological quest of achieving security and anxiety reduction by creating systems of intellectual activity that achieve a certain relatively superficial sense of meaning through rational analysis, and thus give the impression of control through logical categorization. The fruits of philosophy are important for our understanding of ourselves and of life, but while they gratify the mind, they do not make the psyche wholly satisfied. Rationality and a sound orientation is essential for a good life but leaves the psyche hungry for the things of the spirit.

An important derivative of our development as philosophers, however, is the formation of ethical needs and notions. Psychologically, we long for a sense of coherence, authenticity, and clarity in our posture in the world. We seek a proper perception as to how we ought to carry ourselves in life, and this moves us to grow into mature, ethical persons, unless we are psychologically stunted by unfortunate influences, circumstances, or inherited psychological illness. From our ethical principles, we form our moral codes of responsible behavior, conforming to social requirements, doing our duty, seeking a destiny of responsible individuality, and acquiring a creative flexible style of dealing with the unfolding situations and relationships of life.

When this noetic process,[2] that is, the unfolding of the deep psychological mind-set, comes finally to fruitful maturity, it affords an awareness of the aesthetic need that is irrepressible in the human psyche, our psychological longing for beauty. We learn the gratification of celebrating sensitivity, prizing the good, true, and beautiful wherever we find it, and by this means, we develop a transcendent sense of the meaningfulness of all things.

Communication is the matrix in which society functions, in which we progress along the noetic continuum as just described, and in terms of which we endeavor to create communal relationships with those who share our place and quest on that continuum, experiencing reality somewhat in the same manner as we do. When that endeavor succeeds, we are twice blessed: it facilitates our understanding of our own meanings and engenders the bonding of real relationships as we sense others understanding, sharing, and enhancing our meanings.

The significant driver and conditioning force in all this is our psychological needs, not our logic or rationality. Moreover, though we generally think of ourselves as very logical, only 20 percent of the human community scores well on the simplest tests of objective logic, regardless of right or left brain dominance. Moreover, emotionally conditioned inferences function much more prominently in our perception of things and our progress through the phases of the noetic continuum than anything else. Inferences also are a great jeopardy to efficient communication because each of us draws his or her own inferences from a situation, stimulus, or message, based on his or her own private set of experiences, psychological needs, and personal projections. Inferences fill in the data gaps to let us make meaning out of limited information or experience, but they therefore also have the potential to create enormous misperceptions and misunderstandings.

There is an obvious and important reason for this. We are fashioned as persons with a desperate psychological need for reducing our primal and situational anxiety by increasing our sense of meaning. We grasp for it in everything we do or experience. When someone gives us a message, it is usually just part of a whole worldview. To make it of maximum meaning, we immediately set that message in our own context of insight; fill in the information that was not there; build a complete, coherent picture around the minimum data the message contained; and then interpret the other person's communication in terms of the total meaning picture that we have created out of our own imagination, to serve our personal lust for the story to be fully meaningful. So out of our own personal psychological need comes our theological outlook, those formulations and perspectives that best meet the longing to settle our anxiety and afford us security, satisfying our predominant brain preference. Out of our theology, our philosophical worldview is projected, and thence our ethics, morality, and aesthetics.

COMMUNICATION AS PSYCHOTHERAPEUTIC

Some forms of communication help more than others to build efficient interaction with fellow humans, develop communal feelings and shared insights, and enhance progress along the maturing road of the noetic continuum. If communication is to generate psychological health, we must pay attention to the forms and styles that help most in moving us along that path. Two of the greatest tools for doing that are genuine listening and precise articulate expression. Genuine listening is a skill that we acquire only by intentional development, and it depends on our willingness to listen not only to what another is saying, but to hear the emotion that lies beyond the words. That gives us the ability to solicit further expressions of the ideas and feelings cherished and intended by the other person. This solicitous approach may be called *active listening*. It is a process of responding to the other person's communication with affirming words and gestures, remarks that invite further comment and elaboration and contributions that expand the insights of the other in a way congenial and gratifying to both.

We are often surprised and gratified when we fall in with another person who seems to sense our meanings even before we have quite completed our message. At other times, we suffer the agony of conversation with a person who seems to catch on to nothing we mean, even though we elaborate it at great length and in great detail. In any case, the most effective way of improving communication and so creating healing relationships is to develop an exchange of expression and active listening. The word for that is a simple but profound one: dialogue. Achieving effective dialogue is the most important communication goal, tool, and style for ordinary human relationships, the healing relationships of the helping professions such as psychotherapy, and the proclamatory requirements of pastoring.

The Psychology of Pastoral Communication

The primary function of a pastor is that of priestly and prophetic healing. There can be no legitimate escape from the fact that in the final analysis, everything a pastor does, whether Jewish, Christian, or Muslim, that is authentic in terms of his or her office and vocation is effective and valid only in terms of its healing consequences. The criterion most basic to judging effectiveness of preaching, counseling, or pastoral administration is the concrete and practical quality of its healing impact. "Have I communicated with pastoral effect?" is the most necessary and painful question with which the rabbi, minister, and imam must live.

Pastoring is shepherding the anxious, needy, inadequate, guilt-ridden, confused, and restless folk that all humans are. We all are hungering and thirsting for righteousness, consciously or unaware, each in our own private way and style. To be a pastoral person is to aid compassionately the humans in one's own personal world to find a resolution for the emptiness each feels in his or her own soul: the need for the security that comes with belonging in the fellowship of our parenting God and of the community of God's children. To pastor is to help humans perceive that fellowship to be the answer to the hunger for meaning, security, and destiny that drives all of us. To pastor is to assist such persons in discovering these consolations in the unqualified commitment of God to each of us in our own peculiar needs. To pastor is to communicate the meaning of God's affirmation of us all when God says to us, "I will be a God to you and to your children, forever!" (Gen. 12 and 17). That affirmation has no qualifications, no strings attached, no limiting conditions. Pastoring is communicating that grace and thereby the good news to the poor, release to those who are victims of themselves or their world, insight to the blind, liberty to those under duress, and the announcement of the timeliness of God's personal acceptance of all of us needy persons (Luke 4:18–19). To be a pastor is to communicate healing relationality to anxious and anguished humanity. The same is true for a responsible psychotherapist.

Practical Considerations

How does a psychotherapist or a pastor do that? What is the nature, dynamic, method, and character of this healing? Communicate. Listen and articulate. There never was a good substitute for good preaching, profound and vital, or for incisive caring therapy that illuminates the patient with good news. Insight heals. These qualities and forces are irreplaceable in people care. Pastoral and psychotherapeutic communication cultivates insight and incites inspiration; it can afford remarkable consolation as it incarnates the caring acceptance of the healer and unconditional acceptance by God. However, if the pastoring or therapy is only a one-way communication, it cannot be as effective as when it is in dialogue, either with the receiver as a person or with the receiver's real troubles. If the healer simply communicates in a lecture-teaching-sermon mode, he or she leaves the hearer at least one level of abstraction from the actual communication. Even if the communicator is superbly skilled, the best he or she can do in one-way communication is create or describe an imaginary need situation, before the insight and consolation can be applied to it or a course of action can be suggested to meet the need.

Direct dialogue with the other human being, person to person, in which both become communicators and listeners, empowers both to address the real needs of the needy person. In the process, both discover their individual neediness, and it becomes a dialogic process of growth in both. When the receiver is empowered to articulate his or her need, pathology, suffering, or heartache, and if the healer is sensitive and sensible, dialogue offers a built-in basis for response directly to that specific problem.

How can a therapist or healer make his or her communication a healing relationship between him or her and the people individually, and communally? How can he or she personify God's presence, in God's style? That style, as we have seen, is communication by *incarnation*. To pastor or do therapy means to heal as a healer who also needs healing—as a wounded healer, as a needy person, in a way that represents in relationships, methods, attitudes, objectives, concerns, compassion, and grace God's disposition and style toward us all. In developing as an incarnating healer, of course, one can never get to Easter morning except through Good Friday. However, there are better and worse ways to do it.

Psychotherapeutic Dialogue

The genius of Socrates, the noted ancient Greek philosopher of the fifth century B.C.E., was his appreciation of the communication value of dialogue. The genius of dialogue is that its healing power is in the mutuality of hearing, expressing, sharing, and bonding that it offers. Sharing meaning that succeeds in communicating God's graciousness must be a communication process that gains its form, content, and structure from the human need to which it speaks. Therapy and pastoral care do not begin in the sacred scriptures of any faith, but in the world and in the hurting hearts of troubled humans. It is centered in persons, though it moves out from God through healing persons.

How shall psychotherapy, preaching, or pastoring address the real factors, the specific human problems of fear and faith, if it is not a dialogic process of active listening first and well-tuned expression in response—expression of the caring response that incarnates God's unique grace. The power of communication through well-chosen questions, soliciting the heartaches of real people, was so evident in Pericles's Athens that Socrates had to be done away with, lest he change the society. He saw that carefully focused questions achieved more than wisely designed answers to questions that remain unasked. It was obviously his design to communicate ideas and meaning sensations, which he possessed and cherished, not simply by announcing them for public or private consumption, as is usually done in education. It was his design to communicate his meanings by inciting in his students, through provocative queries and parries, a perception of the real issues and the real insights, applicable to specific hungers he had incited in them. This is a kind of style we must adopt, if we wish to heal efficiently. This is the kind of incarnation of grace required if we wish to be efficiently therapeutic or pastoral.

Dialogic caregiving is adaptable to most forms of psychotherapy and pastoral ministry, including clinical work, preaching, and education. The design can create a relatively comfortable communication process in which the openness insures a low level of emotional stress in which each person functions alternatively as expresser and listener, thus being afforded occasion to evidence his or her specific kind and size of need.

The context of a dialogue is important, as is the presence of a perceptive initiator, such as the therapist or pastor, who can really hear and see what human need is being surfaced, and by whom. This makes it possible for such an initiator to elicit or provide responses that sustain the process of verbalizing and relating in a fashion that brings increased perception of and response to the healing graces of the therapist or pastor, and God's grace. In such a setting, grace is not an abstraction, but an experienced and applied resolution and fulfillment of the needs expressed. Therapists and pastors can further this process of the individual or group by soliciting interaction between the persons involved, probing for deeper insights, suggesting reflection from new viewpoints, and the like. This is a design for providing insight by guiding the reflective processes of persons until their inquiry discovers what best serves the needs expressed. The effect of such discovery is greater as a source of learning, insight, retention, growth, and gratification than is a communication of neatly packaged answers or declarations to imagined questions, not shaped directly by the need expressed by the sheep to be shepherded.

Humans learn in terms of what they already know. We grow in the degree to which we can build on past experience. That is why a broad communication encounter front is so important. The best way to create a large scope of overlap in experience between a therapist and his client, or a pastor and his people, thus affording maximum mutuality, is dialogue: real listening and expression responsive to real or felt needs.

CONCLUSION

The dialogic style of the Socratic method affords us a relevant way of creating a common universe of discourse and a common channel with anyone with whom we relate. Efficient active listening in that dialogic process will insure that real communication can happen. Since we learn little more than what we can verbalize, we grow in insight, wisdom, faith, and peace only in terms of what we are led to confess or profess. We are healed only in the degree to which we can express our needs and affirm the solutions.

Educators have long insisted that we retain 20–30 percent of what we hear, 40–50 percent of what we see, and 80–90 percent of what we enact. This is the statistic that challenges the efficiency of one-way communication and affirms the potential efficiency of Socratic dialogue as the healing communication or relationality. Moreover, that is the incarnation model of communication and relationship—incarnating in our personal style and method God's way of handling all of us in God's grace.

NOTES

1. See the graphic models of these aspects of communication in J. Harold Ellens (1987), *Psychotheology: Key Issues*, Johannesburg: UNISA, 65–67.

2. A graphic model of this concept may be found in Ellens, *Psychotheology*, 69.

CHAPTER 8

A PSYCHOTHEOLOGY
OF COMMUNICATION

This chapter focuses very specifically on important aspects of the psychology of spirituality. In fact, it is particularly oriented toward issues of Christian spirituality, though this volume generally takes a broader psychological and religious perspective. However, while at this point, it is the function of Christian forces that are analyzed and described, it may be seen readily how the insights emphasized here can be applied to some degree in the experience of Muslims, Jews, and other faith devotees, as well.

Christian conversion and psychospiritual development depends on the providential structure of personality growth and on significant emotional events in our lives. Both of these are heavily dependent in the way they unfold and affect us on crucial insights gained from what we are taught and what we experience. Those insights arise mainly from what is communicated to us by others, by our sacred scriptures, by our education, and by God.

The development of a psychotheology of communication is therefore an imperative for the Christian community today. The matter is of special urgency for Christians in the helping professions, particularly counselors and pastors. Communication is basic to humanness and humaneness, as we discerned in the previous chapter. It is also at the center of our being made in the image and likeness of God. Though it is basic and natural, communication is surprisingly inefficient in humans. While our knowledge explodes, our communication deteriorates with the rise of cultural tribalism in our society. This chapter explores the definitions, assumptions, and contentions in terms of which a sound thesis about the nature of Christian psychotheological communication can be formulated and the question of a sound psychotheology of communication can be developed.

THE URGENCY OF THIS IMPERATIVE

The Christian community has been ambivalent about a number of things for some time: the institutional model of the church which is most appropriate; the form of a proper theology of scripture as the word of God; and the nature and function of communication processes within the community of believers, viewed in the light of the last half century of psychosociological research in the communication field. The communication issues involve the entire scope of the life of the psyche and the spirit. Therefore they shape the forms of clinical and pastoral work that are done and the institutions in or from which they are performed. The issues impact equally on the entire range of concerns essential to Christian roles in the psychospirituality in church ministries and in the helping professions.

Moreover, as we have previously noted, these psychosociological considerations impinge on Christian professionals precisely in terms of the concepts of the nature of humanness and of God's intentions regarding our humanness, which are at play in our worldviews. Therefore the matter demands a careful psychotheological investigation. That makes the development of a psychotheology of communication imperative. This chapter can only set the stage, assess the question, and hardly exhaust the matter. Others will be able and motivated to undertake the detailed development of aspects of the problem suggested here. Thus the Christian community may be able to come to a psychotheology of communication that is both sound and articulate.

One of the most important things humans hold in common is our urge and need to communicate. For many of us, that goes beyond the ordinary need to relate to others and involves our professional roles as communicators. A definition of communication in precise and generally applicable terms is not easy. One can start, however, by emphasizing that communication is a significant form of interpersonal relationship, as noted at length in the previous chapter, that all of us by nature want to do. We start very early doing it, quite without a great deal of prompting. We continue to do it all of our conscious lives, and ultimately, we realize that nonetheless, we do it rather inefficiently.

Though it is a natural instinct and faculty, communication between humans is always a problem, the source of considerable intellectual and emotional quandary, and as complex as human personality itself. That fact is not at all decreased in size or urgency by the fact that today, our culture is apparently caught up in the knowledge and communication technology explosion. Scholars have reported for a half century that as our society gets more complex, it is also reverting in some crucial ways to a communication decline.

Some question whether the brain function necessary to simple conversation is being engineered out of our cerebral operations and memory tracks.

We are experiencing, in the Western world, as hinted previously, an increase in cultural tribalism, coincident with our increased information base, our expanded internationalism, and our exponential multiplication of technology. It is now equally easy to telephone Moscow, Mumbai, and Madison, New Jersey, and relatively difficult to say good evening to one's spouse with the correct inflexion. Increasingly, our society is achieving that situation in which engineers are limited to speaking to engineers, physicians to physicians, psychologists to psychologists, and professionals from other tribes to their own colleagues in their own jargon. The ability to cross these tribal boundaries is eroding in our present-day cultures. Communication between people of substantially different orientations and different interests seems under siege.

That says important things about the nature, function, role, and duty of persons in our world who have as their primary function the obligation to communicate well. It implies that communication and its problems is a psychotheological matter. The term *psychotheology*, properly employed, describes a scientific enterprise. It is in that fashion that it must be taken here. It is the science of analyzing and describing the way in which human nature, particularly the function of the human psyche, reflects the nature of God, and the way in which this divine and human nature impacts the nature and destiny of the universe in its various facets and functions, and our human role in it.

It is of some value to investigate this science and its import for communication under four headings. First, we must set down some definitions. That will be followed, second, by the description of some important assumptions in terms of which the psychotheology of communication must be formulated. Third, we will endeavor to isolate some of the contentions that will likely arise and that must be taken seriously. Finally, some questions will be raised that will suggest the proper formulation of a sound thesis for the quest of a psychotheology of communication.

DEFINITIONS

Not only is it true and important to consider that psychotheology, properly so called, is a scientific enterprise; it must also be understood that such an enterprise is one that requires the discipline of discerning and disclosing data that have the warrant that scientific data ought to have. Moreover, it is necessary to take account of the fact that psychotheology is a certain kind of thing in terms of which, legitimately, a science may be developed. To put it simply, psychotheology, however one conceives it and in whatever context, is really nothing more or less than a worldview—a way of viewing or conceiving of human beings before the face of God. It may express itself as a worldview of a microcosm: one individual person or some specific aspect of that person's function or nature. Or it may be a worldview of the macrocosm: the whole universe, this planet, or a function of this world as we know it socially, culturally, or otherwise. In any case, psychotheology has to do with the formulation of a perspective on reality. A psychotheology is a worldview that takes its shape in terms of some perception about the nature and behavior of God and the manner in which that shapes us and our world.

There are other kinds of worldviews. One may have a philosophical, rather than a psychotheological, worldview. Camus and Sartre may be said to have had philosophical worldviews, for example, in terms of which they were interested in differentiating their perspective from a Christian psychotheological worldview that takes its shape in terms of precommitments about the nature and behavior of God in his world and in human lives. So psychotheology is one thing and philosophy is another; although at this point, one must note that it is impossible to develop a philosophical worldview that does not imply certain psychotheological assumptions or precommitments about God and the way in which his nature is reflected and functions in the human psyche and spirit. Whatever one says about the world in terms of its ultimate meaning implies some type of faith statement regarding God's existence, nature, and behavior. Perhaps, therefore, every philosophical worldview is also a psychotheological one. A psychotheology, in any case, is a worldview of the whole or part of our world, which takes its shape in terms of a perception about the nature and behavior of God as one who is engaged in the material world and its history and who engages us personally as psychospiritual persons.

Communication will be defined in general terms in this chapter. Usually, it means an exchange of information in the form of spoken or printed words. That, of course, is too limiting. A very significant part of communication is nonverbal; perhaps that is the most important part of our communicative interaction. Human communication is the registration of any change in the conscious or subconscious mind or psyche of a human being caused by some function of another human being. There are other kinds of communication: animals communicate with humans, humans with animals; some say plants communicate or express emotion. Here we are concerned with people relating to each other by sharing messages: a registration of a change in the mind or psyche of one human being as a result of action taken by another person. This is communication conceived of in terms of a very broad scope process and effect.

ASSUMPTIONS

Some assumptions, then, in doing a psychotheology of communication, should be set forth. First, doing psychotheology is a matter of describing the form, function, and meaning of the world or a facet of it, in terms of what that form, function, and meaning *ought to be* before the face of God. Psychotheologically, we are concerned with what *can be* in God's world and hence our own, not just what is *functioning* at the present time.

Second, communication is a facet of our world that is imposed on by and answerable to God's design for his world. These first two assumptions are obviously related. The second implies that humans, as described in a proper psychotheology of communication, will need to be described in terms of conscious, subconscious, unconscious, verbal, and nonverbal communication with each other. This needs to be detailed, moreover, in terms of our potentials and responsibilities in communication as God has equipped and empowered us to do it. Our activity of communicating in all these ways constitutes our style and technique for handling each other, and therefore directly involves the *oughts* of life.

Third, insights about reality—humanness, group function, interpersonal relationships, God, the world—gleaned from and by natural and social sciences are essential to the achievement of a proper psychotheological science. Doing justice to the truth of biochemistry, physics, archaeology, psychology, sociology, and the like, is as essential to the formulation of a psychotheology as are the data gleaned from sacred scripture. Whatever we say about creation on the basis of sacred scripture may not violate what we know about the universe through the natural and social sciences. Whatever we say about the living human document on the basis of sacred scripture may not violate what we know about human nature from the natural and social sciences. Doing justice to the truth of psychology and theology is essential to a proper and defensible psychotheology of humanness, a proper theology of communication, and, indeed, a proper interpretation of scripture regarding a Christian view of human nature.

CONTENTIONS

Human communication, for Christians who take living in the presence of God seriously, is not just a psychological or sociological matter, but also and significantly a theological matter, as implied in the term *psychotheology*, which we have used throughout this chapter. To say that it is a theological issue means that it involves matters having to do with God. It is a theological issue in three ways. First, it is theological because of the fact that the character and destiny of human beings are facets of those who are created in the image of God. It is crucial when a psychotherapist or pastor sits down in a counseling session that he or she takes account of the fact, in technique and content, that the person with whom he or she is dealing is a divine image bearer. That preconditions what he or she goes about doing and how it is to be done. So human communication is a facet of a person's theological operations because of the fact that human character and destiny are those of a divine image bearer. Our native need for relationship, as God-designed persons, must be taken account of in a quest for understanding persons as communicators, as must our native dignity as beloved children of God, for whom God has specific intentions and expectations, and for whom God intends freedom for self-actualization and self-realization.

It is not self-evident, of course, precisely what that means in each case. The issue needs considerable work. What are the parameters of human freedom within the context of grace? Does a person have the freedom for self-destruction? What are the theological constraints on psychological dynamics, if any? What is the scope and what are the limits of the freedom for the pursuit of selfhood or self-imposed destiny that one has as an image bearer of God? The import of this will become more specifically evident in subsequent chapters, in which we address the application of psychotheological concerns to clinical practice.

Second, human beings are not only in relationship with each other, but also with themselves—as those destined to experience the relief of grace, forgiveness, and unconditional acceptance. Communication is also a theological enterprise because it must take seriously the fact that God is *for* humankind; thus grace means God's radical and unconditional acceptance of persons and our acceptance of each other just as we are. That contention is central to a theology of communication. Moreover, the obverse of that fact is that each person is potentially a grace expresser who takes seriously our possibilities as recipients of God's grace.

Third, present in humans is a large incongruity between the possibilities and the experienced realities of any person, between human vision and human character, between what we can imagine and what we are able to create. We tend to be naively and insatiably utopian in what we reach for and imagine, but finite and disordered in what we grasp. What is this about human beings? Why is it that we live perpetually in the tension between the once and future paradise we imagine and that seems to be embedded somewhere very deep in our psyches, on one hand, and the frustrating practical reality of life's limitations and failures that we cannot transcend, on the other? Because that is a central question for us all, human communication is a theological enterprise. It is the analysis and expression of incongruity between our human limits and our godlike transcendental qualities. Thus since humans, who live in the presence of God, constitute a fundamentally theological consideration, human communication is, for all the above reasons, a theological concern—and therefore a psychotheological process in all circumstances.

SUGGESTIONS

Communication, as a psychotheological matter, requires honest and comprehensive attention to three things. First, attention must be paid to sound doctrine: if we are to have a reputable psychotheology of communication, we must fashion it in terms of an accurate and concise description of the nature and destiny of humans understood in terms of the real nature of God in so far as we can discern that.

That is an easy and traditional thing to say. What has been less traditional is the recognition that a sound psychotheology of communication requires equally honest and informed learning theory. In developing a psychotheology of communication, one needs to deal seriously with what happens in group process, and why. What is the character of healing therapeutic technique, and why? What is successful as proclamation in worship liturgies, and why, and what is effective in interpersonal conversation, and why? What happens to persons in those situations is a psychotheological issue, crucial to a psychotheology of communication.

Sound learning theory hinges on understanding human rationality: how people think. Why and how do humans remember? How do those matters relate dynamically to human personality? What does that have to do with being a divine image bearer? It is readily evident why a careful and honest account must be taken of what can be gleaned from and by the natural and social sciences for a proper psychotheology. Techniques of handling people in directive and nondirective counseling, in psychodynamic psychotherapy, or in transactional analysis, for example, imply a precommitment about the nature of humanness. Therefore it implies important things regarding our assumptions regarding humans as beings before the face of God, so to speak. Unfortunately, those assumptions are generally not carefully analyzed or critically evaluated. Communication tends to move along on other paths than a conscious awareness of what is implied in its method and style about the nature of human persons. That is a serious matter, of course. Some ethical philosophers have felt that psychological sensitivity sessions, for example, are suborgasmic orgies rather than therapeutic communication. There is enough truth in that to make the notion humorous and a little sad. From a psychotheology-of-human-communication point of view, how should one design a sensitivity program? Such issues have far-reaching consequences.

Consider the state of affairs in the field of education today. Numerous different psychotheologies of human nature are evident, and most of them with little critical awareness on the part of the educators. The educational theories of John Dewey and Abraham Maslow are unconsciously pervasive in American public institutions. These perspectives imply a specific psychotheology of human nature and communication, but one would be hard-pressed to find a teacher who is aware of that. One's psychotheology in these matters should be conscious and intentional, not accidental, since it shapes what we do and how we do it. The elite rational humanist Robert Hutchins proposed an educational process designed in terms of Plato's notions about philosopher-king ideals. An important psychotheology of human nature and communication is implied in his perspective. If we go about the business of education as our public high schools do today, structured by the discipline of nondiscipline, that implies an important psychotheology of human personhood and of what makes effective communication work with the kind of persons we then imagine humans to be.

In the field of politics, part of the difference between laissez-faire democracy, controlled capitalism, socialism, and totalitarianism as ways of handling people is the difference in the psychotheological precommitments concerning the nature of humanness and thus useful human communication methods.

Finally, a proper psychotheology of communication must take seriously a thoroughgoing communication theory. It is necessary to learn from those for whom communication is a scientific inquiry. For a psychotheology of communication to be correct and relevant, it must insure that the discrete facets of the communication process are taken with conscious appreciation. The potential of communication processes for producing wholeness in persons and groups is crucial. Communication processes answer the question as to who says what to whom with what effect. As we have noted in previous chapters, the intentive behavior of the communicator or sender; the encoding behavior of the speaker, in which his or her intent is verbalized or symbolically acted out; the message encoded; and the language channel in which it is sent as well as the decoding behavior of the receiver and his or her internalization of the experience incited by the message all reflect the function of human beings who have natures like God's communicating nature.

Those are the basic elements, and they may be graphed like the wiring diagram on the back of your stove: informative source, message-encoding process, transmitting vehicle of words or actions, receiver, and decoding process. While this process is happening, there is always a good deal of static in the system, produced by distractions from the communication setting. We noted in chapter 7 the fragile character of human communication and the numerous junctures and reasons it may break down. Static or noise in the system is one of those reasons.

If, for example, I injected a curse word or obscene symbol into this paragraph at this point, it would take some time before the average reader would be able to pick up the ongoing line of thought. The reason is that this is a book, and particularly a chapter, about religious and spiritual issues and about efficiency in psychotheological communication. Such words or symbols would be wholly out of place here, though there might be a setting in which that would not be the case. Those words and symbols would produce static for most readers who would choose a book like this. They would be incongruous with the message of this chapter, as would be a curse word in a sermon. Static injects emotional overload in the line of thought, cutting off communication by channeling our psychic and spiritual energy into dealing with the extraneous and inappropriate information. That would reshape the actual message the reader would receive here. Psychological noise, so to speak, or the static factor, is a crucial element in communication.

There is a great number of sources of influence and distraction on any given message in each of our communication processes. They involve our entire psychic, social, and spiritual worlds in greater or lesser ways. As a result, communication between two persons is really the process of two worlds meeting and attempting to overlap in some significant way by means of symbols or signals, verbal or nonverbal. That fact is crucial to understanding communication theory and so must be taken quite seriously in the development of a sound psychotheology of communication. People who care about humans, as those for whom God cares greatly, must be intentional and wise in the way we communicate with each other. We cannot afford to neglect careful attention to our effectiveness and our communication impact. It cannot be left to accidental processes or thoughtless modes.

BASIC QUESTIONS

Where, then, do we stand in the pursuit of a psychotheology of communication? What are the key remaining questions? First, what do our sacred scriptures say about the nature and behavior of *God*, which concretely suggests or describes the nature of humans, so as to define the purpose, style, and imperatives for the content of human communication? Second, what do our sacred scriptures say about the nature and function of *humans* in and of themselves, defining the purpose, style, and imperatives of human communication? Third, what does current psychological theory contribute to or detract from our understanding of the relevant scriptural data concerning humans as communicators? Fourth, what does current communication theory contribute to or detract from our understanding of the relevant psychological teaching concerning humans as communicators? These questions constitute the framework around which a responsible theology of communication must be developed. Wrestling with a wide variety of implications of these questions is the theoretical and applied work of the rest of this volume.

CONCLUSION

The relevant scriptural model for shaping a psychotheological model of communication is that of *incarnation*. "God, who in various ways and times, in bits and pieces, spoke to the fathers by the prophets, has in these last days visited us in his Son" (Heb. 1:1). God employed a limited and limiting communication method for speaking to us and developed it into a new and finally definitive self-expression. He came and visited us, and enacted his message and nature in a man: Jesus. Whether your theology prompts you to claim that he was utterly divine and not human, or utterly human and not divine, or some *tertiam quid*, the statement is still true. As Marcus Borg reminds us, he was a man with a life full of God. That is an adequate definition for any of us. Most of us recognize that from his mouth came divine wisdom. God visited us. That is the controlling model for a Christian psychotheology of communication.

What does that mean? What does that say about our theology of communication? What does that imply about us as communicators? It says something important about communication as deference and adaptation to another person or to the community. That stands against every form of manipulative communication. It speaks of communication as the enactment of the message, rather than expressing abstractions. It proposes sharing, rather than imposing, and *ethos:* the responsibility to be believable, to incite confidence by authenticity, to engender trust and security, to convey and inspire certitude. Incarnation, as a communication model, says a great deal about sharing security and the quest for meaning, as opposed to communication as the employment of power strategies, coercion, or threat. The incarnation model says a lot about communication as sensitivity and deference to the freedom of persons for achieving full fledged personhood in God's image, rather than the expression of authority and pressures to conformity to arbitrarily imposed requirements.

The incarnation model has its shape essentially in the process of grace and graciousness. Grace is a technique for handling people that maximizes taking the person seriously, as he or she is, not as he or she can be or ought to be. Finally, therefore, a psychotheology of communication, whether that has to do with proclamation in worship, healing in psychotherapy, counseling in guidance, or other kinds of interpersonal relationships, must be a description of what Christian communication should be in purpose, style, and responsibility—since God is God and grace is grace. A sound psychotheology of human communication acknowledges the other person as the object of God's profound care, implying our responsibility to enact God's kind of generous and solicitous care for him or her, by incarnating and enacting toward that person unconditional acceptance, forgiveness, and grace, as needed for the enhancement of his or her growth or healing, with a view to facilitating that person's robust self-actualization, before the face of God. The rest of this volume teases out what that means in the clinic and in life.

CHAPTER 9

STORY AS PSYCHOTHERAPY

The driving engine of human personality development is that set of dynamic forces that makes up the life of the human psyche. Those are psychological, spiritual, social, and intellectual functions of our humanness. They include all the experiences in each of those categories that operate on our conscious, subconscious, and unconscious levels. If we fail to take any one of them seriously, we shall certainly misunderstand what we need to do in the care of one another, particularly in professional roles such as psychotherapy or pastoral care. In these professional roles, we are responsible for providing people with the kind of insight that heals them.

One might say that the task of the psychotherapist or pastor is that of information handling and of conditioning human experience in such a fashion that people gain insight and growth. This requires wise forms of communication, cast in terms of a deep understanding of the real nature of persons. The information and communication for which persons in the helping professions assume responsibility are usually those necessary for interpreting the pain and perplexity of troubled and needy people. To put it more concisely, the calling of the helping professions is to wholesomely handle people so that they come to that truth and insight that brings faith and wholeness to them as persons.

TRUTH AND HEALING

The dynamics of faith and wholeness, then, turn on the fulcrum of truth and insight: truth about our selves, feelings, needs, goals, defenses, strengths, and pathologies. Just as crucial is the truth about how human personality functions, what psychology teaches, what our sacred scriptures offer, how the world is fashioned, and the way actions have consequences in our lives. For example, when a therapist, counselor, patient, or parishioner abuses himself or herself or another person, or violates the decorum of society, what is the most important truth about that incident? What insight may be the healing or redemptive one? What is the real story in that situation? Is the main fact that he or she has failed morally or spiritually, or is sick psychologically? Is the potentially healing and saving perception that such a person has broken some kind of law, human or divine, or that he or she has fallen short of his or her own divinely designed destiny as an image bearer of God? Perhaps all of that is true somehow, but which is the truth that can heal?

If one is to focus on the moral failure, sinfulness, or breach of a human or divine expectation or requirement, little healing can come of it until it is acknowledged that the failure of duty involved is an incidental consequence of the larger and more central issue. That central matter is the person's failure to achieve his or her best destiny. Moreover, that failure of destiny is a consequence of the psychospiritual pathology that is the driving disorder in that person's life. If healing is to come, *that* fundamental truth must come to the surface, and it must be *the* truth that conditions the redemptive or therapeutic intervention.

I have noted that it is frequently the case that pastors who have an excessive concern for meticulous attention to dogma, correct procedure, orthodox traditions, heresy hunting among their colleagues, and vociferous emphasis on intense spirituality also are the pastors who tend to fall into misbehaviors destructive to their ministry. Of the eight theologian-pastors who aggressively opposed me regarding the views expressed in this book and accused me of heresy, all were put out of the ministry because of adultery. Similar pathology often afflicts psychotherapists. It is too often the laity in congregations and secular communities, however, who are the most aggressive in pressing those claims of authority and rigid standards. Persons with such so-called righteousness needs are usually the ones who are morally and psychologically the most brittle and unstable. That should tell us something. What is the truth that it suggests and that might be the potentially healing insight? It is likely to be something like the following.

In such an instance, we have in view a person who is rigid and insecure, fearful of not being accepted as he or she is, by fellow humans or by God. That likely comes from inadequate parenting as a child or from a fear-filled religious upbringing or acculturation, which left that person feeling that life is dangerous and that one's own worth is questionable and precariously held. As a result, that person is incapable of easily and naturally receiving love and affirmation. The result is a deep inner hunger of the heart for love and tenderness, a desperate need for some affirmations from others as well as the assurance of God's love and grace. Such a feeling is a primal level doubt about one's own worthiness to be loved. That person seeks love by proving that he or she can be more right and good than anyone else and so adheres to or imposes on others various rigid and constraining codes of expectation, ethical conduct, liturgical practice, or intellectual ideology.

In such a mode, a person seeks the affirmation of fellow humans and the assurance of God's goodwill by being the most perfect of all around, a creed and code of conduct that one cannot measure up to in the long run. This posture toward God and other humans leads to inflexible interpretation of religious dogma, political ideals, ethical requirements, and behavioral codes, particularly as they apply to others—to the society in general. When someone who is equally neurotic and perhaps somewhat hysteric crosses the path of such a rigid person, looking and longing for the same kind of affirmation, personal fulfillment, and cherishing, a very seductive situation is afoot.

If the latter person is able to express what feels like intense tenderness, caring, cherishing, esteem, and nurturing, both will experience, perhaps for the first time, a deep sense of connectedness. This binds them to each other in feelings of gratifying acceptance of each other, a thing neither has experienced before. When the bonding breaches standard regulations of marriage or social decorum, the newfound seductive nurturing can be destructive. The fact that this cherishing is driven by ulterior motives of personal need fulfillment makes little immediate difference. Paradise seems to have been gained, and all else may seem worth sacrificing for it. The defenses against inappropriate relationships are eroded at all levels—spiritual, psychological, social, and intellectual—and the personality structures of both persons are in danger of disintegration under the pressure of the long-standing psychospiritual pathology both have brought to the relationship.

Many patients and parishioners, perplexed by their own human limitations and pathologies, as well as pastors and psychotherapists, exhausted from the burden of perpetually caring for others, while receiving little care from their loved ones and family, have found themselves in this type of life situation. Inappropriate and self-defeating behavior often results in compromised integrity, disaffection from those from whom strength should be counted on, loneliness, isolation, adultery, social confusion, and legal complications. Sometimes, of course, those that one should be able to count on for strength and nurturing are themselves deeply pathological and incapable of real relationships—more a part of the problem than a part of the solution. The needy person is then in a very vulnerable and precarious position. Sometimes the newfound alternative relationship, however dangerous, adulterous, and compromising, is the only thing that saves his or her emotional and psychospiritual life.

How can healing be brought to this kind of suffering? By dismissing the professional person from his or her role or function as a healer? By condemning the patient or parishioner for failure of character and integrity? By demanding confession of sin and iniquity? By public chastisement? By legal action? What is the truth that must take control here? Is it not the deep need for psychospiritual renewal? Perhaps such a wounded human is just the person who should be a healer for others. Perhaps such a failed psychotherapist or pastor is just the one who should be kept in his or her job and role as healer, once psychospiritual healing and renewal has been accomplished.

Such a wounded healer, who has been through the fires of humanness, inadequacy, failure, and restoration, is equipped for better care of others than those more perfect ones who have never found out about their own limitations and the flawed and tragic nature of their own humanness. If psychotherapy can bring insights about the psychological and spiritual truth of matters like this, and these insights are able to restore wholeness to that person, such a wounded healer will undoubtedly be superior in quality as a caregiver, compared with those who have not visited this shadow side of their own personalities.

That is to say, the issue here is the healing of the psyche so that the whole life of that person may be placed on a new foundation of psychotheological or psychospiritual wholeness and reintegration. That healing of the psyche depends on honest address to the truth that can heal. When truth and wholeness are so joined, health and faith can flourish, and a restored life can thrive. Perhaps it is just at this point that we should emphasize that our notion of healing, renewal, redemption, or salvation may often be somewhat distorted. Many of us tend to isolate such human processes to highly personal and private psychological or spiritual experiences. This is likely to be a limited and inadequate notion of psychological and spiritual healing.

Healing involves the restoration to function and wholeness of fractured persons within a community of fractured humans, in a fractured human world. It is not just getting right with God or receiving definitive psychotherapy. Healing is the restoration of the whole person, within a community that is moving toward wholeness, in a world in which we are all contributing to the achievement of the best cosmic destiny for our world. This healing that restores wholeness in persons, communities, and God's world is complex. Growth and wholeness, which deserves the name, is psychological in that it functions through the insights that correct psychopathology. It is social when functioning through the insights and actions that correct the distortions and oppressiveness of our institutions and sociocultural structures. It is intellectual when enacted through the insights that provide us a wholesome and complete worldview. It is emotional when it is expressed through the insights and experiences that afford appropriate inner satisfaction and relational security and fulfillment. It is spiritual when realized through the insights that assure us of God's unconditional, radical, and universal grace to all of us, just as we are right now, at this point in our human pilgrimage.

Jesus drew no line between healing of the body, mind, or soul. Any good psychotherapist would agree with him immediately. When he was preaching in Capernaum, he was presented with a paraplegic, whose underlying disorder was a classic hysteric paralysis, apparently derived from an extreme neurotic sense of guilt. Jesus said to him, "Your sins are forgiven you! Get up and walk home." The man did so. The man's paralysis was obviously psychological in source. Jesus perceived immediately that the psychodynamics were related to the debilitating effects of neurotic guilt. Cure the psyche by resolving the guilt, and the rest will come along naturally. Wholeness was restored.

Jesus was, in effect, saying that this man's salvation was a restoration of wholeness. It comes from getting to the bottom of our disorders. Getting to that root of things means getting at the truth—about us, the created universe, and God. When we know the truth and act on it, it leads to the freedom we need for growth, faith, and wholeness. Frequently, our inherited body chemistry must be corrected with medicine before we are capable of seeing that truth or acting on it. It is a short logical leap from that insight to the realization that healing requires the incarnating in the healer of the full range of the various kinds of concern, like God's concern, for human suffering and human wholeness. This incarnation must shape our care of others as friends or professional therapists and pastors. That is the required style of our teaching, nurturing, healing, friendship, guidance, forgiving, and encouraging. Grace and truth incarnated in us saves lives and is, psychotheologically, the reign of God in this world.

TRUTH AND STORY

How do we get at the truth? Plato thought we got at truth through that rational thought which leads toward understanding the universe, life, and the human enterprise, in terms of the way in which God views all of that: in terms of transcendental ideas. He thought it was a function of the head or intellect. Aristotle saw Plato's rational idealism as too speculative. He urged that we find truth through experiment with tangible, empirical reality around us and within us, keeping careful records of our results, constructing hypotheses regarding the meaning of the data we find, and then testing those hypothetical perspectives against more experience with data through our five senses. Rene Descartes, David Hume, Francis Bacon, and August Comte followed on Thomas Aquinas's enthusiasm for a combination of Plato and Aristotle: a kind of rational empiricism. Thus the positivist school of Western thought grew up and has dominated our modern era since the eighteenth-century Enlightenment. This perspective is frequently referred to in recent years as foundationalism, the method for getting at truth by positing a rational or empirical foundation for our search for truth and deducing from that foundation the necessary insights and conclusions for building an entire philosophy or worldview.

It is quite interesting, and of considerable importance to our psychospiritual perspective, that this outlook of foundationalism has shaped the formulations of both the sciences of psychology and theology in the West since the days of the Roman Empire. That was not accidental because the Roman Empire shaped the mind-set of the West along the lines of the notion that truth is logical, propositional, nomistic, and normative; that is, it is empirical, rationally structured, and principial or lawful. Natural laws of life and how it functions can be discerned in life itself. The Romans derived that idea, in great part, from the Greek Aristotelian view that what is true is that which is evidential, that which we can stand objectively outside of and view with dispassion, letting the evidence or the argument speak for itself. Evidential truth is always the same, eternally true, as long as the situation or conditions are the same.

Some have suggested that the Hebrew people of the Bible had quite a different view of truth, but that claim is highly debated. It is said that for the ancient Israelites of the Hebrew Bible, truth was not objectively evidential, but confessional, not objective, but subjective. So truth is less what can be demonstrated as having necessary and eternal significance or warrant outside of us, and more what can be experienced from the inside as faithfully or predictably trustworthy; that is, one can only see truth by standing inside a life experience and testifying to what can be discerned and how things look from that inside perspective. It is a view of truth more *affective* than rational and intellectual. Whether that was the mode of the Hebrews is indifferent since this perspective is another way of seeking and seeing the truth nonetheless.

So the Greeks and Romans, together with their modern counterparts, the positivists, wrote philosophical essays, treatises on logic, case studies, and laboratory records of their empirical evidences. The Hebrews wrote their notions about truth in the form of stories about their experiences with life before the face of God, life in relationship with each other, life as their quest to understand their own history and history in general, and life as the unfolding of their inner and outer story. Their story is about the covenantal faithfulness and trustworthiness of experiential truth, particularly of God and his truth for them. Their truth was always in some way consciously the story about their psychospirituality. The truth for them had to do with meaning and purpose, while truth for the Greeks and Romans remained mainly about mere cause and effect.

FOUNDATIONALISM

Two decades ago, Nicolas Wolterstorff wrote a fine little book titled *Reason within the Bounds of Religion*, taking the title of Immanuel Kant's *Religion within the Bounds of Reason* and neatly inversing its foundationalist thrust. Wolterstorff pointed out that positivism, and its foundationalism, is no longer a satisfactory perspective for getting at truth. Positivism could never deliver on its claim that it was founded on unassailable rational-empirical truth because behind its entire approach were always beginning faith assumptions about the nature of reality, the function of logic, or the character of the palpable data studied; that is, such a system rests on initial faith assumptions just as surely as a religious or psychotheological system does. So the truth value of that system is no better than its initial assumptions. Those assumptions are always to some extent speculative.

Wolterstorff was on the right track. Philosophy today is turned upside down, so to speak, by the limitations of positivism and its foundationalism and has sought to find new ground to stand on by experimenting with semantic and linguistic functions in getting at and conveying meaning and truth. The problem this raises is nowhere more acute than in the field of psychology and theology or spirituality. In both these fields, great effort has been expended to develop each respective science on the model that the natural sciences, particularly physics, have used, that is, the model of rational empiricism, or positivism.

Philosophy and the natural sciences are thrown into confusion because of the discovery of the limits of that model to get at truth in the fields dependent primarily on issues of meaning and purpose, though the model was quite effective in the fields of cause and effect: the natural sciences. The model worked well enough for physics and astrophysics, chemistry and biology, as well as other natural sciences, as long as the issues studied were merely the cause and effect issues in those fields. Now that astrophysics has crossed the boundary into cosmology and the study of the origin and destiny of the cosmos, cause and effect issues tend to become absorbed into the questions of meaning and purpose. In that arena, positivism seems to have little value. Thus rational empiricism has proven less than satisfactory as a model for understanding the disciplines that have as much to do with meaning and purpose as with cause and effect such as psychology and spirituality.

We are thrown back on the question of how to get at the truth that brings psychospiritual wholeness. I have a number of friends and some patients who are engineers in the automobile industry. They are very good at what they do. They build excellent automobiles. They achieve great efficiency in production systems. They program things successfully so that industry is profitable, and they demonstrate that they have the wisdom and character that insures success in what they do. They are responsible and effective people. However, they come to me for help because they are failures at home with their wives and children. Why should that be? How can that be? Wise, responsible, and effective people who can run mechanical systems and human teams, but cannot maintain wholeness and joy in their homes and families?

The problem is that at home, the issue is not cause and effect dynamics, as it is at work. At home, the important things have to do with meaning and purpose in relationships. At work the objective is production; at home the function is growth. Work is like a factory that takes in raw materials and puts out a finished product: a quantifiable input, a calculated and controlled process of production, and a predictable quantity and quality of output. Home is like a greenhouse, where tender plants are carefully planted, watered, fertilized, pruned, guided, sustained, and protected from too many harsh conditions. None of the family processes are quantifiable, nor can quality be measured by prescribed standards.

Running a greenhouse requires a lot of preparation of the conditions; careful planting of the seeds; waiting and praying to see how many of the seeds germinate, how many of the plants survive, blossom, and bear fruit; and lots more waiting and praying about the quality and quantity of the outcome. In the meantime, considerable attention needs to be given to the atmosphere, the teasing of the vines in the right direction, and the feeding and watering of the burgeoning growth. Greenhouses are a fragile business requiring tender care and long seasons of nothing but hope. Factories require no hope, only certainty; no prayer, only controlled processes; no waiting, only immediate gratification; and no preparation, just turning on the switch.

Moreover, there is an inherent difference between men and women in this matter. I did an experiment with a number of my university classes. I presented a case about a man stealing a loaf of bread and some other food from a bakery. I asked each person to describe how this destitute man who stole to feed his hungry family should be treated. Uniformly, the men asked questions about what the law required and how justice might be gained for all involved. On the other hand, all the women raised issues about relationships: between the thief and his hungry wife and children, between the baker and his own family and creditors, between the baker and the thief, and regarding the level of resources the baker had compared with what the thief had. In the end, the men decided for justice and the women for caring relationship solutions for both the thief and the baker.

There is ample research literature to demonstrate that the difference between these two solution patterns is related to the fact that 70 percent of all men in the world are left brain–dominant and 70 percent of all women in the world are right brain–dominant. Left-brained people acquire meaning from life experiences through linear logic and computer-like problem solving, creating mathematical and mechanical processes that lead to a bottom-line resolution of any problem. Right-brained persons acquire meaning from life experiences through the color, texture, emotional content, aesthetic or artistic quality, flavor, relationality, and pleasure of any process of life. Left brain function is oriented toward cause and effect issues and mathematical forms of problem solving: good at fixing faucets and toilets. Right brain function is oriented toward meaning and purpose issues and relational forms of problem resolution: good at nurturing little children. The 30 percent of persons not primarily right or left brain oriented, both male and female, tend to be high on both scales and generally function better in all areas of life's challenges.

It is clear, then, that in matters of psychological development and spiritual maturity, where life and growth are the primary focus, we are dealing mainly with meaning and purpose issues. Those are not readily illumined by left brain rational empiricism. To get at the truth that counts here, we need to find a way to get more of a right-brained grasp of what the story really is with human growth, healing, and wholeness. Insight is the critical issue for achieving these objectives. Insight stimulates growth. Insight heals. Mere information is not enough for the required quality of insight. Just the facts about the thief and his illegal act, or about the sick patient's misbehavior, or about the engineer's incapacity to relate to his family do not equip us for healing. What the information *means* in its human setting and in terms of its human dynamics—spiritual, psychological, social, emotional, and intellectual—is the real story: the truth that heals. The healing truth is in the story.

I believe that 70 percent of what makes a good therapist is that he or she has suffered enough and sufficiently integrated that suffering into a wholesome life that he or she never sees a patient without having the sense that the travail of the patient is in some way a personally familiar perplexity for the therapist. The other 30 percent of what makes a good therapist is academic training. We may inform our children, patients, constituencies, or parishioners of a great deal of data about psychology, philosophy, theology, and spiritual truths, but that is not going to be for them the truth or insight that heals. That is head knowledge. When it is incarnated in our persons and conveyed in our story or in other relevant stories, it has a chance of being internalized by them as healing insight and truth for their psychospiritual experience and growth. We may produce informed psychotherapists or theologians who have the science down thoroughly but who have little apprehension at the affective level of what human suffering, relational healing, or the relief of God's embrace of us in his grace are about. They are not likely to incarnate the required capacity for healing others.

The effective healing impact of psychotherapy and of incarnated grace in us is that profound sense of relief, integrated into the root and foundation of one's personality and character, expressed in unconditional positive regard for the needy person: *our caring regard and God's*. If that sense of things is truly integrated into our persons and characters, it will permeate everything about how we see ourselves and the world, forming and informing everything we do with ourselves and with those in need of us. That is the healing power of a grace-incarnating person. It is interesting that ancient scripture was already aware of this. It declares that formerly, God spoke to humans in bits and pieces, now and then, and finally visited us in Jesus, who sat down with shamed women, touched street urchins, ate with disreputable men, and called multitudes of heartbroken and sick people to him. With his words, presence, and touch, he afforded them the relief of unconditional positive regard—personal caring, grace. He got the truth across to them. They could see what the real story was with them, with God, with his world, and with their fractured world.

The issue of psychospiritual growth and wholeness is not first of all and certainly not exclusively the experience of knowing intellectual information through the analytical left hemisphere of the brain. Comte and the positivists thought it was. They forgot that such a notion is a faith assumption about cause and effect analysis being the most important or exclusive experience for getting at truth. Behind that assumption is a prior faith assumption that truth is propositional. Such assumptions are philosophical leaps that the positivists take to land in positions that they wish to hold because of the psychological need that predisposes them to this form of security. It makes them feel secure to have all of life under apparent logical control so that they never need to deal with their own vulnerability to error and with the vulnerability of the truth question itself, as it always stands under the shadow of doubt. That is their kind of psychospiritual need to reduce anxiety and increase security by increasing control. Its fulfillment of the need for accuracy is only secondary to the fulfillment of the psychological need for assurance. Indeed, psychological anxiety motivates us to the drive for logic, accuracy, control, and that kind of strategy for anxiety reduction.

Information, of course, can convey truth. Scientific information in psychology and theology is necessary for our self-understanding. Understanding requires intellectual and analytic approaches to truth. Analytic exploration of the truth demands left brain function and logical thought. However, one may achieve all that and experience no healing or capacity to heal others. Logical philosophy does not provide growth-inducing relationships with oneself or others, or renewal of one's person at the root and foundation of the self. Yet that is where change must take place to overcome psychopathology, alienation, guilt, anxiety, distorted attitudes, dysfunction, isolation, loneliness, and moral disorder. There, at the deep levels of the self, lies our human inadequacy to the responsibilities of life and the challenges of godliness. These are, after all, the dysfunctions in us that call for healing and wholeness and to which real human care and divine grace are directed. How shall we get beyond mere information, beyond the controls of logic, beyond the left brain, into the heart of our humanness—to truth, faith, healing, and wholeness?

THE PSYCHODYNAMICS OF STORY

Stanley Hauerwas has given us a significant clue. He has written such works as *Vision and Virtue, Character and the Christian Life, Truthfulness and*

Tragedy, and *A Community of Character.* He agrees that foundationalism is dead and can never be revived, that it simply does not help in the arenas that count most in the quest for the truth that heals and redeems humans. As a consequence, we are left with something that seems on first blush to be too subjective, too much like rank individualism, too much like situational truth and ethics, too privatistic a notion of truth. Hauerwas says that all we really have for the pursuit of truth is the psychodynamics of story.

What can he possibly mean by that? He means that if I am to convey to you truth that makes a difference in your growth, healing, and wholeness, the best I can do is to tell you my story. That is what I have been doing thus far in this book. I have been telling you my story as I understand it and as it has taken on meaningful and healing dimensions and contours for me. That is to say, I have been letting you know that I have looked around the world of psychology, philosophy, theology, and the like; that I have investigated rather thoroughly vast regions of that world; and that the search has illumined my sense of how psychospirituality functions in my life. So I have been telling my story about how, in that context, the unconditional positive regard of others has enhanced my growth and healing as a fractured human being.

That story is, inevitably, also the story of how the central experience of God's unconditional grace has functioned in that growth and healing process, as the most critical and formative psychological factor. I have been suggesting all along how, in my judgment, that experience can usefully illumine your quest for truth, healing, growth, and the faith that is at the core of psychological wholeness. *I have been telling you my story.* I have been saying that I believe that the nature and shape of things, as humans can properly understand them at this moment in human history, is largely as I have described my experience of the quest and its consequences in my life. That is my story, and that is the best I can do in getting across to you what the real story is in human existence.

Of course, this sounds very subjective. It may well be, but is that inherently as unfortunate as the positivists thought it was? It also sounds as though this method of storytelling will never get us back to the ultimate foundation of irreducible truth. Of course, that is quite correct. Hauerwas insists that the human condition, philosophically, psychologically, and spiritually, is such that we must settle with the fact that we cannot get to irreducible and ultimate truth. Perhaps there is such a thing as ultimate truth in God's perception of things, but we have no access to it. We have only access to story: our stories, the story of mankind, and that part of God's story that is woven into history or that we can imagine or extrapolate from scientifically investigating this created world.

Most religious traditions are sure that they stand on a solid foundation of truth and authority, usually enshrined in their sacred scriptures. Each tradition acts like its scriptures are a dependable source of all the data necessary to establish a true philosophy of life or a faith system. That easily leads to the notion that truth is in scriptural propositions about human and divine nature and behavior. In my tradition, the Reformed Faith, the assumption is that God is the sovereign ruler and director of all things. From this principle, theologians have deduced the entire Reformed system of God's truth and therefore what they claim to be the truth about all things. The entire system, of course, is human conjecture.

However, there are glimmering elements of truth throughout that system of thought, as in all such faith formulae. The creeds and other statements of faith that preserve faith traditions for posterity are the story of special moments in the life of a faith community. They give us baselines in terms of which to pursue our quest for truth and insight and against which to react as we test the development of our own personal story. The glimmering elements of truth in a community's story can be determined by what works for growth and health for needy humans. If the community's story has many sound glimmerings of truth that work for maturation and healing in our stories, that will help in our quest for God's story and the relevance of God's story to our personal stories.

Things go wrong in this quest when we forget Hauerwas's main point, namely, that the question of psychospiritual truth is much more complicated and precarious an enterprise than mere philosophical deduction from foundational principles. We are always tempted to overlook the point that the quest for the truth that heals is not primarily an intellectual exercise about philosophy and theology. It is psychospiritual, a matter of the psyche—of the heart of a person. Truth that counts for the healing of the psyche and the soul can only be conveyed by an *I believe* statement, even in the science of psychology, where much of what we know is empirically demonstrable. Intellectual analysis is always important in any matter, but it is merely a part of the puzzle in our quest for truth that grows us and heals us.

In the end, all we have is story: our own stories, the stories of human history, the community's stories. The stories of science are an important part of the human community's story and of God's story. Hauerwas wants us to remember that scientists, philosophers, research psychologists, and theologians are not telling us God's story, pristinely packaged and complete. They are only telling us their own stories. If the truth of human nature or the truth about God, derived from the natural or scriptural sciences, is wrapped into their stories, that enhances their work of telling us the stories of their own quest for useful truth wherever they have sought and found it. Their stories will describe their intellectual quest, their psychological quest, their theological perception, and their degree of psychospiritual wholeness and authenticity.

John Cobb is a process theologian. He is sure, for example, that God's story is not static, finished, or captured in philosophical propositions. God's story is in process. God is growing in his experience and therefore in his nature and character, just as are we. Each new day brings for God a new set of circumstances to which to adapt, a new set of perceptions to integrate, an expanded volume of data to take into consideration, and new decisions to make. This is true because history unfolds and changes, and so do we. Cobb insists that God is in a growth process and that God's story continues to develop as ours does. So God's truth is expanding, as is ours. God develops from the impact of our stories on God just as we grow from the impact of God's story on us. This notion is very helpful in illumining our quest for the truth that brings healing and wholeness to human life. It certainly correlates and comports well with Hauerwas's idea of truth as story.

What you and I have to say to each other, therefore, is not some objectively quantifiable and definitively packaged statement of psychospiritual truth, but personal testimonies each of us can make about our own story of life, insight, scientific understanding, faith, growth, and wholeness. I walk out of my intellectual and psychological house, so to speak, and I meet you walking out of yours. I tell you my story—truth that works, as I see it. I say to you, "This is the way things look to me, after due consideration, scientific reflection, and appreciation of all the relevant stories I have been able to investigate. In the light of the illumination, growth, and healing this has given me, I believe that the truth which works has the following nature, dimensions, and contours. I believe that this is the real story about things." Then you respond by saying, "Well, my perception comports well with yours in this way and that, but differs in the following ways. Moreover, in my reading of the historical story of human experience and perception, I find the following confirmations of my perspective."

As a result of such an encounter, informal or scientific, your story cuts across my story, and my story cuts across yours. Both our stories have been altered, expanded, and illumined by the other's. From that moment on, irrevocably, you are part of my story, growth, and wholeness, and I am part of yours. A significant, creative, existential event has taken place in both of us. It is never merely an intellectual encounter, but is filled with psychological process and content—the stuff of growth and healing. Each of us goes away from that event a different person at the psychospiritual level. That difference is not necessarily a matter of the propositions about truth that we exchanged. It may have much more to do with nonverbal communication shared in the event, or with implications of the way something one of us said stimulates an exponential expansion of what the other already seminally perceived. In any case, it is a moment of truth for us. It is life changing—in minute or massive ways.

Moreover, if it is the case that my personal odyssey, my quest for knowledge, truth, and wholeness, has been shaped by some psychospiritually illumining person or scripture, leading me to the conclusion that the most healing psychological truth is God's unconditional grace, some significant aspect of

God's story will be interwoven in my story as I tell it to you. Then it is inevitably the case that in the life-shaping psychospirituality of my story, something of God's story will cut across your story, further altering, expanding, and illumining it.

So the history of human experience is simply the story of stories cutting across and illumining each other. The quest for the truth is a search for the stories that can most satisfyingly expand and illumine our own stories. The truth that brings healing, wholeness, faith, and hope is that illumining set of stories that gets at our deep sense of dysfunction. It deals with our human anxiety, guilt, alienation, distortion, isolation, loneliness, and inadequacy to the responsibilities of life and the challenges of godliness. These are the factors that keep all of us fractured, unwhole, and unwholesome. God's story of grace riding in your story and insinuated into my story brings the illumination of the truth that heals.

It is relatively easy to illustrate the reality of this claim about the psychodynamics of story in the quest for growth, healing, and wholeness as well as for truth, trust, and faith. We all have experiences frequently that witness to the authenticity of it. I graphically remember discovering early in my work as a psychologist and parish priest how little there is to say that makes a definitive difference to people in the times of their most intense crises, and inversely, how little needs to be said to them at times like that. I discovered that when a family is grieving the loss of a loved one, perhaps a child untimely dead, it is not time for philosophical rationales or theologically weighty sermons about death and eternity. People cannot hear propositions about truth at such a time. Grief's wounding anguish does not drive us into the left hemisphere of the brain for analytic processing of the experience of bereavement. Grief, anxiety, stress, rage, and fear propel us into the right side of our brains, into the place of perceiving the meaning of things in emotional gestalts, the center where the unconscious, subconscious, and conscious minds meet.

Frequently, I have gone to a funeral parlor or to a family home and discovered that the bereaved were not hungry for words, but for nonverbal relationship. A touch, the way one grasps the sorrower's hand, a warm and sustained embrace often say more at such a time, reach more deeply into the grief, than words can ever do. Emotional connections at a deeper level than sentences and thoughts form more real connections. These establish more authentic and relevant bonds between us in such moments of confrontation with the deep brokenness of life.

I have noticed that this is particularly true of families that have lost children. I have watched concerned friends express their hopes and wishes for the bereaved, with little apparent effect. I have noticed that when someone who has likewise lost a child approaches the forlorn, bereaved parents, suddenly something new and deeper takes place. A communication of understanding, of healing truth, transpires at the very root level of the loss and grief. It is as though there is a sudden recognition of truth deeper than the data, knowledge more profound than information, sharing beyond words. It is a sudden awareness that each has been in the same place of awful aloneness and impossible pain. What really happens, obviously, is that the story of the veteran griever cuts across the story of loss in the newly bereaved. At a fundamental level, this new story is illumined in meaning by the old story.

Healing truth illumines both. The healing truth is that grief can be survived, impossible loss can be sustained, and pain can lead to healing and growth. The healing truth is that such isolating trauma of loss is not unique to these newly bereaved. Such loss of loved ones is not total aloneness, but is a shared human experience for those who have walked before through the valley of this kind of shadow. Some deep and significant sense of meaning and purpose is exchanged at that secret moment of encounter. One old story cuts across this new story, and the two illumine each other. From that point, each is part of the other's life-shaping story, and neither is so much alone in the lonely vigil of grieving and life. Now both stories are new and renewed stories and both persons a little more whole.

This works even better, experience demonstrates, when a healthy God story is riding on one or both of the human stories. God's story has cut across our human stories in human history. It cut across our story especially in the events, the presence, and the incarnation of Jesus as well as in the impact of other great spiritual figures. The Bible is a report of how God's intriguing story unfolded as it intersected the story of that believing community in its progress through history. It is the witness to the way in which that intersection illumined their traditional communal stories and gave them significance. This afforded that community insight into the real story of the world, spelling out the truths that bring forth faith and healing. The results of such intersection of God's story with the human story also illustrate how crucial it is that the God story is a story about a healthy God. Sick God stories make sick people, leaving us in our brokenness, and usually worsening it.

I once believed that the most touching healing afforded people in times of crisis was that shared between two Christians who experienced similar bereavements. However, God's story enters our stories from the most unexpected sources. When my father was dying at age 93, I was not alerted to his impending death. He was, by a wide margin and without exception, the very best man I ever met. I love him deeply. His death is a severe loss to me, multiplied by my grief over not having been able to visit him at the end or be present at his passing.

As I tried to get life back on track after the funeral, I went one morning to my usual breakfast spot. The manager saw my grief and sat down with me at my table. He carefully solicited from me the story of my sadness. Then he shared his feelings with me for a half hour or so, relating his own similar experience of losing his father and speaking about how his sense of God's presence in his life had helped and healed his grief. Of my wide range of friends and family, this relative stranger gave me the wisest and most caring words, insights, and feelings of consolation. He was a Muslim from Iraq.

He spoke more wisely of God's grace and providence in our lives than my Christian friends. I realized that it is not the shared faith group that makes the difference. It is the depth of spirituality and the degree to which the God who crosses our story in the story of another is a really healthy God, that is, a God of unconditional grace and caring positive regard, not of threat or conditional love. Moreover, these conditions for a truly healing impact are true not only in times of lost loved ones, but also in times of crises caused by mental illness, failed relationships, and the myriad dead-end streets of the human odyssey.

My eldest brother's second son died suddenly of a congenital brain tumor that became active at the age of 18. The funeral was held in a conservative Reformed church of a rather philosophical-theological orientation. The preacher preached for 47 minutes, detailing the intricacies of life, death, eternal life, salvation, heaven, and hell. When he was about 20 minutes into the sermon, my second daughter, a staff artist for *Time* magazine at the time, leaned over to me and said, "For death, poetry is better than philosophy." She put her finger on the issue. The preacher was busy revealing what he supposed was God's story for this moment. He seemed not to have learned three crucial things: first, that in our grief, we could not hear with our heads at the time. We could only hear with our hearts. Second, God's truth is not the preacher's or the church's philosophical speculation, but God's story in the story of the believing community. Third, had the preacher simply told us his own story, into which God's story of consolation and grace had cut its way, it would have touched us with God's consolation and grace. It would have touched us not in the head, but in the heart.

Telling the stories that count is more poetry than philosophy. Doing therapy is first listening to the poetry, healthy or sick, in the story of the patient, and then telling the healing story that fits that person's need. These things are things of the heart, of the psyche, of the soul. I came away from my nephew's funeral wondering whether the preacher had ever suffered, whether he had ever told or allowed himself to sense his own story, whether his story really carried any of God's real story and its healing consolations. Sometimes I get patients who are the wreckage of other therapists' failures. They fail just like that preacher did.

The poetry of telling one's story and of thereby incarnating God's real story into it is authentic therapy and true ministry. The story of the man from Nazareth cuts across all of our stories, and we cannot get around him in history. In him God's story is incarnated in its epitome. As Marcus Borg reminds us, he was a man with a life full of God. One day, that man's story cuts across your story, and then you and I encounter each other, and his story in yours illumines mine. That is the poetry of life, ministry, therapy, healing. That ministry goes through and gets beyond cognitive preoccupations of the intellect. It goes further than propositions about theology. It reaches the psychological structures that form our personalities and characters. It even penetrates more deeply than that, into the very essence of our psychospirituality, where our greatest terror and disorder wait in our unconscious minds. There it longs for the supreme resolution of knowing that we are unconditionally accepted and affirmed by another person and by God, just as we are—and for the sake of what we can be freed to become as God's imagers and God's compatriots in building the good things on earth. In that sense, and at that level, the grasp of truth can generate security, faith, and the fruits of healing and wholeness in humans.

STORIES THAT REALLY COUNT

It is for all those reasons that in the lives of humans who have suffered from the most abject dysfunction and have destructively affected the lives of others, the most important question is whether they have found psychospiritual healing through the grace of their fellow humans and by the illumination of God's grace and providence. The most important thing is that through their suffering, God's story has cut across their stories a little more deeply and thoroughly than ever before. If so, those people are all the more completely equipped to be the purveyors of the healing story for others: as friends, therapists, pastors, or mentors. We should put a battle streamer on such a person's cowl that says "This one has been there where the tragedies of life happened. He or she has seen the human story and God's story in ways that most of us cannot imagine. It has become part of the fabric of his or her own story. This person has something very special to give us. This is a wounded healer who knows what wounds mean and what they tell us of God in his grace and healing. This one knows a healthy God and thus is a healed and healing person."

If this seems like to a private and individualistic view of truth, there can be no apology for that. We cannot boil down the truth in our several and combined stories to a finite and quantifiable packaged story. Story only works if it is incarnated in a particular person. The lust to boil it down to a tradition is merely another way of trying for some new kind of foundationalism. It is our perpetual temptation to touch bottom, rather than simply remain in the swim of life and of our personal quests. We cannot claim that our story is God's story unless it becomes God's healing story for someone else. It must work, or it is not dynamically true, that is, real. When it works to heal, that makes it compelling and persuasive, relevant to the human predicament.

The great risk that truth takes in that sense is the same as the risk that God has apparently taken in his decision to stop shouting at us through the prophets and begin speaking to us instead through a visit, an incarnation in Jesus, the man with the life full of God. Preaching, conversation, and therapy are brief incarnations of the real story for our world, and they all participate in the same risk: they are not real or authentic until they work real healing. These modes of communication participate in God's truth telling and in God's risk that the truth will not work—that it may be imprecise, incomplete, or distorted by human process, lost in the weave of human history or transmuted into any erroneous story humans may conjure up.

The truth that heals in the mental health clinic is not the propositions about psychology, the intellectual information from psychological sciences, the cognitive process of learning. It is, rather, the therapist's touch of the wounded psyche and soul, the distorted spirit, the sick imagination, and the hurting heart. Truth is not, in such cases, a page from the textbook, with all of its warrantable authority and documentation. The truth that heals is that insight which comes from the therapist's story intersecting the patient's story and illumining it. Whether it is God's story from the material world God created, as we know it from the natural and social sciences, or whether it is God's story from the sacred scriptures of a believing community, it is God's story illumining ours. Truth that heals is finally in incarnation, by incarnation, and for incarnation only. Truth is not for standing objectively out there in the wind, shimmering in its inherent and pristine brilliance, worshiped or esteemed for its inherent symmetry, coherence, or ultimacy. Truth is for healing. Truth is God's grace reflected in the wounded healer.

That reflection of God by incarnation in our persons can be misunderstood. I am always impressed by two things about Jesus, as one who incarnates God, and about the place of God's story in Jesus's story. The first is that he walked all around Palestine, and most people did not notice him or God's story reflected in him. Most people did not notice that God's story was intersecting their human stories in that man from Nazareth. Only a paradigmatic few noticed. That was the risk God took and always takes. The second is that Jesus absolutely refused to resort to spectacle or manipulation of people and their thoughts or imagination to get their attention. He did not develop a worldview of philosophical propositions or harangue the crowds from the temple wall with persuasive sermonic logic.

He might have come in the twentieth century, I suppose, and taken advantage of the worldwide TV networks, as some who operate in his name are prone to do today. Even so, I feel he would have rejected the invitation to be a televangelist, garishly seducing or hypnotizing a massive following for his kingdom. Presumably, he did not do that for the same reason he turned down the three great temptations he encountered during his retreat in the wilderness: he was absolutely against the notion of truth as a manipulative lever.

The invitation to change stones to bread was surely a consideration of the phenomenal psychological allegiance he could have gained, and the worldwide power he could have wielded, had he appealed to the stomachs of humanity and solved the problem of poverty and starvation. The invitation to jump from the temple heights into the arms of the angels was obviously a thought about how captivating a psychological spectacle he could create to gain the wondering allegiance of humanity, hypnotized by his supernatural magic. The suggestion that he bow down to the powers of political and military force to gain owner-ship of the kingdoms of the world was certainly a consideration to become the new Alexander the Great.

Had he resorted to the crass advantages of raw power for commanding the attention and controlling the allegiance of humans, undoubtedly, he could have managed it successfully. Presumably, he could have made any one of the three temptations work effectively, if his objective and mode had been to benefit people by controlling them. He discarded all three options because they were manipulative of people and unreflective of the story of God and his healing relief of grace. God's story could not ride well on those kinds of human stories.

So Jesus took the risk of simply living out the life story of a thoughtful and contrarian rabbi. Perhaps 80 percent of his contemporaries did not notice his story or God's story in his story. The real story is not different today, but just as then, where people are telling their stories to each other with passion and compassion, in professional roles or personal friendships, God's story from science and from sacred writings is riding on those human stories. There the truth is breaking through to faith, and faith to healing, and healing to whole-ness. That is the generative and leavening role of story.

PERSONALITY MODELS AND STORY

Story functions in this process in a very special way. It can be understood readily when one looks at the role of story in the light of how human per-sonality develops and functions. Salvatore R. Maddi has given us one of the best books on this matter, titled simply *Personality Theories*. In it he describes the spate of theories that psychology has given us. His emphasis is specially focused on the interaction of the core and peripheral forces of human per-sonality. He suggests that all personality theories fall into three categories: those that see personality development as the thrust toward conflict resolu-tion, those that see it as the movement toward fulfillment, and those that see it as persistence in maintaining consistency in the psychological state of the person. His distinctions are very helpful; however, it is possible to catego-rize the whole matter of personality theory in much simpler ways: theories that assume that humans are primarily rational, primarily relational, primar-ily emotional, or primarily biological.

Each of these categories has significant truth in it. Each carries with it, as well, important implications regarding the role of truth and truth telling and thus the function of information and story. If I assume that human personality is primarily rational, I will assume that moving a person to understanding, education, therapy, healing, or salvation requires informing the person more completely with the facts or data necessary for correct thinking, sound cognition, and increased intellectual precision. I will claim that humans must be taught truth, conceived of as an objective set of facts, propositions, and conclusions.

If I assume that human personality is primarily relational, I will further assume that moving a person to growth in understanding, education, therapy, healing, and psychospiritual wholeness requires helping that person build healing relationships so that the desired growth will take place under the stimulation of such relationships. This design intends to give persons that experience of constructive relationality in which alone, it is then supposed, persons can realize their real and true selves.

If I assume that human personality is primarily emotional, I will expect that moving a person to increased understanding, education, therapy, and wholeness requires freeing his or her emotions for more complete self-awareness and self-expression, thus integrating his or her affective world more wholesomely. Humans must be made free to feel their real and necessary feelings.

If I assume, however, that human personality is primarily biological, I will conclude that growth in all areas will require refinement and correction of the stimuli bearing on this person, to produce appropriate classic conditioning and the necessary responses that afford maturation, function, healing, and wholeness.

Since all these formulations are true in certain profound ways, the address to human development in self-awareness, self-expression, and self-actualization requires a comprehensive approach. When that is done, it is clear that truth has been found and has functioned as truth intends to function: for growth and wholeness. Presenting and sharing story is a channel for the multiple facets of truth to address and stimulate human development comprehensively, on all four levels at the same time, without giving priority to any one of them. Story addresses the entire person and mobilizes the entire person to respond in growth and wholeness. Incarnation is the way for the story to infiltrate the screens of defensiveness on all the levels of personality function: cognitive and intellectual defenses, affective or emotional defenses, relational or interpersonal defenses, and physical or instinctual defenses.

CONCLUSION

When you, as a rational, relational, emotional, and biological person, tell me your story, you intersect my story at the biochemical level, at the emotional level, at the relational level, and at the intellectual level. You meet me at each level of my existence. If you do that, instigating comprehensive growth in me at all those levels, and God's story is interwoven with your story, you insinuate his story into mine at all the levels of my person. You may profit me by teaching me my catechism, but you do better by insuring that in the process, you become for me the incarnation of God's redemptive story of grace and acceptance. Then I can grow because in you I can see the truth of science or sacred story and the importance of both for my story.

We are inherently psychospiritual people—at center we are psyche, as God is spirit. Growth and wholeness cannot come until it comes to the spirit and thence to the whole unified person. Bringing that comprehensive growth to the whole person is the enterprise of ministry, in the mental health clinic, the parish, and daily social life. The psychodynamics of story are the forces of truth incarnated in a wholesome person, addressing humans as total persons, affording growth, healing, and faith.

CHAPTER 10

PSYCHOLOGICAL STRESS AS A WAY TO SPIRITUALITY

Life is often like an ice cream cone. Just when you think you have it licked, it drips all over you. Perplexity is as much a part of human existence as is pleasure; and often, in many ways, the perplexity seems not only more prevalent than the pleasure, but sometimes deteriorates into real and devastating pain. Human existence is generically a stressful process. Daily human experience is regularly distressing in unavoidable ways.

The secret to happy and fulfilling living is not to find the strategy or tactics to avoid distress or rid life of stressors. The secret is quite on the other side of things, in the wisdom to manage our stress and distress constructively toward growth. Stress is a function of growth, and distress is a potential growth inducer. Stress management as a way to a psychospiritually healthful life is a strategy for harnessing our stress and distress for growth in all facets of ourselves: spiritual, psychological, emotional, intellectual, and physical. If life is dripping all over you, just when you think you have it licked, remember the words of James 1:2–4: "Count it an advantage when you find yourself in stressful situations. Remember that distress in your life produces the growth called endurance. Moreover, as you savor the experience of perseverance, you will find a sense of hopefulness spontaneously rising in your spirit. That mature assurance of being equipped to handle life constructively will make you feel complete." That is the best psychological advice you can get for stress management.

STRESS AND DISTRESS

For many years, I taught university classes in the psychodynamics of interpersonal communication and group process. I always began the course with a generative group experience in which I invited each student to share with the group his or her most intense emotional experience. I was repeatedly surprised that every student in the class accepted the opportunity to share those intimate events. I was pleased that they were always respectful and compassionate of each other, as well. However, the most surprising part of the experience for me was the consistent pattern of the personal stories. Ninety percent or more were stories of the most abject and painful grief experiences imaginable: loss of parents at an early age, death of a sibling or a child, rape, murder of a close acquaintance or relative, overwhelming rejection, terrible disease or accident, and desperate periods of destitution. The patterns and percentages were always about the same from class to class.

I had not asked them to share their most painful experiences, only their most intense emotional ones, but uniformly, those intense processes had the shape of grief. Moreover, all that grief would have gone unnoticed and unknown during the entire four years of the students' university lives if it had not been for that class. Is it any wonder that the people around us act strangely at times? Is it a surprise that there is often so much distance between us at the real level of the soul? Indeed, is it not surprising, instead, that humans function as well as they do, considering the size of the anguish most of us carry in us? An old Dutch proverb declares poignantly, *Ieder huis hat zijn kruis.* Every house has its cross; none of us gets clean away from the bite of the stress and distress of life.

For some, that stress and distress proves destructive, while for others, it proves providential and growth affording. The task of therapists and healers must be the enhancement of the possibilities for human stress to become constructive. Each of us is responsible for employing the stress of our lives for wholesome personal development: increased function and effectiveness in body, mind, and spirit. How can that be done? More particularly, how can that be done as an experience in enhanced psychospiritual wholeness?

STRESSORS

In previous chapters, we explored the intricacies of human communication and examined the ways it can serve us almost miraculously in our quest for healing and wholeness. We also noted the numerous junctures at which it can break down. There is no greater stressor for humans than the experience of the failure of communication and the destructive effects on relationship that result from it. Nearly every person who seeks psychotherapy or pastoral counseling because of interpersonal distress reports that the heart of the problem is a lack of communication.

Communication Breakdown

Many who suffer from personal instead of interpersonal pathology acknowledge that a central issue for them is the inability to communicate
effectively, particularly their difficulty in sharing feelings or emotions.
Nearly every person who seeks psychotherapy or pastoral counseling because of interpersonal distress reports that the heart of the problem is a
lack of communication. Many who suffer from personal instead of interpersonal pathology acknowledge that a central issue for them is the inability
to communicate effectively, particularly their difficulty in sharing feelings
or emotions.

Of course, it is never true that people have no communication with each
other, even though they often express the problem in that manner. Frequently, couples who say they have no communication with each other are, in
fact, communicating vigorously with each other, but it is all a destructive exchange. They will sit together in my office with their faces turned away and
their backs toward each other. One of them may sit in stony silence, forcing
the other to do all the work at healing, all the time glaring with a shaming
gaze of disapproval at the person attempting to gain some ground toward
repair of the relationship. Such nonverbal communication speaks volumes, all
of it destructive. Silence can be a very articulate and brutally manipulative
mode of communication: intense communication, but none of it healing or an
enhancement of constructive relationship.

Silence is particularly powerful. It is a very effective way to manipulate
others. It speaks more loudly than words, and unless it is constructively interpreted, it is always inevitably destructive. We communicate constantly.
What people mean to say when they complain that they lack communication
is that the process has turned sour for them, verbally and nonverbally, shift-
ing wholly toward hostile or alienating experience. They mean to say that
their communication mainly increases their stress and distress and does not
fulfill the proper function of interpersonal relationship, namely, amelioration of distress. They mean that the dynamic spiral of relating has turned
severely downward toward the swamp of loneliness. They hunger for it to
be restored to its proper upward spiraling thrust, which gladdens the heart,
tantalizes the mind, challenges imagination, and changes distress into
growth-inducing stress.

Considering the inherent differences between men and women, or any
two individual humans, in such characteristics as brain hemisphere preference, problem-solving styles, and personal agenda; it is a miracle of providence and love whenever human communication succeeds at all. If we assume
it is succeeding or will succeed, we have signed the charter of its certain failure.
The inevitable result is a significant increase in stress and predictable expansion of distress.

It is likely that if we could solve the communication problem for humankind, 90 percent of all psychosocial illness would disappear. It is imperative that if we are to succeed in constructive stress management, we cultivate the requisite skills and work with great effort for the development of effective communication. The rewards in interpersonal relationships will be incalculable.

Ego Threats

The second major stressor for humans is ego threats. Many kinds of experiences can be ego threats. When we experience real or imagined rejection, especially in a relationship that we prize in some way, our stress level must greatly increase. Likewise, circumstances that give rise to feelings of unworthiness or perceived challenges to our worthiness are always highly stressful. When we perceive that we are not viewed with high regard or are not greatly needed in our job or chosen vocation, we must experience stress. When our job performance is in question or our job satisfaction is decreasing, when we fear that we are not measuring up to expectation, stress greatly increases. When we face responsibilities or problems and we are in the impasse of seeing no courses of action to take, stress follows as sure as the night follows day.

A peculiar instance of job stress in our corporate world in recent decades is that of the Peter principle. This is the experience of being promoted up the corporate ladder until one has reached the level just beyond one's capabilities. There one finds that all the esteem previously earned and that propelled the promotion to that exalted level is progressively eroded and replaced with disrepute, dissatisfaction, and defeat. The stress of these dynamics can be disastrous. It is at least overwhelmingly painful and unjust. Nearly as stressful is the even more current situation now common in commerce and industry in which a person who has given his life and creativity to a company in the expectation of a good retirement at the end of a normal career is suddenly retired early with less resources as a result of a company's arbitrary downsizing.

Frequently, such experiences result in feelings of loss of ego strength, self-esteem, and personal ability to control one's own destiny. Feelings of futility, abandonment, hopelessness, and even panic or terror can result. On some occasions, those losses need not be real, but merely anticipated, in order, nonetheless, to be devastating. Anticipated loss is as real and painful as the experience of the actual loss itself. One of the most painful forms of loss experience is the loss of the sense of a satisfactory relationship between one's real self and one's idealized self. When we perceive others as viewing us vastly differently from our cherished ideal self, we inevitably feel significant loss, perhaps even grief and fear. When we discover our own inadequacies and are forced to judge ourselves as falling far short of our idealized self, we may feel equal stress and distress.

Losses of many kinds contribute to human stress. They may be losses of treasured objects, familiar haunts, cherished or important relationships, convenient settings, predictable security, or a usable vision of the future. They may be personal losses such as health, youth, fame, or fortune. They may be communal losses such as threats to one's nation, defeat in war, economic depression, or defamation of trusted leaders. All of these constitute major personal ego insults and high stress.

We may even experience a high degree of stress merely from realizing that we are finite persons with human limitations who are called to a divine-sized task of contributing to the decency, beauty, hopefulness, and healing of the world. Sometimes we feel a little like the Mesopotamians must have felt, caught in a destiny for which we are not fitted, challenged to a vocation for which we have been ill equipped. Stress is the inevitable response. High stress is almost inevitably the matrix of human existence in our troubled time. I remember a sign over the desk of my battalion sergeant major in Vietnam. It read, "If you think you have this situation figured out, you just do not begin to understand the problem."

Recently, I preached a sermon in which I described the degree of stress most humans must endure throughout the world. My point had to do with the sensitivity and compassion we are all called on to exercise. I was surprised and saddened when a wealthy lady from a rich suburb came up to me a few weeks later and said that she was offended by my exaggeration of the human predicament. She said her husband refused to return to church because of my sermon since it bore no correspondence to their experience and their lives. She remarked further that they were insulted by being forced to view such a sordid and unrealistic picture. I responded by saying, "If you do not recognize the picture I painted, you belong to that dubiously lucky 10 percent of the human race that is not plugged into reality." If a person does not know that high stress is almost inevitably the matrix of human existence, he or she does not know what is going on, or does not care.

A third source of human stress is intimacy. The deep longing for intimacy, loss of intimacy, anxiety about intimacy, and the fear of failed intimacy all produce stress. The radical sexual promiscuity prevalent in many societies today is, undoubtedly, an overcompensation for the anxiety we feel about intimacy—a subconscious drive to desensitize the sharp pain of failure in intimacy by overwhelming oneself with exposure to intimacy-like experiences that, however, require no real connection, no real relationship. Frequently, the stress about intimacy arises from ego involved anxiety about one's sexual identity, prowess, or skill. As the distance increases between our sense of psychospiritual integrity and sexual authenticity, stress rises exponentially. As those two are reintegrated, stress returns to appropriate proportions in our intimacy experiences and needs.

A final major source of stress is our mortality. It is likely that humans are the most self-reflective of all animals and also more consciously aware of our own mortality than all other creatures. We can contemplate it in advance, recognize the way it relates to our moral imperatives, and live every moment with the awareness that no one gets out of life alive. Probably the specter behind much of our psychospiritual illness is the presence and awareness of the unresolvable matter of our mortality. The potential for stress that our sense of mortality brings to every person is very great.

STRESS MANAGEMENT

As the task of the therapist and pastoral counselor is not to remove the patient's or parishioner's pain, but to interpret it, so the object in stress management is not to reduce or remove the stress, but to interpret it, manage it, and channel it into productive achievements. Stress is not the enemy. Because stress is designed into our lives as a stimulus for empowerment and growth, and because in that life system, God is God and grace is grace, pain and stress can be our friends. Stress is not the enemy. That is the reason this chapter is about stress management and not about stress reduction.

Many stress seminars are focused on the physiology of stress and emphasize a variety of exercises and diets designed to reduce the experiences stress produces. Those strategies treat the symptoms and not the problem. Moreover, they are usually self-defeating in that they create behavioral regimens that tend to increase the subject's anxiety about getting the regimen correct. When there is a little neurotic anxiety present in the person in unusual stress, as there almost always is, these regimens promote increased neurotic compulsivity. That in turn raises the stress level over the long term, rather than reducing or wholesomely channeling it. This leads to failure in stress reduction, resulting in the subject experiencing an increase of dysfunction, helplessness, and hopelessness.

Stress can be our friend. When one injures a finger, the body rushes blood to the site to cleanse the wound, increasing the oxygen available for healing the wound, engorging the tissue with healing blood cells, and raising the temperature around the wound to kill any foreign bacteria that may have invaded the tissue. The result of that physiological response to the injury is to set up a state of inflammation around the wound. The inflammation makes the wound look red and irritated and ugly. The inflammation presents a feverish condition and can be painful. It would be easy for an uninformed person to conclude that the inflammation is the enemy, while in fact, it is a friend. Now, admittedly, if the wound is massive, the inflammation can become flagrant and run away with itself, so to speak. Then one may lose tissue as a result of the inflammation. However, under normal conditions, the inflammation is the enemy of infection—the body's way of fighting the danger, preventing infection, and healing the injury.

Likewise, when the psyche is traumatized by a significant loss experience, such as the death of a loved one or the failure of a plan one heavily depended on, that loss is met by a grief response from the emotional world of the person. Grief is not the enemy, but a friend. It is the psyche's way of responding to significant loss or psychological trauma so as to prevent more massive insult to the whole feeling system of the person. Grief is to the psyche what inflammation is to the body. It is a mechanism for limiting the damage area and introducing a process of healing.

Just as inflammation can get out of hand and become a source of damage to the body tissue—so stress of grief can become so massive and endemic that it takes over the personality, entrenches the psyche in the stress or grief process, and prevents the psyche from healing itself. However, normally, grief, for example, introduces a three-stage process of healing. Stress functions comparably to empower us. The initial stage of grief is denial, a way in which the psyche buys time, so to speak, for the person to prepare to deal with the actual trauma or loss. What is sometimes referred to as the bargaining stage of grief experience is really only a special part of that denial phase. Eventually, in a healthy grieving process, the psyche moves along to the second, or acknowledgment, stage of grieving. This is the stage at which the reality of the awful situation penetrates the conscious world of the person and must be dealt with realistically. The final stage is integration, when the healthy psyche is able to acknowledge again that life can go on wholesomely, constructively, and meaningfully, despite the awful loss. Grief is the healing inflammation function of the healthy psyche. It is not an enemy, but a friend.

So also with stress. Stress is the reaction of the total organism, body, mind, and psyche, to significant threat to the organism. It functions for the total organism as inflammation and grief do for the body and psyche, respectively. When some aspect of the organism of the human person is beginning to feel that it is overloaded, the organism reacts with the physiology, psychology, and cognition of stress. Our blood pressure rises, we perspire, our heart rate increases, the adrenal glands begin to pump their secretions, the entire endocrine system is mobilized, and we begin to breath more deeply and rapidly, introducing more oxygen into the body. The pancreas produces insulin to metabolize the sugar that is in the system, insuring maximum available energy for quick reaction to any danger we discern. Stress alerts every facet of our physiology for appropriate response to the threatened overload.

Similarly, the psyche responds with a psychological alert, and the mind quickens its reactions of attention, perception, decision making, and integration of stimuli, creating interpretation and meaning with regard to the nature of whatever threat it is that we are perceiving. Stress mobilizes the total organism for response to a special challenging situational demand. Change always brings pain of some sort. Pain brings stress of some degree. This stress calls up our inner resources of response, and we grow by coping with the change. Moreover, since we grow more from our pain than from our pleasure, stress may well be welcomed as a resource for growth, providing great potential for energizing us, provided we can discern how to use it well.

We can treat the symptoms and thus suppress the stress process, just as steroids suppress inflammation and thus endanger the wound by its becoming flagrantly infected; or we can manage the sources, dynamics, channels, and consequences of stress so as to enhance growth and healing. How shall we proceed to make that difference?

TOOLS FOR STRESS MANAGEMENT

We have numerous tools for constructive management of stress. As has already been suggested, the first tool is *understanding* the stress and its sources so that we can accurately interpret it and what it is telling us about ourselves and our situation. Stress that is well interpreted begins immediately to take on and provide meaning in terms of which we can see our way to new courses of action. Second, we can accept the *friendship of stress* and recognize it as a mechanism for our healing. That permits us to work with it, rather than fight it as an enemy, thus reducing at the outset much of the neurotic anxiety usually associated with the experience of stress. We must remember that management of stress is a total-organism process. Befriending it frees it to work constructively for us. Befriending stress means that we do not respond to it by being terrified by it, but rather by recognizing it as a natural part of life and appropriate to the situation we happen to be in.

Third, much stress management is really a matter of *anger management*. There are only six ways to channel anger—only six things that one can do with anger. One can internalize it and experience the inevitable consequence of depression. One can displace it on those who are not the rightful sources of the anger, thus increasing the damage area and expanding the reasons to be angry and stressed. One can *destructively* confront the source of one's anger and again increase the damage area and expand the number of stimuli for anger and stress. One can *constructively* confront the source of the anger and so move toward resolution of the impasse. One can channel the anger into *hard work*, particularly large muscle activity such as running. Or one can express the anger in a therapeutic setting, with appropriate *catharsis* of the emotion.

The first three strategies for anger management are inevitably and inherently self-defeating, containing self-destructive elements; that is, they are actions that really end in the anger being reflected on oneself in harmful ways. The last three are constructive courses of action for managing anger and the stress that prompts it, moving a person toward utilizing the energy generated by the stress for growth and problem solving. These channels for anger constitute available courses of action in every anger situation and channel stress constructively.

It seems clear that anger is normally a healthy emotion and that it is not destructive to us or others as long as we can perceive a constructive action through which to act it out usefully. That is also true of grief and stress. These experiences do not become constipated, internalized, and self-defeating unless we cannot see or imagine a clear course of action to take. Moreover, when we cannot see how to find a course of action for our grief and stress, they tend to turn into anger. If we can find a course of action for them, they tend to dissipate. If they turn to anger and we cannot discern a course for resolving it, it will be internalized automatically and produce depression. Management of anger, therefore, is a crucial tool for stress management.

Fourth, *awareness* of the forces and phases of grief can be an important tool for management of stress. We all experience some degree of stress each day. Every loss experience, however great or small, activates the grief mechanism to heal the wound inflicted on the psyche by the loss. When we do not understand grief, it induces a secondary insult in the form of anxiety, which raises our stress levels significantly. Awareness of the grief process frees us to allow it to follow its natural healing course from denial, to acknowledgment, to integration into ongoing life and health. Then stress is constructively channeled, and function is normalized.

A fifth important tool for handling stress is *forgiveness*. Few people are sufficiently aware today of the remarkable resource forgiveness can be for us. No day passes in which each of us is not insulted in some way by the neglect, thoughtlessness, insensitivity, or blatant injury inflicted by the behavior of another person. These events generate a great deal of stress that, because of the inadvertency of most of those occasions, is offered no clear way to problem solving and channeling the stress constructively. Forgiveness is a resource over which we have total control. We can decide that we will forgive that which cannot be excused, understood, explained, compensated for, or forgotten. To forgive that which can be explained, understood, excused, rationalized, compensated for, or forgotten makes no sense because such things need no forgiveness. They make sense somehow. It is precisely those things for which there is no help that must be forgiven. They can be resolved by an authentic decision for an act of forgiveness, and in no other way.

Lewis Smedes's book *Forgive and Forget* is one of the best on forgiveness. His message is essentially the same as that of Martin Marty, penned many years earlier in response to Simon Wiesenthal's *Sunflowers*. As you remember, Simon Wiesenthal was the man who, after World War II, ran the institute in Austria that hunted down Nazi war criminals who had perpetrated the deaths of 6 million Jews and 12 million Germans, Poles, and Russians. In his book, *Sunflowers*, he related the story of being called to the bedside of a terminally wounded German soldier. The lad was the disaffected son of a Lutheran pastor. He had called for a leading Jewish person to visit him so that he could ask forgiveness for shooting Jewish women and children as they fled a tenement that the Wehrmacht had set afire. Three times, Wiesenthal visited the blinded soldier, whose mortal wounds had recalled him to his father's faith. Having listened to the young man for four or five hours over three or four days, Wiesenthal walked out in disgust, refusing to forgive him.

Refusing to forgive what could not be rationalized or understood in this young German officer, who was trying to confess his atrocities against Jews, Wiesenthal lost his chance to handle, in the one way available to him, the horrible stress the holocaust caused him. Apparently, he could not get that out of his system. He wrote his book to tell that story and then sent it to leading religious and philosophical professors of ethics around the world, asking if he had done the right thing in failing to forgive the man. Martin Marty said, in effect, "Simon, you should have forgiven him. You needed to forgive him for three reasons. God forgives him and all of us. You were God's man on the spot at that moment. You should have forgiven him in God's name. Moreover, you should have forgiven him, and you should forgive him even now, because you are getting way too much mileage out of your guilt and stress about that event. Most of all, you should have forgiven him because forgiveness frees the forgiver, even more than the forgiven." Lewis Smedes declared that we should always be ready to forgive and then to remember what we have forgiven and remember that we have forgiven it. When we forget that we have forgiven it and revert to our vindictiveness and recriminations, we should forgive it again.

That notion leads to a sixth tool: religion, more particularly, the experience of God's *grace*. Here stress management as a way in godliness comes to full bloom. Stress is induced by ego insult, loss, mortality, inadequacy, threat, unworthiness, and fear of intimacy. The ultimate resolution of all these insults to our psyche or soul, to our identity and security, is the discovery of the fact that God accepts and affirms us unconditionally as we are just now, in all our perceived weakness, perplexity, and dead-end streets. As his imagers and compatriots in pressing the claims of his kingdom in our generation, God sees us as his saints, cherishing us in providence and guaranteeing that he will always be for us what he has always been for us. The very meaning of God's name, Yahweh, guarantees that. God's entire intent is focused on his ambition to afford us the consolation of the Gospel. A life of appropriate *prayer* keeps us continually in a posture of a needy child at the hand of our beneficent divine parent. Prayer offers catharsis of our grief, anger, and stress. Prayer provides insights that correct our vision of our own condition and actual neediness. Prayer generates and expresses that gratitude which makes health and happiness possible. Prayer channels stress energy into directions in which it is appropriate to the situation and constructive for our dynamic growth. Healing therapy and pastoral care facilitates that life of *spiritual sensitivity* as the central process beyond mere restoration of psychological function, to psychospiritual wholeness.

CONCLUSION

One of the great advantages of realizing the relief of God's grace and the spontaneous healing gratitude it generates is the perception that being a Christian, or a person of deep spirituality, does not mean measuring up, but, rather, it means our unconditional acceptance of God's unconditional acceptance of us. Being a person of deep spirituality is not a command to be obeyed, but an invitation to be joyfully and freely accepted, not an obligation to be met, but an opportunity to be seized and celebrated. The reason for being a Christian is not to save one's crippled and fractured soul from hell. The only good reason to be a Christian or a person of any form of deep spirituality is because it is more fun to live life in all of its stressors and vicissitudes, with the full and present realization that God is unconditionally for us and not against us. It is the pleasure of realizing that God embraces us in forgiving love and grace in all our frailty and inadequacy for the responsibilities of life and the challenges of godliness—the pleasure of knowing that we cannot sin ourselves out of God's grace, nor squirm out of his long embrace. We are free in his love and care. In our most stressful moments, we can see the presence of God if we keep an eye open to see how he will show up in our moments of need. Then stress can become God's gift for our growth.

Recently, while traveling to the Republic of South Africa, I was delayed in New York City because my visa was not in order. I had been given inappropriate information by the authorities in Chicago, and as I boarded the airplane, I was informed that I could not make the trip. Normally, such situations exasperate me, particularly since I had a deadline to appear in Johannesburg to preach two days later. I felt an unusually intense surge of stress and could see no course of action to resolve the problem. Before anguish overwhelmed me, for some reason I took a step backward, as it were. I said to myself, "This is a completely inadvertent situation for which there was no prevention, and now there is no immediate remedy. Let me see how the Lord will show up in this impossible situation and show his way of using it as a matrix for his grace."

The person who turned me away from the airplane and insisted that I had to go to the South African consulate in New York was a woman in her mid-forties who seemed proficient and professional in her work. She instructed me in what was necessary to correct my visa and proceed to Africa. I did as she said and tried to keep control of myself while the consular people considered the situation. They repeatedly told me that they could do nothing about the problem. Finally, after numerous transoceanic telephone calls, the matter was resolved by the appearance of an old friend of mine who had been an officer of the consulate in Chicago but was lately promoted to a senior role in New York.

I was rescheduled to board the flight departing Friday afternoon at 3:00 P.M. Since I had had so much confusion in this matter, I went to Kennedy Airport at about 11:00 A.M., so I would have time to check everything and relax a bit before the 17-hour flight via Isle del Sol. When I entered the terminal, I was still wondering how the Lord would show up in all this in his provident grace. It was hard to see any meaning in the entire irrational mess. When I approached the flight processing desks, I saw, once again, the woman who had sent me away the day before. She stood alone awaiting a flight that had been seriously delayed. I greeted her and asked where I could buy flight insurance.

As I spoke, I noticed that she was looking at my business card, given to her the day before. She immediately asked me what it meant that I was the executive director of the Christian Association for Psychological Studies. "What does this mean, Christian and psychology?" she inquired. I told her that I was a theologian and a psychotherapist. She declared that she needed to talk to me. She then told me a long story of grief and pain, the odyssey of her childhood in a series of orphanages in the Netherlands, being passed from foster family to foster family, exploited and rejected, never belonging and always abused. World War II had brought her further tragedy and sorrow. She had finally taken control of her destiny by escaping to the university, mastering three foreign languages, finding sophisticated international employment, shepherding her wealth wisely, and ultimately being able to live well in New York City. Now she could travel widely, enjoy financial security and luxury, collect art, and own a upscale apartment in this lovely cosmopolitan city. Every morning, when she awoke, she was in misery, emotional pain, and stress. She had lived her life seeking meaningful relationship and its security but still felt rejected, abandoned, alone, unworthy, and undesirable. She still did not belong. She felt like killing herself.

We spoke for two hours without stopping. I began to see the presence of God showing up in this strange inadvertency of my visa problem. I do not mean that God causes things like that, but he seems to enter into them when they happen and produce gain from our pain. An old baptismal formula declares that "God averts all evil from us or turns it to our profit." I carried on a correspondence with that lady and urged her to seek help with a psychologist friend of mine in New York City because I believed she was suffering from menopausal depression. That proved to be the case. She achieved an entirely new appreciation of her lovely life with the aid of appropriate estrogen supplement. The Lord was in all that process on my trip to South Africa. He did not cause her suffering or my visa problem, but he entered into it, and he had in mind a dangerously distressed airline official in New York. Faith, or deep spirituality, is the assurance that God will show up in our stress, that he really will be for us as he has always been for us, and that he will see the process through to its redemptive end. That is undoubtedly the most important tool of all for stress management and surely clearly reveals how stress is an opportunity on the way to psychospiritual health.

CHAPTER 11

THE ESSENCE OF PSYCHOSPIRITUAL HEALTH: LIFE AND GRACE

In the cool silence of an early spring morning in 1963, the steel gray hull of a U.S. Navy ship loosed its moorings in its berth at Groton, Connecticut, crept quietly out of the harbor, and knifed its way keenly into the dark swells of the North Atlantic. It was the world's first nuclear submarine, the USS *Thresher*, under way for its final shakedown cruise. It was manned by 167 fine, young, red-blooded American men. The *Thresher* made its rendezvous with the mother ship precisely on time and proceeded immediately with the preliminary sea trials. All went very well. In mid-afternoon, the time came for its most demanding mission, the deep swift dive to a still-classified depth, somewhere below 2,000 feet beneath the rolling waves of that turbulent sea.

Suddenly, at 3:14 P.M., the mother ship intercepted a frantic call, apparently an SOS from the *Thresher*'s radio room. The message lasted for mere seconds, was broken in the middle, and then silence. The mother ship responded immediately to reestablish communication with the *Thresher*; the tension grew, but still only silence remained. The U.S. Navy's Atlantic Headquarters, which was monitoring the progress of the sea trials, recognized the frantic efforts of the mother ship and flexed its muscles. The whole range of power and resources that it could bring to bear in an effort to reestablish contact with the *Thresher* and its gallant crew was mobilized. Still only silence. Woods Hole was alerted for the deployment of its deep submersibles, but there was still nothing but silence.

Silence all that afternoon, *silence* all that night. Only *silence* all the next day, while wise men of power around the world wracked their brains for something sensible and useful to do. *Silence* all that week. *Silence* to all eternity!

For that valiant ship and her dedicated men had gone down into the depths of the sea. What is lost in the depths of the sea is not recoverable. It cannot be rediscovered. It cannot be resurrected. Lost! Gone! Erased! Expunged from the record, almost as though they had never existed, 167 fine young men and their magnificent submarine.

Micah, the biblical prophet, declared that God has cast all our sins into the depths of the sea (Mic. 7:18–20). Erased! Gone! As though they had never existed! Expunged from the record of God's memory! They cannot be recovered or resurrected against us ever again! That is the most relevant and healing psychological fact ever conceived on the face of this planet. It is also the most central and significant theological truth ever understood. It is stunning to think that Micah revealed it already in the eighth century B.C.E. He prophesied both before and after the Assyrian invasion destroyed five-sixths of the nation of Israel in 722 B.C.E.

MICAH'S METAPHOR

It is a memorable and meaningful metaphor Micah manages to insinuate into our consciousness in those words. "Who is a God like our God?" asks the prophet. "He pardons iniquity, he passes over transgression, . . . he delights in steadfast love, . . . he tramples our iniquity under his feet, and he casts all our sins into the depths of the sea!" Moreover, Micah assures us that God had taken this action before we were born and guaranteed it to us through our ancestors, "from the days of old."

Micah had available to him other metaphoric options. He might have said that forgiveness and grace in God is like God taking our iniquity and pouring it into a space capsule and firing it off into the nether regions of outer space. Micah knew that such a picture would not carry the precisely honed message that he knew humankind really needed, then and now, to relieve their spirits of neurotic guilt, exaggerated anxiety, compulsive self-righteousness, and self-defeating fear, shame, and disorder. People knew already in the eighth century B.C.E. that what goes up must come down. If you know the direction and velocity of a space capsule, you can track it, recover it, retrieve it, and use it if need be in court evidence against any manufacturer who has produced a malfunctioning product. It can be resurrected against you, if you are the perpetrator. Remember *Apollo 13*, the spaceship damaged near the moon and gingerly but successfully brought back by Houston Control. The metaphor would not work for Micah's message. God has cast all our sins into the depths of the sea. That is the only thing that works to free us from our inherent fear, guilt, and shame.

The prophet might have chosen instead to say that for God, forgiveness is like sealing our sins in a pirate's chest and burying it in the sands of the sea at low tide. In the nineteenth century, it was common in the oaths of secret societies to declare that if anyone betrayed the oath, he would be killed and buried in the sand of the sea at ebb tide. That was supposed to imply that he would never be found, recovered, or justified. But Micah knew, as do we since our earliest childhood memories, how pirate's chests are washed up to land by the incessant hammering of the waves. How many pirates in fable and in life have been brought to bar by the inadvertent appearance of the evidence of their dastardly deeds, which they had so carefully hidden? That metaphor would not work either for Micah's unique purposes.

Micah needed a way to say that with God, forgiving is forgetting. He needed a way to say it that we could not forget, even if, in our preference for self-righteousness and self-justification, we genuinely wished to forget the profound character of divine grace. He needed a way to say it that would get past our cognition and rationalizations down to our affective level. He needed to outflank our theological defensiveness and philosophy and hit us where we could not vomit it out—where it would infect us with spiritual freedom and psychological relief, where it could heal us before we could nullify it with our religious excuses for rejecting unconditional grace and replacing it with our addiction to conditional relationships.

Micah chose the only way that would work, the only metaphor that would be adequately memorable. God has cast all our sins into the depths of the sea. The Apocalypse of St. John says that is the sea of God's eternal forgetfulness. Micah chose his metaphor carefully and consciously to say what humankind always needed most to hear. His metaphor defines God's disposition toward us. "He delights in steadfast love. He will not retain his anger. He will have compassion. He will be faithful even when we are not. He does not focus on transgression. He promised this to us from the beginning, from the days of our ancestors."

MICAH'S MESSAGE

If that is Micah's memorable metaphor, what is Micah's intended message in it? Micah's message is theologically simple and psychologically profound: the center of the good news, psychologically and theologically, is grace. Not just any ordinary kind of grace, implied in the easy and superficial way we throw that term around. This is a very special and precise kind of grace. It is unconditional, radical, and universal. That is why this central biblical fact is called *good news—Evangelium.* All other conditional messages, which require us to shape up, repent, change our behavior, or prove ourselves to God in some other way to receive his goodwill, are always bad news. They only address the superficialities of our symptomology or dysfunction. They do not get at our problem, that is, that *we cannot shape up* until we are freed by God's radical and unconditional acceptance of us, as we are. Only if his grace sets us free from what we are, congenitally anxiety-laden humans driven thereby into pathology, can we be empowered to become what we have the potential of being.

That is the only therapy that gets at our final and fundamental problem. Only unconditional grace takes our problem as seriously as it really is. Carl Rogers knew long ago that it is only unconditional positive regard that frees the patient to grow and heal, to be free to choose wholesomeness. Why has it taken Jews and Christians so long to hear Micah clearly? God has cast all our fracturedness and distortion, all our inadequacy for the responsibilities of life and the challenges of godliness, all our dysfunction, into the depths of the sea. They do not count. They can never be counted against us, ever again.

Bishop Oxnam of the Methodist Church is reported to have said at the beginning of the twentieth century that the God we see on the pages of the Hebrew Bible or Old Testament is a big bully who is in no sense the same God whom we see in the face of Jesus Christ. That is not much of a commentary on the Old Testament, but it is a significant comment on Mr. Oxnam. It clearly indicates that he never read the Old Testament, or at least did not know how to read it. He obviously never really heard the words of Micah. Moreover, the entire main stream of Old Testament theology is this same message of radical grace.

Think of David, the murderous adulterer, of whom in the end God said, "A man after my own heart." Think of Zechariah's dream (Zech. 3:2). He envisioned Joshua, the high priest, standing in God's eternal judgment hall, hailed before the divine tribunal for the sins of the covenant-breaking and God-forsaking people whom he represented, his filthy clothes symbolizing their degradation. On his right hand, where the defense attorney should have stood, was Satan himself, reading into the record of the court the sonorous history of the humanness, sin, fracturedness, and distortions of the people of God. Your story and mine!

Satan never missed a beat in this story, nor forgot a datum or date. He had it all there. As you watch the scene, you can feel the tension build, the climax approach, when the hammer of judgment will come down, with Satan declaring, "God, these are not your people. They are my people. They act like the devil, feel like the devil, think like the devil, and they are beginning to look like the devil! They are my kind of people, not your kind of people." Joshua seems somehow filthier and smaller as the proceedings unfold. Satan looks better and more like an honest man with constructive social intent the further he progresses to the climax of condemnation.

Then, suddenly, in the middle of the unfolding transcendental drama, the Angel of the Lord steps onto center stage and makes a momentous announcement. He declares, "The Lord rebukes you, Satan. The Lord who has chosen humankind rebukes you. Humanity is like a charred pine knot that God has plucked from the fires of hell. He is going to clean it, polish it, and set it on the mantelpiece of the universe, as a grand work of art for all the world to delight in. Satan, you have an incredible mind for detail. Like the American mass media, you have an admirable memory for dates and data, particularly for negative and tragic stories, for the worst possible interpretations and the grossest possible distortions and manipulations of reality. Your research skill seems inexhaustible. You surely have done your homework and prepared your brief with consummate thoroughness, in terms of your distorted concept of reality. Your case is so comprehensive that I almost feel like apologizing for spoiling your apparent triumphalism. You have not missed a fact of all the history of dysfunctional humankind. However, you have unfortunately forgotten one point, the one point that really counts: I love them. They are mine, in spite of themselves. I have chosen humanity, even when they have not chosen me. I love them, even when they are unlovable. The Lord rebukes you, Satan, and throws your case out of court. You forgot the only fact that counts. You could have saved yourself the time and trouble. The facts are *for* you, but the *law* and the *precedent* are against you. God's law is love. Of course, you can never comprehend that. You were destined from all eternity to fail here. You should have gone for a vacation to Miami instead."

"Who is a God like our God? He pardons iniquity, he passes over transgression, he will not keep his anger forever, he delights in steadfast love. He is faithful to us when we are unfaithful to him. He tramples all our iniquities under his feet and casts all our sins into the depths of the sea of his eternal forgetfulness. Moreover, he has guaranteed this to us through our ancestors from the days of old" (Mic. 7:18–20).

Surely that is just what Jesus had in mind in his very best story, the parable of the prodigal son. Of course, this parable is incorrectly named. It is a story about two sons. It is really the parable of the waiting father. You know the story well, I am sure, but remind yourself of the central moment. The son prematurely and self-destructively spent his inheritance and wasted his life in worthless behavior, landing at last in a pig pen, as so many American kids did during the three decades from 1965 to 1995. He had enough brains to realize that his father's servants lived in luxury and dignity while he, the son, lived like a pig.

He did the sensible thing. He went home to his father's bounteous house. What he did not count on was that his father had been waiting for him all this time, looking down that road every day. When he rounded the curve and came over the hill, his father was looking, waiting, longing for him, and his father saw him before the son recognized his father. So his father ran to him, embraced him in all his filth, kissed him on his dirty cheek, and instructed the servants to clean him and clothe him in royal garments.

The son could hardly protest quickly enough. You can see him pushing his father away, declaring, "Just a minute, you do not understand. I have been an offense to heaven and before your face. I am unworthy to be called your son—to wear your royal garb. I want to be taken back into your household as a hired man. I want to have the chance to prove myself to you, to earn my way back into your favor and goodwill. I want to prove that I have come to my senses finally, that I can be a responsible and industrious person, that I can justify myself over the years to come. I want to make up for my failure and demonstrate that I am really a good guy after all, deep down inside. I have discovered that what I need is your care, largesse, friendship, and esteem. I want to be your hired man."

You can just imagine his father drawing back in astonishment, looking at him quizzically, and then, with a hushed voice, saying, "You want to be my servant? How can you be my hired man? You are my son! Oh, it is clear that you do not look like my son anymore. You have not been acting like my son. You do not seem to feel like my son. After your time in the pig pen you do not smell like my son. Apparently, you do not think like a son of mine anymore. But you are my son—in spite of yourself. Your sonship does not hinge on your character and behavior. It depends on my character and behavior as your father. You are my son as long as I go on being a father to you. I will not abrogate my prerogative to be your father. You are my son because I insist on continuing to father you, in spite of yourself—and I will never let you go."

The story continues as a great party is thrown to celebrate the return of the Prodigal Son. So much noise can be heard that the elder son, in the back of the farm, inquires what is happening. Greatly disturbed by the occasion, this diligent older brother returned from his work but would not join in the festivities. Indeed, when he was urgently invited, he furiously refused. Typical of God, therefore, the father went out to him. He sat where his son sat and tried to put himself into his son's shoes. Can you see the father putting his arm around the fellow, cinching him up close and saying, "Why won't you come in?"

The elder son said fiercely, "All these years I have done my duty and you have never thrown a party for me!" Spitting it bitterly through his clenched teeth, he continued, "I stayed with you and responsibly cared for the estate and the family, and you never celebrated me! Now this wastrel comes home like a pig, and you act like it is some epiphany of God. This is not justice!" Well, that sounds like a good argument. Is that not the truth? That is your and my argument, is it not? We are the people who have done our duty. I have been a vigorous, even sometimes heroic, self-sacrificing, faithful churchman for 50 years of ministry. That should surely count for something. I should have accrued some leverage by now. God must, surely, be taking notice, don't you think? We are the respectable and diligent ones who keep alive the reign of God's grace that works and love that heals. Mainstream Christianity, these days, is big on justice. If justice is the issue, the father's failure to celebrate that faithful son who always did his duty does not look like justice.

Well, in a hushed vioce the father asked, in effect, of that elder son, "You have done your duty? You thought I loved and esteemed you because you did your duty? You think you are a son to me because you do your duty? You are as badly off as your wretched brother. *You* need to learn exactly what *he* needs to learn. You are not my son because you did your duty. I do not love you on account of the fact that you did your duty. It is not the record of *your* character and behavior that makes you my son. It is *my* character and behavior on which your sonship hinges. You are my son because I insist on being your father, in spite of yourself, no strings attached, and I will never let you go. You must come in to celebrate your brother's return to family life and to our healing world of love, grace, and forgiveness. Can you not see that what counts here is that he is my son? He was dead to me, and now he is alive again. He was lost me, and he is found. Nothing else counts! It is imperative that we have a great big raucous party of celebration, love, and relief."

God's grace is rooted in God's character. Our relief and freedom do not depend on our characters or behavior but on God's faithful, fatherly acceptance of us unconditionally. That is why grace is *radical*. It cuts right down to the central malfunction in us. It gets behind our defenses and self-justification needs and gets at the fundamental anxiety and sense of disorder that drive our psychological sickness and dysfunction.

That grace is also *universal*. Paul says repeatedly that in the end, "Every eye shall see God and every knee shall bow and every tongue shall confess the Lord, to the glory of God." We cannot sin ourselves out of God's grace, nor can we ever squirm out of God's long embrace. That is the message in Micah's meticulously chosen and marvelously memorable metaphor.

MICAH'S MEANING

The memorable message in Micah's marvelous metaphor has practical import for our work in the clinic and congregation. That is where the meaning of it becomes operational. I have noticed in my work in both those arenas of healing that people tend to be sick and dysfunctional in very similar ways. Moreover, I have observed that they are sick about in the same way that I am sick. At the point in time they seek my help, life may have rendered them a little more distorted and dysfunctional in one way or another than I might be at that moment, perhaps, or perhaps not. Perhaps we are both in the same boat at that moment.

In the universal human frenzy to deal with our inner sense of disorder and our outer sense of the derangement of things, most human pathology tends to fall into two categories: the urgent need to measure up to some perceived standards that press down on us, on one hand, and the aggressive inner need to resist such pressure to conform, on the other. That resistance represents the healthy desire to be free to live up to our own personal inner standards of achievement. The former pathology derives from the correct or incorrect perception that parents, church, society, the establishment, authorities, or God demand of us that we conform to certain challenging principles or codes of conduct in order that we may have a right to be loved, esteemed, certified, approved, or cherished and accepted. People who try to win that game of life begin to notice quite early that however much we strive and achieve, we never believe or feel that it is going to be quite enough to give us full certification. We can never quite do enough.

That pathology makes us compulsive, filled with neurotic guilt, laden with exaggerated anxiety, sometimes obsessive and driven to the meticulous rituals of perfectionist behavior in our daily code of conduct and in our religious prescriptions. It leads eventually to hostile independence needs, which deprive us of wholesome relationship and interdependence. It may even lead to our inability to trust God. We slide further into narcissistic isolation and paranoia, further from a sense of well-being. The primary dynamics in our psychospirituality then become fear, guilt, and shame. All of these make us more dysfunctional. Those really unfortunate persons whose dysfunction is rooted in disturbed biochemistry have even more intractable forces driving their needs for measuring up, or resisting that pressure. They cannot experience grace until their chemistry is corrected.

If we have some strand of healthy psychological tissue in our souls, as most humans do, we must soon develop an urgent need to resist such pressures to measure up, a need to throw off such constraints, for we are all made in God's image, and that means that we are designed inherently to be free agents: free to do as we please; free to decide our own destinies; free to take charge and create meaningful and joyful lives; free from fear, guilt, and shame. If we cannot achieve this real freedom, how can we be free enough to really love God, to really want to celebrate his goodness, providence, and grace to us? If I cannot be my real self, how can I be God's authentic person? It means nothing to choose for God if you have no freedom to choose against him. It means nothing to say yes to your loved one if you have no freedom to honestly say no. So if we are healthy, we will resist the pressure of constraints on our hearts, souls, minds, and psyches.

However, the second pathology in our world grows directly out of this healthy need to resist psychospiritual oppression, taken to sick exaggeration. I see people with poor interpersonal skills, lacking in idealism and aesthetic dignity, distorted by the pressures to measure up to feel worthy to be loved and cherished as persons, who are rebelling so hard that they are burning down their own psychological worlds, so to speak. You have seen people who are ramming their independence down the social throat of the community so hard that they are killing their own support systems. Our social system can become as sick from this as the persons are themselves. We tend to diagnose such folk as suffering from moderate to severe borderline syndrome. When they corner themselves in the extreme, they often seem to move across the line into temporary psychotic episodes. That is really quite crazy.

We are living with the results of that process in the West today. It was an epidemic in our society during most of the last three decades of the twentieth century in America. It is now manifesting itself in the form of the radicals who are hijacking the inherently peaceful and dignified religion of Islam and terrorizing the world to settle their feelings about being unempowered and pressured by what seems to them to be a dysfunctional tradition. A narcissistic moral order of rebellion, insurrection, terror, and self-indulgence is flourishing in the world community almost everywhere. The driving forces behind this horror are everywhere the same. Real or imagined oppressive systems of constraint, forcing God's free creatures, sick or well, into distorting conformity to what are perceived to be inappropriate standards, and the oppositional terrors that the consequently pathological people and communities are perpetrating on the body politic, arise from the fact that few seem to be really hearing Micah's unforgettable metaphor.

We live in a time of confused values, self-defeating individualism, fascistic exploitation of other people, entrepreneurial systems used for immediate personal gratification, and fear of failing to be adequately approved, accepted, successful, powerful, or safe. Twenty-five percent of the world is fat, fit, and fashionable. The rest of the world is skinny, scared, and skeptical. Neither condition improves the sense of security and adequacy, of peace and love. All of us wonder whether we are worthy to be loved or if we are really loved and cherished.

That is a universal tragedy, psychologically, socially, and spiritually, for the meaning of Micah's memorable message addresses exactly that psycho-spiritual enigma. His real meaning is that *measuring up* is not the issue in the universe. It never has been the issue. Neither is our guilt the issue, nor is our shame the issue, nor is our real or imagined inadequacy or fear the issue, nor is our failure the issue, nor is sin an issue. There is only one issue. The issue is God's grace, unconditional, radical, and universal, as Micah clearly understood 2,800 years ago.

The reason to be a godly person or a Christian is not to escape threat or to buy insurance against the fires of hell. The only reason to be a godly person is because it is so much more fun. It is much more fun to enjoy the relief of life in our father's house of forgiveness, as it were. That is why St. Paul can say in Romans 15:13, "The God of hope fill you with all the fun and relief of being a believer, that you may spontaneously overflow with a sense of the hopefulness of things, by the power of God's divine spirit." I believe that anyone anywhere who *really* hears Micah's word of unconditional acceptance by God, and is able to *take it in* at the affective level, spontaneously responds by declaring, "If that is how God really feels about me, I want to be his kind of person." That turns the motivation for being, and for being healthy, wholesome, and godly, 180 degrees around. Instead of our being motivated by a sense of divine threat, we can live with a sense of the opportunity to be God's kind of grace-filled persons.

Christianity or godliness is not an obligation to be labored under, but an opportunity to be seized and celebrated, not a command to be obeyed, but an invitation to be accepted with relief and joy. It is a freedom to live through the precarious and painful changes and perplexities of one's entire existence secured by the relief of grace: the assurance that God's message through Micah's metaphor intends to prompt us to stop wasting our psychospiritual energy on fear, guilt, and shame, all of which God has ruled out of the equation of our life before his face. The obvious intent is that we should be free to use all that psychospiritual energy to grow in body, mind, soul, and psyche.

When we are motivated by fear, we are always getting psychologically and spiritually sicker. When we are motivated by grace, we are always getting healthier and growing psychologically and spiritually. People who can be grateful for that can be psychologically and spiritually healthy. People who cannot be grateful cannot be psychologically and spiritually well or wholesome. People with a sick God whom they perceive as inducing fear, guilt, or shame, rather than eliminating it, must inevitably be very sick people psychospiritually. Most forms of fundamentalism in all religions are afflicted with that pathology. That is particularly evident just now in Islamic Fundamentalism, but it is no different in that regard from Christian Fundamentalism. Driving a plane into the World Trade Center is the same psychopathology as shooting doctors and nurses at abortion clinics. The former is just a bit more clever, grandiose, and devastating to the community, but if you are the nine-year-old son of one of those dead doctors or nurses, the devastation for you, personally, is worse. Moreover, the psychospiritual pathology, the insanity, is the same kind of thing in both cases.

CONCLUSION

Frequently, I have asked people directly whether they believed that Micah's metaphor, message, and meaning are true, namely, that God's grace is so unconditional, radical, and universal that it urges us to give up our fear, guilt, and shame completely. I ask them whether they believe the consequence of that, namely, that persons who are grateful for that grace can be healthy, and those who cannot feel that gratefulness cannot be. They all say they believe it. They believe in the grace of God, of course. Then I scratch them a little more deeply, and I discover that they are just like me. They do not want to believe in such unconditional grace, for the same reason that I inherently resist it.

It is the same reason that the church and all other religious communities have resisted this central and pervasive fact of good news throughout the centuries. To believe that grace is that radical means that I must do two things that I inherently do not want to do: I must take my hands off the controls of my desire for conditional self-justification—of working myself into favor, esteem, and approval by God or others—by proving that I am really a diligent and reputable character who is willing and able to do his *duty*, as in the case of the two sons in the parable of the waiting father. I cannot any longer say to God, as it were, "I have done my duty, and you owe me your goodwill, so get off my back." I must cast myself into his arms and on the mercy of his court.

Second, if grace is as radical and unconditional as Micah claims, I must give up my need to keep you under control by making my relationship with you conditional. I must stop saying that as soon as you have the right color skin, you can sit in my church or participate in my government. I must stop saying that if you wear the right clothes and smell right, you can belong to my club or sit next to me at a fine restaurant, or in church. I must stop saying that if you have enough money, you can have as good an education or medical care or housing or future security as I have. I must stop saying that if you are the right kind of friend, you can have my tenderness, generosity, and decent concern. I must stop saying that if you have the right kind of morals or psychological makeup, you can be my brother or sister before the face of God.

Nobody wants unconditional grace at that price, does he or she?

Well, God casts even those sins into the depths of the sea. What is lost in the depths of the sea is not recoverable. It cannot be rediscovered. It cannot be resurrected against us. Lost! Gone! Erased! Expunged from the record as though it had never been. We may see some of our flaws or neurotically celebrate our fracturedness and inadequacy, but when God looks at us, he does not remember we are sinners. He tramples our iniquities under his feet and has cast all our sins into the depths of the sea. He thinks we are saints. We are charred pine knots that he thinks are like beautiful sculptures, reflecting his image, and that he is busy trying to polish up and illumine so we can be ornaments of beauty on the mantelpiece of the universe.

I could not have had the temerity to try to fashion a marriage out of my own limited nature and the humanness of my wife, or try to raise seven children through all the changes of childhood and the craziness of adolescence, or try to make sense out of the work of healing in clinic and parish—playing God with other people's lives—if I could not have known in advance that God has cast all my sins into the depths of the sea of his eternal forgetfulness. I could not face my own mortality and the impairments in my own morality today if I could not believe that God is God and grace is grace. It is that fact that has healed me. The reason I know that Micah's message of unconditional positive regard for me, in spite of myself, is the most important psychotherapeutic fact ever perceived on this planet is that it is the insight that heals my neuroses, frees me to grow, embraces me in the security of knowing that I belong, and so is saving my life.

My only comfort in life and in death is that I belong to that kind of grace-filled God. I live and move and have my being from him. He holds firmly the thin golden thread on which my life is hung. This book endeavors to interpret that healing insight psychotheologically and psychospiritually. The following chapters explain how this dynamic psychospiritual force works at the applied and operational level in the healing professions.

CHAPTER 12

RADICAL GRACE: PSYCHOLOGICAL IMPLICATIONS AND APPLICATIONS

As I have repeatedly emphasized in this volume, the fact that divine grace is the most therapeutic psychological concept ever hatched on this planet has life-shaping implications and applications for the healing professions. The mainstream of theological thought in the entire Bible, as I have noted earlier, is the unique idea that God is a God of unconditional grace, not a God of threat. There are serious divergences from this mainstream within the Bible itself, but they are, indeed, aberrations and do not undo the fundamental theme and message of our sacred scriptures. Bishop Oxnam, also previously mentioned, apparently overlooked the key psychotheological passages that dominate the whole fabric of the Bible from Genesis 3:15 to Exodus 12 and 17, and on to the reverberant themes of the finest Psalms and all of the prophets, as illustrated by Micah 7:18–20. Having presented this in the narrative form earlier, permit me to tell it again in the original Hebrew structure of the text:

Who is a God like our God?
He pardons iniquity.
He passes over transgression.
He will not stay angry.
He delights in steadfast love.
He will have compassion upon us.
He will tread our iniquities under his feet.
He will cast all our sins into the depths of the sea.
He will be faithful to us when we are unfaithful to him.
He will show mercy to us.
He pledged this to our ancestors right from the beginning.

The Bible sounds a clear and singular trumpet. The theme it plays is good news. It is the good news that first uniquely exploded in the Judaic theological tradition, in Abraham's soul and psyche, and that is epitomized and incarnated in the person and work of Jesus of Nazareth. It is the good news that God accepts us as and where we are in our life pilgrimage of development, for the sake of what we can, therefore, become. It is important to repeat this central theme here as we prepare to set forth its implications and applications.

Grace is unconditional because it is not merely something that God does, but what God is, an attribute and disposition inherent to his character, defining his very nature. It is therefore inevitable in God and God's relation to humans, as it radically thrusts to the center of our pathology: our anxiety-driven self-preoccupation that is both the cause and the result of our alienation from our true selves, and the sickness and sin or dysfunction that comes from that. Moreover, the Bible makes clear that such grace is universal in its scope and intent. God is in the enterprise of healing humans and bringing wholesomeness and wholeness to the entire creation.

THEOLOGICAL OBSERVATIONS

As described in detail at the beginning of this volume, life is a tragic adventure from the outset. From the moment that the first uterine contractions signal our impending birth, until our last enfeebled breath, life affords anxiety-inducing threats to vital existence, stability, goal achievement, and fulfillment. As hinted in previous chapters, our brief span of living is a conscious and subconscious endeavor to gain control of our destiny so as to reduce the *threat* we feel against our fulfillment as persons, our goal achievement as volitional agents in God's world and ours, our certification as worth-seeking social beings, our stabilization as psychobiological organisms, and our survival as creatures.

The initial loss of security and the nurturing of the womb engrains in our primal formation a sense of the essentially violent and tragic nature of life's experience. The universal sense of psychological and spiritual fracturedness and alienation native to humans is surely rooted in that primal violent event of birth. We are torn unwillingly and painfully from that setting to which we are committed and adjusted, and which we systemically love in the sense of being identified with it, attached to it, dependent on it, and at home in it.

So birth is the loss experience of separation, perceived as alienation from our natural world and true selves, combined with a sense of fragileness, vulnerability, and disenfranchisement. That is surely interpreted by the newborn babe as rejection, implying personal unworthiness. So that loss induces grief, and it is internalized as a sense of guilt. If that is subsequently translated into a sense of alienation from God and all things godly, as persons and as a community of humans, it continues to reinforce pathologically that awareness of loss. We are, as it were, orphaned: wrenched from our mother's womb and out of touch with our father's hand. That is why the story of being cast out of paradise in Genesis does not surprise us. It illumines our most fundamental awareness, that is, that we are creatures of loss, experienced as alienation, and which feels like powerlessness and unworthiness. Moreover, that experience of loss is so close to our essence, chronologically, psychologically, and logically, that we perceive that we are not merely inadequate and lonely, but lost souls.

That myth of paradise lost depicts our first parents in a psychospiritual experience akin to a combination of birth trauma and the trauma of adolescent disengagement. The separation anxiety, ambivalence, and undermined certification as a worthy person are all there. Hope, meaningfulness, the worthwhileness of things, and our naive integrity are all threatened. Guilt, depression, distortions of perception, and hostile, inappropriate behavior must result. This sense of loss is the engine driving our sickness and sin.

I have previously contended, however, that our sense of loss has a constructive side in that it drives us to quest. Likewise, the trauma of birth and adolescent disengagement brings with it the promise of hope, pregnant with new possibilities, filled with fresh air and growth—so also does the biblical myth of paradise lost and the scriptural odyssey from creation to redemption, the long historical experience of humankind. The biblical narrative is a paradigm of the development of each of us as a person. Naivety, pain, risks, loss, growth, resilience, and transcendence are the changing scenes of the drama. Driven by anxiety, the whole process moves from incompleteness and pathology to maturity and wholeness. Trauma and loss move toward hope, tragedy is always driving toward denouement, pained and distorted life reaches for wholeness, anxiety lusts for reduction in tranquility, and dissonance is always hungering for resolution and *shalom*. The growth and development process of human maturation is an increasing transcendence over chaos, primitivity, naivety, fear, and idolatry (fixation on false sources of security). In this growth, anxiety is reduced constructively as the cosmos and as we as individuals mature and come into the self-actualization God designed for us as his imagers and reflectors.

Religion that seeks to reduce anxiety by placating or manipulating a supposedly threatening God inhibits growth, maturation, and psychospiritual health. Grace religion enhances the entire process for persons and the cosmos, for religion rooted in God's radical grace perceives that even in the myth of paradise lost, God did not abrogate his certification of humans as his compatriots in building his kingdom, nor their characters as his image bearers destined to divinely ordered self-realization of all their God-given potential. Enhancing our growth was obviously God's agenda, not strategizing judgment and condemnation. Grace means the inherent inviolability of

God's design for humans as reflectors of his nature and builders of his reign of grace that works and love that heals. We cannot escape his grace, nor his long embrace.

The predicament of human existence, therefore, is not our *real* lostness, but our *perceived* lostness. Our destiny is not that of achieving a successful power play to get right with God or get the right leverage with God. Our destiny is to *accept* and *realize* the benefits of our *real* status: divine compatriots in the enterprise of his kingdom coming in this world, in and through and around us. We are invited, urged, in relief and freedom, to accept God's unconditional acceptance of us all, and hence of each other. In the parable of the prodigal son or the waiting father, the greatest difficulty of the prodigal son was his problem of unconditional acceptance of his father's unconditional acceptance of him. That is why he is such an effective epitome of our human predicament. In that unconditional acceptance is the generic root for a primal-level freedom from the need for our universal anxiety, both systemic and situational. That was St. Paul's insight when he spoke of the progress from our primordial state, through the experience of acknowledging our dysfunction, to the destiny of the person free and empowered *in Christ*.

It is unfortunate that it has been so difficult for all branches of biblical religion to keep the healing vision of this grace theology in focus. This failure is clearly evident throughout the entire history of the three great Abraham religions: Judaism, Christianity, and Islam. As I have mentioned, even Dietrich Bonhoeffer, who understood grace so well in so many ways, inadvertently sold out to a pernicious notion of conditional grace in his remarks on so-called cheap grace. In that unguarded moment, he lusts again for legalism, obscuring the fact that grace is free; can be presumed upon eternally; and is radical, unconditional, and universal. Anything short of that is no grace at all, no good news at all, since it fails to get at the heart and center of our pathology and its consequent hopelessness. Conditional grace is no grace at all. Conditional grace, moreover, is arrogant. It fails to appreciate how pervasive and profound our problem of perceived lostness really is.

As the radical nature of our disorder of psyche and soul is adequately appreciated by the theologians, and as they grasp more clearly how radical is the intervention of grace, their service to the psychologists will substantially increase. As psychologists take with increasing seriousness our fallenness as the source of human pathology and the healing dynamic of the experience of grace as its resolution; as they appreciate the illumining value of the biblical narrative in understanding human disorder and clinical function; and as they realize how crucial to good psychology is the insight of biblical anthropology, their service to the theologians will be greatly enhanced, as well. Together, the psychologists and theologians will add greatly to our understanding, defining, and explicating of grace at the applied levels of research and clinical therapy. Was Aquinas right, perhaps, in his notion that what we know by faith in divine revelation we would have come to anyway by social science, if we had been able to track only the empirical evidence of human nature and its healing to its sources and center?

PSYCHOLOGICAL OBSERVATIONS

The suggestion that the biblical story is a paradigm of the human psychological odyssey implies that the experience of God and humans intersect in history and mutually reshape each other. For us to talk about God, therefore, we must have some sound understanding of ourselves, and to talk about ourselves, we must have some sound understanding of God. Social science and theology, as disciplines and as models for understanding the nature of things, therefore, are intricately and inevitably interrelated. To do either thoroughly forces one to open a clear eye to the other. Religion is barren without a comprehensive appreciation of the natural and social world, and creation cannot be deeply understood without being illumined by the insights of religion. A hint regarding how inevitable this process is may be seen in what has happened to the most exquisite of the natural empirical sciences: physics. Physics has pushed its quest to the very limits of its possibilities, and there it has found the significance and necessity of joining forces with astronomy. Astrophysics, in turn, in its irrepressible quest, has crossed the boundary of empirical science and landed in the rational idealism of cosmology. In the end, we cannot resist raising the questions of meaning beyond the empirical data, and truth beyond our comprehension.

Since psychology is an applied social science with a base in the natural sciences, it does its work by assembling data, formulating theories for managing it, and applying it to the practical concerns of clinical therapy. Clinically generated insights are then brought to bear on theory development. That process of the hermeneutical circle begins with certain assumptions derived from the worldview of the psychologist. Those assumptions are faith assumptions, whether they are theistic, naturalistic, idealistic, rationalistic, empiricist, or positivist.

Because all that is so, many serious scientists have been concerned lately about the way one's worldview shapes one's science, and vice versa. This is one of the crucial concerns of postmodernism. Christians have been concerned about how the science of theology interacts with the science of psychology, how faith impacts work in the social and natural sciences, and how one's religion, or lack thereof, shapes one's professional life. I will remind you that some have suggested that the answer to the question lies in portraying theoretical and empirical psychological principles as consistent with theological understanding of biblical texts. Others suggest that the interaction is merely a matter of the psychologist incarnating in his or her person a Christian lifestyle and value system in his or her daily work. As noted previously, this latter has been referred to as embodied integration of psychology and theology, of faith and work. Still others have suggested that the two sciences intersect at various levels of work or inquiry, mutually illuming each other's perspective on life and work in the healing professions and in the treatment of the living human document: a person. This perspective recommends itself well, and it is imperative that psychology and theology discern how much they can illumine each other, indeed, how much they need each other to be authentic and complete, each in its own discipline.

Surely the biblical claim that humans can be understood only if the human nature of God-imager and the human status of God-compatriot are taken seriously is an assumption about the nature of persons that will significantly shape psychological perspective. Moreover, if in that context, the vision of the healing function of grace is taken into account, psychological investigation and application will be influenced in truly important ways. Our beginning assumptions make enormous difference in the outcome of our work, and therefore, whether in theology or in psychology, it is imperative that our theoretical formulations and research methods are warrantable and our clinical applications and conclusions have integrity, in terms of reflecting the light shed on our work by both psychology and theology. Warrantable theory and method is that which is empirically, philosophically, and psychologically valid in the sense that it effectively manages the full range of data from all sources: empirical evidence, philosophical and theological insights, biblical claims and contentions, and psychological perceptions.

As the interaction of theology and psychology proceeds at each level of intersection, it is scientifically imperative that a continual interaction is carried on throughout the system of inquiry so that the applied clinical experience informs and forms theoretical development as much as the latter does the former, and so forth. Thus the hermeneutical or interpretive circle can continue to form and inform itself as it spirals to increasingly improved perceptions of the real state of affairs in our human world of dysfunction, healing, and growth.

CLINICAL OBSERVATIONS

A brief overview of the import of all this for clinical operations is useful at this point and will be treated more completely in a subsequent chapter, specifically given to the implications of a grace-oriented psychotheology for clinical psychotherapy. As the total range of insight from psychology and theology, in their common quest for truth, shapes our developing concept of the nature of humanness, and psychology and theology thoroughly form and inform each other, very important clinical applications must be expected. The clinical enterprise is the work of inciting and enhancing human growth, while assisting the patient in the harnessing and appropriate reduction of pathological anxiety. The objective is to produce the fully actualized person God designed all of us to be. Christian or godly therapy, therefore, looks for more than a mere return to psychological functionality. It anticipates and works toward holistic self-realization for every patient. That means maximum growth in body, mind, and spirit, as the image bearers of God and his compatriots in the work of his reign of grace and love on earth.

Health is the state of having achieved wholeness or of being in the process of achieving it, and of having achieved that degree of it appropriate to one's station in his or her process on the growth continuum at any given time. To assist patients in achieving such health, a well-developed Christian or godly psychotheological model of illness and healing is imperative in clinical practice. As explained in detail in the chapter on illness and health, it must incorporate an adequate appreciation of our real sense of universal lostness, expressive of the distance between our destiny and our daily function, our potentials and our problematic state of underachievement, our imagination and our performance, our reach and our grasp. It must appreciate the physical stress and distress, the psychopathogenesis, and the spiritual defeat reflected in and generated by that distance we sense between our perception of God's vision for us and our own realities inside us.

In the light of that concern, the development of a Christian or godly therapeutic strategy, which adequately reflects the kind of Christian anthropology implied in a thoroughgoing grace theology, will include the following applied aspects. First, it requires the incarnation in the therapist of the unconditional acceptance of the patient, where the patient is at the moment in his or her pathology. That means valuing the patient as a cherished human being, despite his or her dysfunction. This reflects the divine paradigm of unconditional acceptance, implements it as a reality in the patient's life and experience, and implicitly holds it out as a significant healing insight for the patient.

Second, a profound empathy is required that places the therapist inside the psychological frame of reference in which the patient experiences the pathology or suffering. This will enhance the therapist's ability to see or sense the sources and nature of the obstructions to health and growth as well as the possibilities for reinitiating growth that exist within or for the patient. This empathic incarnation of God's grace empowers the therapist to affirm the patient as a person, not just as a patient. God also affirms us in the same manner in taking us and our alienation or dysfunction so seriously as to visit us in his son. Such verbal and nonverbal mediation of God's unconditional acceptance of persons, including the patient, is a crucial baseline experience for the patient's recovery of a perception of self-worth, power, and destiny that rings true to his or her real nature as a potentially whole person, fulfilled in all the possibilities that the arbitrarily imputed states of a compatriot of God implies.

Third, the Christian or godly therapist will provide the patient with a sense of a mutuality of the quest for wholeness for the patient on which the patient-therapist team have embarked. Fourth, it will be made evident in the therapy process that the therapist, too, is wrestling with his or her own humanness, with both its pathology and its potential. Fifth, it will become evident in a sound Christian therapeutic strategy that the therapist's worldview expresses a comprehensive ambition for the wholeness of the whole world of humans and things and that the patient's wholeness is sought in that setting. Sixth, the possibilities and expectations for the patient's wholeness inherent in that worldview will become apparent.

Seventh, the grace-imputed status of the patient as a compatriot of God in building a healed and wholesome world will become evident to the patient as the underpinning reality of the worldview. Eighth, soundly established techniques for countering defensive patterns of resistance in the patient will be utilized to defeat any obstruction to the progress of growth to wholeness. Ninth, the patient's physical, intellectual, psychological, and spiritual needs and status will be taken seriously as functions of a whole-person concern. Tenth, the effectiveness of therapy for body, mind, and spirit, in the light of the expectation that the ultimate achievement of health will be the arrival at spiritual as well as psychological maturity and integration, will shape the entire process.

CONCLUSION

The consequences for psychotherapy of a thoroughgoing grace theology and the Christian or godly view of human nature inherent in it may be summarized briefly. To operate clinically from the view that humans image God and are his inviolable compatriots in making this world whole and healthy is to envision them as infinitely valuable, esteemed, and dignified. They possess a preestablished identity accorded them by God and certified in spite of themselves and their illnesses or dysfunctions. Moreover, this view holds up the notion that the root of pathology is alienation from our true selves and from God.

The more we learn about the intricate, two-way switching mechanism of the hypothalamus in the relationship between endocrine chemistry and psychological states, the more likely seems a relationship between spiritual disposition and physical illness. This alienation indicates the need for the therapist to express a godlike acceptance and affirmation of the patient. That acceptance must be unconditional and must recognize that our dysfunction or sin is more a failure of destiny to grow and actualize the God-given self within us than it is a failure of duty to measure up to some standard of function.

Under this model, the goal of therapy and the course toward wholeness may become, together with the unconditional affirmation of the patient, a

significant instrument for defusing neurotic guilt, anxiety, remorse, hopelessness, helplessness, grief, self-pity, low self-esteem, compulsivity, and obstructions to restoration of a sense of the inherent dignity and freedom God affords
the patient and all of us. This model is also likely to defuse the therapist's
panic about the responsibility to play God, as it were, making decisions about
bringing health to the patient. This should free the therapist to make meaningful steps toward constructive anxiety reduction for the patient, who then
can perceive that he or she does not need to get well to be accepted and cherished, certified and honored by the therapist or God. The patient can perceive
that he or she is free to get well in a naturally unfolding, unpunished growth
process, that his or her worthiness is inherent and not earned by measuring
up to the therapist's expectations, his or her own expectations, or God's.

This godly or Christian clinical approach provides a base of trust for the
risk taking necessary for growth as well as decreased danger of the pathology of the therapist getting in the way of growth. Thus the therapist and the
patient are freed to take themselves and each other with an appropriate sense
of the humorousness of being human, even pathological, yet potentially God's
full-orbed person. Our mortality, the specter behind all psychopathology, can
therefore also be viewed less heavily. The therapist and patient together can
learn to cherish each other as dying persons in a generation of dying persons,
but cherished redemptively and eternally, and held firmly in the gracious
hand of God. This sense of the resolution of all things empowers a person,
therefore, to live with a sense of joy, freedom, and wholeness.

CHAPTER 13

THE PSYCHOSPIRITUAL HEALTH
OF THE HEALER

All of us are products of our childhood. None of us needs to be a prisoner of it. Our early developmental years set many of the courses and biases that we follow the rest of our lives. However, we are as equipped to grow through and beyond those early influences as we are to remain victims of their distortions. We choose our characters and destinies. I once heard that by the age of 40, we have the faces we deserve. In a similar manner, by the time we advance into the years of maturity, we usually have the nature and destiny that we have decided we are willing to live for and cultivate.

In many important ways, my life has been one long gasp of grief. I experienced a relatively neurotic childhood in consequence of specific events and circumstances that made an impact on me. They included my mother's frequent illness and inaccessibility; her high level of anxiety; her compulsivity, especially premenstrually; the devastation that the Great Depression wreaked on my entire childhood world; the threat and eventual outbreak of World War II; the draft of my oldest brother for the war in the Pacific; the untimely death of a number of my playmates by fire, accident, and congenital disease; and the loss of my first sister and third brother by childhood disorders. So my life has been a 75-year-long gasp of grief. The obverse of it, however, has been an odyssey of growth, mediated by precisely those events of pain that proved to be so grievous to me.

My childhood was not all neurosis; moreover, the neurotic anxiety often became just the appropriate impetus to motivate action. The abject deprivation of my rural culture during the depression drove me to take charge of my destiny by seeking a superior education. My father repeatedly spurred me on with the adage, "That is the one thing they cannot take away from you." I chose the ministry, military chaplaincy, and psychotherapy as a professional vocation because I determined at seven years of age that I was going to do something definitive to relieve all the human suffering I perceived around me in those early, desperate years.

My sense of vocation was a mixture of neurotic anxiety, fanciful wish fulfillment, heroic idealism, dedicated godliness, imaginative vision, confident faith, and a tough-minded commitment to hard work with the expectation that it would bear fruit. I determined to get as far beyond the suffering that McBain, Michigan, represented for me in those years as I possibly could. That road led me into Christian ministry, into the helping professions. It afforded me a high degree of professional success and a profound sense of satisfaction in life. The driving engine of that achievement has consistently been the distortions and strengths that my childhood afforded me. I might have become a mere victim of its pathology. I chose to employ the deficits and distortions as drivers for taking charge of my own destiny. In retrospect it is clear to me that without the shaping of my psyche by the divine spirit, I would never have been able to make those critical choices.

So I have always been very much aware of and interested in the problem of the therapist's own mental health, with particular regard to the manner in which it shapes his or her sense of vocation and forms and informs the resulting healing work in clinicians and pastors. I have been specifically intrigued by the challenge to understand my own mental health and the way it has influenced my work, my life, and my family.

THE HEALER'S STRESS

My clinical work over the last 50 years persuades me that the role of therapist and pastor are the most highly stressed roles in our society today. I have had extensive responsibility and opportunity to be the therapist for other pastors and therapists. It is increasingly surprising to me that these professional practitioners survive as well as they do, psychologically. They tend to have an urgent sense of vocation, a sense that is shaped by many different influences. Some of these shaping influences are healthy, some neurotic, some misunderstood, and some understood only in retrospect.

Generally speaking, it seems clear that God calls us to the healing professions by three specific instruments in his divine wisdom. He calls us through our talents; he calls us by the providential setting in which our lives take shape; and he calls us to a style of life that is unique to those specially called to be healers. This does not mean that the calling to the healing professions differs in these regards from callings to other vocations. John Calvin was certainly correct in his perception that all vocations are divine vocations, and each of us in his or her profession, task, or labor is called into that role as surely as a therapist or pastor.

God calls each of us to whatever vocation it is in which we find ourselves, by means of the peculiar talents we possess and can bring to the task. No one should feel called to clinical work or ordained ministry who does not have the basic abilities required for it. Nobody ought to feel called to the role of therapist or pastor who has no essential talents for healing others. God shepherds us into our callings by means of the native talents with which he has invested us.

Moreover, in his general providence, our lives unfold in their own particular settings and circumstances. Each setting carries within it inherent potentials and constraints which make possible or impossible the pursuit of various vocations. God does not call us to work in care for others for which the opportunities and resources are not available to us and cannot be acquired. The circumstances in which we find ourselves speak to us for God regarding what possibilities or limitations for vocation prevail upon us. This providence in practical things must be taken seriously in our wish to know God's vocational will for us so that we do not attempt to push the river of life or swim constantly against the stream, so to speak, thus demeaning or destroying the quality of our lives as they unfold in God's providence, spiritually, emotionally, and physically. For it is less that God calls us to a specific palpable task in life and more that he calls us to a certain style of living, compatible with our natures and talents, and which may be realized in the labor of a great variety of specific tasks.

God calls us to a style. Divine vocation is less a call to what to do in life and more a call to how to do in life. I may be effective as a parish pastor, an army chaplain, a university professor, a psychotherapist, an astronomer, a chemist, a farmer, a politician, or an auto mechanic. However, in any case, I am called to be God's man in whichever role I choose or whatever role unfolds for me. *What* I am to do before his face is secondary and situational? *How* I am to be and do before his face is primary and essential? The former remains always somewhat of an open question and a developmental matter, depending on the circumstances that unfold in my life. *How* I am to be and do is a matter that is endemic and definitive for me as a way of life for one called by God. The former depends on my God-given talents and what the providential setting suggests ought to be done. The latter depends on my vocation to be God's person. God calls me to carry myself as a healing person in whatever role or task I find myself.

God does not effect the call by supernatural means. We need to take a realistic view of the way God apparently operates in history so that we can interpret this matter of vocation in terms of God's apparently preferred *modus operandi* in the human arena. The evidence of history is preponderantly in the direction of the fact that God's operation in history is natural. He created the world with order, laws, and a trustworthy cause and effect function. He shepherds its unfolding story but does not intervene periodically to rearrange or straighten out the process. He assiduously avoids violating the integrity of the cause and effect dynamics of the universe and of human personality or decision making.

He is a shepherd, not a boss. He does not push us around. He is merely among us. As with a shepherd, one can watch him with his flock all day long and never quite be able to tell whether the shepherd is leading his sheep or following them. He is simply among them. He recognizes their voices, and they his. Neither really needs to look up to see where the other is; if they sidle too near the precipice or too far from the fresh water, he simply slows his stride until they unconsciously regroup around him and nuzzle off into a new direction for the taste of the grass and the sniff of the spring.

When we move too far from the vision of God in history like the shepherd in the flock, we are tempted by strange notions of determinism and divine will. Divine vocation is a developmental and situational thing for God as well as for us: a call by providence to the Christian style in whatever we do, a call to live life, as it were, before the face of God. Remember the parable about the rich and prosperous farmer who decided to build new barns to hold his unexpectedly large harvest? He said, in effect, "My goodness, look what a yield I have this year. This is enough for the rest of my life. I will build barns to store it and then retire early." So he did, and that night he died. As Jesus told that parable, that is all there was to it.

Joachim Jeremias, in his book *The Parables of Jesus*, likely the best one on the subject in his day, argues persuasively that Jesus's point was merely the eschatological one we have been discussing. Life is lived always before the face of God—under the pressure of eternity. The man did well. He farmed wisely. He had God's endorsement of his skill and diligence as a farmer. Jesus obviously admired and commended him. He was God's kind of fellow, and as all of us, he lived daily in the eschatological setting of being every moment in the presence of God. So he worked and planned correctly, but he went to heaven instead of having to put up with a long retirement. A rather advantageous exchange, all in all.

Now the early church could not believe that Jesus had told that bare-faced story just like that, with no moral or ethical embellishments. So the church felt compelled to give the parable a moral weight. They added notes to make the parable suggest that Jesus meant to call attention to fact that rich men are greedy or that powerful men must be brought down. No such thing is the case. Jesus was simply making a comment on God's way of moving in terms of history's natural processes. It is a comment on God's way of moving in human life and our simply accepting its unfolding natural dynamics as we grow and exercise responsible control of our own destinies—with the overriding awareness that we do it all under the pressure of eternity and before God's gracious face.

Psychologists and pastors are often too sentimental and too inclined to expect special evidences of their special role and vocation. This enhances neurotic notions about calling and destiny. Healers worthy of the name are, indeed, special people with special characteristics, led by special circumstances and unique talents into the work of special kinds of caring for suffering persons. Such professionals, conscious of this special kind of calling, are usually good at what they do. But there is nothing supernatural about all of that. God calls therapists and pastors just as he calls assembly line workers and shoe polishers.

Nevertheless, research studies on the typical personality patterns of professional healers and caregivers conclusively indicate that they are higher on the nurturance scale than the general population. Indeed, males in these roles tend to be as high in nurturance qualities as women predominantly are. Effective psychologists and pastors tend to be near the top of the scale in both nurturance and instrumental qualities. Those who are not are usually ineffective. That suggests that people who are called to the helping professions tend to be sensitive, are prone to be rescuers, feel a deep identification with the suffering of others, and typically are tempted to carry more of the burdensomeness of living than the average person. That means that their stress levels are going to be consistently above average.

If you add to that the fact that the role of the pastor in most Western societies today is vaguely defined as the caretaker of all neediness, the potential of increased pressure on his or her mental health can be seen as exponential. Most parish pastors are called or appointed to the parish without an adequately comprehensive contract or job description. Many tasks beyond the obvious ones are assumed to fall within the role. However, the lack of finite definition of his or her contracted pastoral duties leaves the pastor vulnerable to as wide a variety and number of parishioner demands as there are parishioners. Each of these expectations then becomes a pastoral job description in the mind of the parishioner. This infinite scope of expectations shifts and changes daily as the emotional tone, the practical neediness, and the pathologies of the parishioners alter.

Moreover, psychologists and pastors never achieve full closure on their work. Just like homemaking and housework, it is the sort of task that continues to unfold before one, no matter how much gain is made. No one ever gets perfectly well and completely whole, so the caregiving is always a work in progress. The job meets the caregiver week after week with the same kind of human suffering, prospects, possibilities, problems, and perplexities, for the healer is not in an enterprise of production, but in the work of tending a greenhouse full of tender and damaged plants, so to speak. The end product or predictable time table is seldom the issue. Growth in its various and precarious stages, fits and starts and regressions, is always the issue. How gratifying it would be for the pastor or therapist if so tangible an outcome could be anticipated and experienced as some final product, some satisfying closure, some definitive completion of the perpetual vocation, some ultimate victory to end the campaign. Healing work is living in a perpetual process of ambiguity and incompleteness.

Concern for his or her own family and its place in the community or parish life is also a source of stress for the psychologist and pastor in that his or her private life is never completely private. The healer is a public figure, on public demand. Being a therapist, pastor, cherisher, and lover for one's family is an additional full-time job. Protecting one's children from the unrealistic expectations of the public community, facilitating one's spouse's role in that community without acceding to the public expectation that he or she is an extension or assistant to the healer, are challenging shoals to navigate. Spouses are called to different roles and vocations than the psychologist and the pastor. Carving out an immune zone for family life and leisure is a sizable task of planning and logistics that further taxes the healer's mental health, in the best of circumstances.

Today, many therapists and pastors build significant support groups of colleagues and friends. Associations for clinical and pastoral fraternal sharing are available. However, there are specific steps persons in the helping professions can and should take to enhance the quality and resilience of their mental health and that of their families. There are 10 commandants for promoting the psychologist's and pastor's mental health.

THE 10 COMMANDMENTS FOR HEALERS' HEALTH

Commandment 1

The first commandment is identifying the enemy correctly. If you have served in the armed forces, you know how important the identification of friend and foe is. That is no less true in daily life. It is easy for a stressed psychologist or pastor to identify a particularly difficult patient or parishioner as the enemy. In truth, such a person is probably very needy of the healer's care and has built in difficulty about asking for it or trusting it. A therapist who is exhausted from the daily healing schedule may be tempted to displace his or her stress on the family when its needs and expectations are expressed at the end of the day. This may result in anger instead of nurturing arising in the family, so the stressed healer as well as the family miss out on the care both need. The needy spouse or family may be unconsciously identified as the enemy.

There are indeed enemies to the effective function of therapists and pastors. However, the people are never the enemy. The enemy is always the unresolved problem. The problem is the enemy, and all the people around, even the irascible ones, are potential allies for resolving the problem. They may not look like allies, but they are resources for gaining ground and growth in the healing of both the patient and the healer. People are God's children, made in God's image, no matter how badly distorted, sick, miserable, uncooperative, nasty, offensive, or inadequate they may be. They are not only needy subjects for our care but also those who make up the enterprise of working out God's reign of love and grace in the life of the pastor and parish, therapist and community.

Commandment 2

The second commandment is not to push the river. Therapists and pastors are no more able to push the river of life than is anyone else. If we try to do so, we may distort the flow, force it out of its banks and out of bounds, drown in it or foul it up, but we can never push it. We must acknowledge that we must go with the flow. The river of work, the river of time, the river of the spirit, and the river of growth will find their own authentic steam. When we impress our agenda on them, we only hamper the flow of growth and healing. It is important to remember that every time we try to push the river, we are erroneous; that is, we indicate that we have stopped believing that we can trust the general natural dynamics of providence in the universe and in personality. God trusts them and takes them seriously, and so he has tied his own hands from intervening to let the process of natural cause and effect, and of our decisions and their consequences, flow. He takes us more seriously than we take him if we choose to push the river.

I am impressed by the leisurely way Jesus went about promoting the consciousness of God in human society. He never seemed in much of a hurry. He did not try to heal everybody, but only a paradigmatic few. He never seemed to be in a panic. All he had to work with was a motley band of 12 rambunctious Galileans and revolutionaries. God does not call us to do any more work than we can *comfortably* do. He does not call us to do what we are not *good* at doing. Jesus manifested an incredible lack of agitation about what he was up against. He vacationed regularly on the Sea of Galilee. When he felt like taking a day off, he did so. When he felt like staying up all night with his friends or in prayer with his heavenly father, he stayed up all night. He was willing to trust the flow of the river of work, of time, of the spirit, and of growth.

Most of all, therapists and pastors should not push the river of their children's lives. One of the real dangers to the stability of the healer's health and that of the healer's family is the temptation to expect his or her children to become more mature, more complete, more perfect, or more Christian, and at a more efficient rate, than anybody else's children. We may entrust them to God's spirit and providence, avoid panic, and keep out of the way, while providing them a context of cherishing love. I suppose we all delay or distort the growth of our children in some degree by getting in the way of the natural flow of God's way for them. God's way will be adequate for them if you and I facilitate it, rather than obstruct it. It will come through to them, just as it has to us. It will be all right if it takes as long for them as for us and moves by as precarious a channel and as circuitous a stream.

Pray, hope, love, be gentle and kind, take time, and trust God's grace and Spirit. Believe that time is always on the side of the person of trust and faith. Divine providence is the mainstream of time and life.

Commandment 3

The third mental health commandment for therapists and pastors is to remember that life is for growth and not for production. Home, parish, and community are not like factories, but like greenhouses, as noted before. Healers are in the work of carefully planting, watering, fertilizing, cultivating, weeding, pruning, supporting, shaping, and leading to the harvest. However, the process is not that of a mechanical formula for raw material input and finished product output. Healers look for buds, blossoms, and fruit, not machined instruments and packaged people. If we get this backward, we are never at ease with what God's real business is with us, our families, our people, and our communities. Our work is not for program, production, and impressing people.

I have seen pastors preoccupied with the numbers game, measuring ministry by the size of the crowd or congregation. I am clearly persuaded that if we care for the health and growth of our people, the growth of the congregation will take care of itself naturally and will achieve that size and scope appropriate to the community situation or setting. When we lose sight of that, as pastors, we impose on ourselves many unrealistic goals and much excessive stress. Then we load ourselves with burdens that do not belong to us and that jeopardize our own mental health and put our families under unnecessary duress as they watch us suffer. Sometimes this causes them to bear the brunt of our displaced distress spilled over on them in our times of pain. This is equally true of psychologists. Healers need to seek tranquility and celebration as well as success. The role of the healer is for enhancing the quality of growth and healing. Let God, in his providence and grace, worry about the measures or standards of success.

Commandment 4

Commandment 4 is to remember that the method and mode of the true healer is that of incarnation. That means that to facilitate the growth and healing of others, we need to express in our nature, style, and method the unconditional acceptance and profound care for the wholeness of the person who needs us, as is epitomized in the person and work of Jesus. To maintain such a role and method or style requires that one has a well-developed sense of humor. Jesus carried himself with a remarkable sense of humor, as indicated in his stories about the camel and the eye of the needle, the man who coughed up a sand flea and swallowed a camel, and by the wink in his eye at the Syro-Phoenician woman as he bantered with her about the incredible Jewish bias of his disciples. Jesus's humanness meant to him great humor as well as passion. Since we are the contemporary incarnations of his spirit and mission, we should appreciate the healing role of humor as much as he did. The Bible is clear on the fact that God has a great sense of humor. Just think of the play of light in a rapidly developing sunset, or of Jesus likening God to a hen gathering her chickens under her wings. God speaks of himself as a mother who dandles her children on her knees and suckles her children at her breast. Is it not humorous for God to paint a self-portrait with great, milky breasts, preparing to nurture humankind?

We tend to take ourselves so seriously, particularly in the healing and helping professions, while God laughs about himself, jokes, and sees humor in it all. Why should we not take ourselves more lightly? Think of the parable mentioned in the preceding paragraph about the sand flea and the camel. Can you imagine the twinkle in Jesus's eye and the roar of laughter from his belly when he told that story about the Pharisees? He had said to them that they were preoccupied with the details of regulating people's behavior and had forgotten the healing power and essence of love. He said they were like a lonely Arab camel driver making his way across the Arabian desert, huffing and puffing as he led his camel in the midday sun. Suddenly, into his great open mouth and right down his windpipe flies a sand flea. The poor fellow coughs and snorts, pukes and coughs. In the meantime, the empathetic camel is astonished by this sudden fit into which his friend has fallen. The camel comes closer and peers incautiously into the huge roaring mouth to see what is wrong. Just then, with a huge orgasmic cough, out comes the flea, and in goes the camel. If it is God's style to be that humorous, in the face of what he is up against in getting his reign of love and grace established on earth, surely we can afford to be humorful in the face of our awesome enterprise of clinical and pastoral work. If we can laugh appropriately about our own strengths and weaknesses, about the humanness of others, and even about how God laughs about himself, we will be better able to forgive ourselves for our human limitations, preserve inner tranquility, enhance our own mental health, and place ourselves empathically in the shoes of our patients and parishioners.

Commandment 5

The fifth commandment is that we should clarify our expectations regarding our work of healing. It is constantly an amazement to me how much misery humans cause each other and themselves by failing to express their expectations clearly. If we identify our expectations clearly for ourselves, we will be able to express them clearly to others. Most people are very cooperative if they are given an opportunity to understand, without confusion or vagueness, what our expectations really are. People are not inherently stubborn and hardheaded. We become resistant, angry, and compulsively defensive only when we do not understand what is expected or cannot perceive what course of action to take to accomplish it. So it is crucial that we clarify our own expectations and honor those of others.

The expectations that our patients and parishioners have regarding us are infinite in number and variety. That is fine. No therapist or pastor can meet them all. Moreover, his or her expectations weigh just as heavily as theirs. Caregivers who state their own expectations forthrightly will be taken seriously and trusted to honor as many of their patients' and parishioners' expectations as is appropriate and humanly possible. Healing professionals who require those they care for to honor the healer's expectation must in turn honor those of the needy persons for whom they care and negotiate the differences and conflicts between the two. This can never be accomplished unless all of the relevant expectations on both sides are stated clearly. This fifth commandment is a fulcrum on which much of the others turn.

Unfortunately, histrionic and narcissistic persons tend to become leaders, motivated by pathological ambitions. It is very difficult to relate to such folk, unless it is possible to clarify expectations, identify specific pathologies, adhere to strictly clinical procedures, and prescribe the necessary medication or intervention.

Commandment 6

Commandment six is to honor individual differences. People all have differences, not only in expectations, but also in preferences, styles, needs, perspectives, brain function, and in the way they have tested and perceived reality during their formative years. They taste their food differently, hear music differently, and shape their hopes and fears differently. When I find a congregation or social community in which there is rigid conformity in the way the people see the truth or express themselves, I immediately wonder from where the flagrant pathology is coming. The significant individual differences people evince in goals, needs, tastes, and ambitions reflect healthy individual notions about self-fulfillment. That sacred goal must be honored if we expect to assist persons to wholeness and health.

If healers can celebrate the variety, rather than fret about incongruities and nonconformity, they will greatly enhance their own mental health and find it much easier to place themselves into the shoes of their clients. That is, after all, what unconditional grace and acceptance is all about, in us and in

God's care for us. If we can avoid pushing the river, appreciate the value of clarifying expectations, and remember the greenhouse metaphor, we should find it possible to celebrate diversity, rather than fear human individuality in taste and style.

Commandment 7

Remembering that feelings follow behavior is the seventh commandment for a healer's mental health. Generally, we operate on the assumption that behavior follows feelings. That is not the primary fact in this matter. We usually think that it is because you have made me feel badly or angry that I treat you badly in return. The primary fact, however, is this: you may make me feel badly or angry, but I decide how I am going to react, and that decision is designed to justify my feeling. If I decide that I am going to turn the other cheek and treat you with gracious generosity and I begin to act out that behavior toward you, I will almost immediately feel gracious and generous toward you.

If, on the other hand, I decide to respond to you in anger and abuse and proceed to do that, I will immediately feel vindictive and convinced that is the appropriate feeling for the situation. My feelings will have been determined by the behavior that I have chosen. It is ever so. Feelings follow behavior. That is how God has given us an advantage over most of the other animals. Animals react largely by instinct. Humans have a self-reflective function by which we are able to decide in any situation how we will behave. The way we behave determines how we end up feeling about the situation, not the other way around.

In doing pastoral or clinical work, therefore, we may develop a great deal of stress, exasperation, fear, or disappointment about the way people dysfunction and treat us. We are not prisoners of those initial sensations. We are in charge of how we decide to respond. How we respond will determine how we feel—and therefore how burdensome to our own mental health the situation turns out to be. In this regard, prayer is a very significant instrument for catharsis of the self-defeating instinctual responses and for the fine-tuning of insight into how we may behave in response to such situations, in a fashion that affords us a constructive and healing feeling pattern.

Undoubtedly, it is the fact that feelings follow behavior that leads the Bible to enjoin us to love one another. Normally one assumes that love is an emotion that is inspired by the loveable nature of the beloved. It is not a thing one expects can be commanded. We feel that if it is forced or ordered, it is false and cannot regain its authenticity. Yet sacred scriptures of almost every faith tradition, especially Christian scriptures, command us to love one another. Obviously, then, that must be an appropriate thing. How can that be? How can emotions be commanded? Precisely because feelings follow behavior, it is true that we can learn genuinely to love anyone we decide to be kind to.

We may find the most distasteful and offensive wretch from the gutters of the world or the most arrogantly abusive person of power we can imagine and find them both intensely undesirable to us. We may despise or hate them. If, however, we cognitively override our initial instinctual response of distaste and dislike and compel ourselves into a decision to be kind and generous to such persons, and then behaviorally act out our decision, we will discover love and compassion growing for that person. That does not mean we will like them, or wish to take them as our bosom buddies, but we will discover ourselves capable of care, kindness, compassion, and grace toward them. God has fashioned us in such a way that we will experience real loving care for anyone to whom we decide to show kindness. So the Bible commands us to make that decision and act on it. It *commands* us to love even the unlovable.

Commandment 8

The eighth commandment is to make love a lot. One of the most painful human experiences is loneliness. Recently, a great deal of research and writing has been done on this subject. We experience loneliness of two types: situational loneliness and existential loneliness. Situational loneliness results mainly from circumstances that separate us from those we love and depend on for warmth and cherishing. We may be separated physically by work and travel. We may be separated emotionally by alienation, by psychopathology, by hurt feelings, or by personality deficiencies in ourselves or others.

Whatever the situation that deprives us of normal cherishing by and for those we love, the result must be a sense of isolation, aloneness, and loneliness. Situational loneliness usually can be handled and resolved with simple steps to increase the time available for sharing, to increase the genuineness of conversation with our loved ones, and to increase the occasions for acts of kindness and affection exchanged with those who care for us and for whom we care. In cases of severe pathology, in which our loved one cannot respond in normal cherishing, only intervention by psychotherapy or chemotherapy can definitively resolve the problem.

Underneath all our situational loneliness is a much deeper and more devastating problem: existential loneliness. For it there is no cure. There can only be some constructive management of it and some amelioration of the intensity of its pain. It is inherent to human existence. It is universal with humans and lasts all life long. Existential loneliness is that experience in which we realize that the central feelings of our inner selves, which define and shape us most profoundly, are feelings or experiences we cannot really share with anyone else. We are, in that sense, born alone, and we die alone. No one can have these experiences for us. No one can really experience our unique individual experiences of birth, growth, and death quite in the same way we experience them. We can never express to others just exactly what it is we feel about those experiences, how they have formed and informed our life, perception of things, and character. At those central places in life, we are alone.

Frequently, we feel anger and resentment that others cannot share with us the pain we feel, or even the joy we feel, at those most intimate of all places in our private odysseys. Moreover, it is often the case that simple, insignificant events transpire that incite situational loneliness that in turn triggers deep reactions of existential loneliness. Perhaps you are not as neurotic as I am, but I experience rejection easily, readily feel abandoned when warm and cherishing relationships are strained, and so experience loneliness during a large percentage of my existence. I always have. When such situational loneliness hits me, it reawakens in me the awful and perpetual loneliness I experienced throughout my childhood, and it triggers deep inside me the resurgence of my existential loneliness.

Losing a button from one's shirt is not normally a devastating experience. However, I have found that if I lose a button and I tell my wife about it and she agrees to sew it back on, but the shirt goes through three washings in four weeks and I have worn it two or more times without the button on it, by the end of the month, the absent button makes me feel lonely. Now I just sew the damned thing on myself, but I miss an opportunity of being cherished that would have done me more good than simply having a button on my shirt. You may have heard of the woman who found the letters her husband agreed to mail for her six weeks ago still sitting in the pocket of the shirt that was hanging behind the door waiting for the button she had promised to sew on it.

The absent button makes me feel lonely, just as the unmailed letters make her feel lonely or neglected; that is, we begin to feel under such circumstances that we are very low on our spouse's priority list. Of course, in the present-day all-American household, everybody or nobody sews on buttons, and everybody or nobody mails letters. My wife and I have had a deal going since we married 55 years ago. It is a simple arrangement for the efficient division of labor in our household. I agree to preach the sermons and do the clinical work, and she agrees to sew on the buttons. If she wants to exchange our set responsibilities, she is free to do so; but for now, I preach, teach, and do therapy, and she sews buttons and does her social work. That is, theoretically! That was the deal. As I said, the system has eroded somewhat. Lately, I notice, I preach, teach, do clinical work, and sew buttons. I am not sure where this erosion will stop.

The absent button used to devastate me eventually because existential loneliness has been a very close to the surface experience for me all my life. This is largely because of its inherent nature, on one hand, and because of specific experiences in my developing years that reinforced the size of the existential loneliness within me, on the other. I am on rather fragile footing as regards this matter of loneliness, as many of us are, so it used to take only the button to make me feel that my needs or desires were a low priority for my wife, whom I love to have love me. That triggers subconscious memories of early devastating experience of perceived rejection, which in turn awakens my deep and vast feelings of isolation, abandonment, and existential loneliness. There were times when I felt that I was unusual and perhaps pathological in these responses, until I discovered that most humans experience life similarly, though their trigger mechanisms for existential loneliness may differ from mine.

There is no cure for existential loneliness, but there are some things that can be done about it. One is to find faithful friends, cherishing loved ones, and a dedicated, caring, warm, and playful spouse. A second thing one can do is to get rid of those friends who trigger more loneliness than nurturing. However, the remedy here under consideration is sexual: make love a lot. Making love, or meaningful sexual communion, does, as a matter of fact, come closer to grounding out existential loneliness than any other human experience does, except perhaps for intense spiritual fellowship. There is a very good reason for that. The sexual connection in a wholesome relationship, just like the spiritual connection in a deep relationship, gets closer to the center of oneself and the other, our identity and selfhood, than any other human experience. It is a connection and communication at the visceral level.

So a sense of playfulness about oneself and with one's spouse is really invaluable in creating frequent and intense intimacy for the establishment of a sustained sense of connectedness and union. Then existential loneliness is greatly reduced and recedes from the surface of one's consciousness and one's existence. Moreover, there will likely be fewer situations that will imply or feel like distance and isolation from one's spouse in a relationship in which meaningful sexual communion is frequent and skillful. Spiritual communion has the same kind of function as sexual communion, requires the same kind of skills, and offers a very similar kind of fruitfulness.

Marriage is hard work, at best, but it can be good fun if situational loneliness can be eliminated and existential loneliness can be kept at bay.

Commandment 9

The ninth commandment for good mental health is to pray a lot. Do not overlook how central a factor of good psychology this is. When Jesus taught his disciples the Lord's Prayer, he prefaced it with instruction that they should not try to manipulate God into doing nice things for them that he would not have the good sense or presence of mind to do if they did not talk him into it. He especially emphasized that they should not expect God to be manipulated by vociferous prayers or ritual incantations, nor should they expect results from verbose performances designed to impress him or the human audience. He said simply, "Your father knows what you need before you ask him."

It is clear that Jesus had a low view of petitionary prayers. That has led me to the conviction that prayer is not mainly for asking God to do things for us, but rather for placing our neediness before God and expressing our gratitude that we can count on his grace and providence, unconditionally. The Lord's Prayer itself is a marvelous example of exactly that. At first appearance, it might seem to be a prayer of petitions, but take another look. It has three sections. The first is a section that extols God, acknowledges his generous fatherhood, and declares our affirmation of it and gratitude for it. In it we declare that we are for what God is for: his rule on earth, of grace that works and love that heals. The second section lays before God our neediness, as a child who recognizes his or her own limitations and celebrates the father's readiness to care for those needs. The third section is a doxology, that is, a statement of praise, that, in effect, declares, "What a grand arrangement you have made for us, father, and we affirm and celebrate it and you."

So what looks a bit like a petitionary section in that prayer is in reality merely a way for us to take our proper posture of trusting compatriots before our father's face. Prayer, therefore, ought to be for expressing our childness in conversation with our father, who is already doing for us all that his grace and providence can supply. Prayer is for acknowledging his generous father-hood and for gratefully endorsing the way he has arranged things for us. This perspective has made prayer most meaningful for me for many years and the source of strength and respite.

I must admit, of course, that just when I thought I had prayer all figured out, I went through a time of extreme suffering because of the abuse wreaked on me by a group of colleagues. I was accused of and tried for heresy in the denomination in which I had grown up and in which I served. In that setting, it meant the end of my ordination, job, income source, professional esteem, and family security. For three years, I experienced deep grief and despair, but in it I discovered an additional dimension to prayer that has continued to have profound meaning to me. It is difficult to define or even to describe precisely. I do not know how to write a theology of this dimension of prayer, but I can let you in on what it came to mean to me and has meant ever since. During those years of existential loneliness and abuse, I discovered what David meant in the Psalms when he said, "This poor man cried and the Lord heard him."

I have found prayer to be a keystone to my sustained mental health and psychological well-being.

Commandment 10

The final commandment for psychological well-being in the healer is to take communication dynamics seriously. I discussed this at length in a previous chapter. Psychologists and pastors should be required to take a number of graduate-level courses specifically in the sciences of communication dynamics. We all automatically assume that we can communicate very well, yet we wonder why our logic seems so different than that of the person next to us. We are surprised when the inferences our spouses draw from a statement, event, or situation are so radically different from ours. Things that seem so obvious to us seem to be so obtuse to others. Things that others cavalierly assume or take for granted we find to be wide of the mark of reality.

Frequently, in seminars on communication, I hand out a four-line statement and ask the audience to mark the correct logical conclusion to be drawn from it. The statement is simple but requires a precise logical insight and sequence of thought. The members of the group are always split three to five ways on the answer to that simple logical statement, which corresponds to those that make up our daily life. I usually follow that exercise with a little experiment about drawing inferences from what others say. Then I hand out a three-line statement from a newspaper story about a man entering a store and getting some money. I then ask 11 questions about what happened in the incident as described in the three-line newspaper story. The group is always divided three ways on almost every question. Humans do not hear, see, perceive, or respond alike to anything. Yet we cavalierly expect our communication to be automatic and complete.

One of the reasons that people draw such differing inferences from the same simple situation is that all of us lust for meaning, and when the message we get is cryptic and incomplete, we proceed immediately to set it in a meaningful context and fill out the world of the message to satisfy our need for its total meaning. We get the material for that enlargement of the cryptic message from our past experience, imagination, needs, and long-standing experience of testing reality around us. Therefore, when we hear the message, we spontaneously build around it our own world of inferred meaning. That will, invariably, be quite different from anyone else's world of reference and meaning because our logic and our inner resources will never be the same as those of others.

Psychologists and pastors, healers of every stripe, ought to be specialists in effective communication, but just as important is the need for us to have a thorough scientific understanding of basic communication dynamics and the need to take those dynamics seriously every day. Only then can we realize wisely what is going on around us, within us, and on account of us in the world of our clients.

MENTAL HEALTH FOR THE HEALER'S FAMILY

The Healer's Children

Marriage and family require much harder work than most of us expect. They also require a great deal more time than we normally realize. A healer's family is therefore in danger of being shortchanged by both since work in the helping professions is endless and consumes all the time available for it. Any dedicated psychologist or pastor is always going to be tempted to do a few extra things for his or her clients or parishioners than time and energy permit. That extra time and energy will almost certainly come out of what his or her family really needs. Perhaps that is one of the reasons why all the evidence so overwhelmingly indicates that of all the healing responsibilities a psychologist or pastor has, he or she tends to do the poorest job of caring for members of his or her own family.

That is an especially severe malady since the healer's family usually stands under unusually stressful pressure from the role expectations of the community or congregation. One often gets the impression, for example, that congregations expect pastors' children to be born as mature adults. That has never happened, as far as I know. Moreover, children who are hardly permitted a childhood worry me with the pathology they are liable to suffer later. One of the most serious, perhaps the most serious, of all pastoral responsibilities is the task of shepherding his or her children through that erroneous world thrust on them by the church. A pastor who succeeds in aiding his or her children through the dangers of defensive hostility toward the church and overwhelming anxiety about the possibility of damaging their pastor-parent's role and reputation is already a successful healer, indeed.

Children of pastors tend to take one of two places in life as regards the church. They either carry on a life as adults of great dedication to the church and with important leadership roles in it, or they tend to be outside the church altogether. Seldom are pastors' children merely mildly dedicated to the church. This certainly indicates that they tend to identify with their pastor-parent's calling and ministry, unless the circumstances in the church or the family are such that they are disillusioned by it all and remember it with excessive pain. A pastor can easily forget that he or she is the only pastor that his or her spouse and children have.

There is, of course, the other side of this coin. It is often a good thing for a pastor's children to grow up in the pastoral family setting and the parish. It provides children with an opportunity to see the spiritual community realistically, compassionately, and celebratively in its more positive moments and characteristics. There are often mature and sensitive people in the church who sense intuitively the problems and perplexities of being the pastor's family and exercise unusually meaningful supportive relationships to the spouse and children. Frequently, such relationships have opened doors of vision, opportunity, and faith to pastor's children that prove to be of incomparable value for the rest of their lives. The same can be said for the therapist's children regarding the needy human community.

The Healer's Spouse

The role of the psychologist's or pastor's spouse is crucial for the psychological well-being of the family in numerous ways. First, if the spouse is the mother in the family, her ability to participate in the life of her husband without being impressed into the role of an appendage of his profession is crucial. If she does become a mere appendage, she will be unable to mother the children adequately. The same may be said if the roles are the other way around. In recent decades, role identification for women was difficult. Professional roles came to be seen as superior to domestic roles. This state of affairs seems to have been improved in more recent times. However, sometimes spouses insinuate themselves into the role of a kind of adjunct to the healer in his or her role, as a way to accrue to themselves some professional status.

Frequently, when I ask the spouse of a psychologist or pastor what he or she does, that spouse will explain that his wife is a clinical psychologist or a pastor, "but I am just a day laborer or an office manager." If the spouse is a woman, she will often say, "My husband is a pastor or psychologist, but I am just a housewife." I feel myself cringing with anguish and fear to note that in our culture, homemaking and mothering can be referred to as the calling of a person who is "just a housewife." I usually respond by saying that she will never in her life do anything more important than mothering her children.

I stopped at McDonald's for a quick hamburger and saw a well-dressed mother in a business suit feeding her four- and five-year-old daughters, both of whom were more interested in climbing and sliding than eating. The anxious mother, evidencing intense repressed impatience, obviously had rushed from her office to spend an hour with her kids before she returned them to child care. She looked like she was near the end of her rope, so I walked over and said, "Never again in your life will you have a chance to do anything more important than what you are doing right now!" Tears fell from her eyes as she nodded assent. Nothing more important ever happens in this world than good parenting. It is a grand achievement that freedom for women to pursue their own destinies has gained such important ground in the last decades. However, it is immoral and criminal that homemaking has been so severely devalued in our time.

It is a truly tragic dimension of the human experiment that children cannot stand on the shoulders of their parents, generation after generation, with regard to the things that count most. Technologically, each generation can advance over the one before. We make better refrigerators today than they made in the nineteenth century, so babies are fed better and die less frequently. That is very good. However, with regard to issues of faith, virtue, moral insight, ideals, goals, education, character formation, and the vision of what life can and should be, each generation must start where the last one began—at the beginning. In moral, intellectual, emotional, psychological, and spiritual matters, children must start again at the beginning and run the same gauntlet and risks of growth and change that their parents and grandparents ran before them.

Consequently, we are perpetually only one generation from reversion to barbarianism. The quality of wholesomeness, warmth, idealism, love, virtue, and steadiness in the home determines whether the children will revert to primitive emotions, goals, ideals, appetites, and styles or reach forward and upward to explore and exploit their possibilities as civilized persons and spiritually mature members of society. The thing that guarantees the appropriate and civilizing wholesomeness of any home is normally the quality of mothering that shapes it. In a healer's home, the quality of parenting is the most important influence on the level of mental health and psychospiritual wholeness that is possible there.

Psychologists' and pastors' spouses, therefore, are not called to be associate or substitute professionals in the healing professions, unless that is their independent vocation. They are called to a style for being a healing presence in the home and family that will enhance the health of the children. If they are parents, they are called to the style appropriate to that healing role. That does not mean that they may not have their own independent occupation or professional role and life. It only means that a professional vocation for father or mother may not be at the expense of the quality of parenting, on the part of the psychologist, pastor, or spouse.

Healers in Their Families

Likewise, professional healers who are husbands or wives have a primary calling to relate effectively to their spouses and families. Many spouses feel that they are in competition with God or their spouse's professional identity, depending on which he or she suggests as the reason for his or her vocation. Such competition for love and devotion can cause the time they have together to be spoiled by grief and complaint about the time they do not have together. When I married, one of the first things I said to my wife was, "You must realize that my sense of vocation to the care and healing of persons and the community is a very high priority in my life." She understood that I meant that I felt called of God to this role. That incredibly stupid remark has stuck in her heart and soul to this day. In retrospect, I see how much damage it has done and the difficulty she has had in seeing beyond it, to say nothing of finding it difficult to forgive it.

The remark was true, of course, but I did not need to announce it as though it would forever take priority over my commitment to her. It was a stupid remark because it was so predictably and unnecessarily damaging. I might, instead, simply have gone about my work, counting on her to be as supportive as was necessary or wise. She might have felt little of the woundedness and would simply have taken one day at a time. After my announcement, it proved impossible for her to experience the special demands of my work on my time and energy in any other way than that she was in competition with my vocation, and hence with God, for my allegiance and love. A woman who feels that she is in competition with God thinks she is always going to lose. A healer's spouse needs to know that he or she is married to a companion and not to the spouse's profession.

I am not sure why I made that strange mistake that wounded my wife so much and so permanently, except that it seems to me that my announcement to my wife reflected a common attitude in the church and in many clergymen of that time, at mid-twentieth century. It is clear that being called to ministry, in clinical work or in the pastorate, is to feel a vocation that deprives one of a normal existence and marries one to the healing profession somewhat more than the vocation of an engineer is married to factory production. People care gets under one's skin in unusual ways. That perspective has not been limited to the psychotheology of vocation in the Roman Catholic Church leading to celibacy for clergy. It has carried over into and persisted in many Protestant communions, as well, and into the view of the helping professions in our society. It is clear, of course, that this is less so today in any field than it was a half century ago in many fields. Young healers today are less inclined to make that mistake, though that may be, unfortunately, more because of an increase in individualistic narcissism than a shift in the psychospiritual understanding of a healthy notion of vocation. In any case, it is important that we see our care of and commitment to our family as our first vocation and to the community and our clients or parishioners, the family of God, as an extension of that.

Our dedication to the care of others who need us can become a kind of idolatry in the sense that the business of it becomes an end in itself, rather than a means to the healing of the specific needs of others. When it does, children and family suffer unnecessarily. When the youthful and formative days of our children's lives are past, those days never return. If we have not cherished them with adequate time and closeness, we shall not ever have that same chance again. In our grandchildren, we do recover some opportunity to relive those days to some extent by proxy, as it were, to the benefit of our children and ourselves. God gives us grandchildren to heal us of those earlier losses, but childhood, once missed, never returns. The best gift a healer can give for the mental health and psychospiritual well-being of his or her family is the celebrative life of love, playfulness, joviality, lightheartedness, and dedication to one's vocation, hard work, idealism, challenge, and professional success. Remember that it only takes one generation of humanity to lose its grip and slide back down the hill into the swamp of some modern form of barbarianism, ending in faithlessness and life without meaning.

Good child nurture requires structure that reduces the child's anxiety and garners all his or her psychic energy for growth, rather than for defensiveness, fear, and self-defeating compensatory psychosocial behavior. A child's self-esteem is closely dependent on a warm, firm, and affirming relationship with his or her parents, particularly the parent of the opposite sex. It depends on that relationship flourishing in a predictable and secure setting that reduces anxiety and wholesomely channels the direction of growth.

Now it is certainly the case that psychologists and pastors cannot do everything. That applies to parenting and family as well as to the care given in their work. We have limited time and energy, infinite demands placed on us, a demanding vocation to tend to, and the well-being of living souls to facilitate and fractured human beings to heal. Sometimes, therefore, shortcuts are necessary. In that regard, it is important for the healer to be able to count on the spouse feeling like he or she is part of the home team. The healer must also be able to trust the truth that quality time is more important than quantity time spent with children and family. If the spouse does not feel like he or she is on the home team, however, the spouse will spoil all the quality of the time that the healer may be able to give to the family. It is not true, of course, that quantity and quality are inversely proportional. As you increase one, you do not necessarily decrease the other. Conversely, it is not necessarily true that as you decrease one, you increase the other. It is possible to have both quality and quantity. However, if one must be sacrificed for the other, quality is more important than quantity and can compensate for some lack of it.

One of the ways to insure quality time with one's family is to insure that one's spirit and disposition in both family and work is generous and gracious. There is no substitute for unconditional positive regard, and kindness will always get you halfway home. Gentleness could get you the rest of the way. Then the normal stresses and grief, disappointments, and weird dynamics that are always present in any community will not fall on the healer and his or her family. It is easy for the healer, a human being after all, to pass along the stresses and disappointments of his or her work to the loving family, thinking this to be useful catharsis, only to discover later that it does a lot of damage.

If the healer can handle the strange and painful sides of such a vocation with grace and compassion, that grace and compassion will come through in sharing and catharsis at home. The family will certainly pick up on that same spirit and thereby grow in grace and knowledge of how a healer handles the weighty business of healing. The results may be a marvelous advantage to the mental health of the healer and his family. It is still true that the most important psychological and psychotherapeutic insight that has ever been perceived on the face of this planet is the realization, and the actualization in our behavior, of the incredible fact that grace works and love heals.

CONCLUSION

While I was going through the heresy trial, three of my daughters were just at that age in early adolescence at which they were most vulnerable to damage from any lack of certification by their father. The demands and anguish of the trial distracted me more than ordinarily from the needs and care of my family. Moreover, the girls witnessed notable persons, who were supposed to be respected members of our community, treating their father as though he were to be discredited, demeaned, and abused. Those persons seemed to have authenticity and credibility. It was very perplexing for my daughters, longing for their certification and cherishing by a father who could be viewed as credible and esteemed, to watch the meat grinder slowly grind him up.

I am still working very hard to repair the damage all that did. It is clear to me now that much of it can never be repaired. Of course, in the end, I was infinitely more credible to them than I would have been had I not taken the necessary distinctive position for which I stood. However, that was only after all those formative years of their duress, quandary, anxiety, deprivation, and fear had passed, leaving their permanent marks. They learned a lot from all that and perhaps are wiser and more mature, more courageous and vigorous, more humorful and independent because of it. But the scars are still there from my distraction and inattention and from the pain they felt at seeing my pain and perplexity. Perhaps if, in my endeavor always to speak the truth with them and to let them see the reality of my life as it was unfolding, I could more often, not only have spoken the truth, but more consistently spoken the truth of love and grace about those who were oppressing us, I could have saved my children from much of the pain and from some of the damage.

In the end, it is clear to me that it would have been completely impossible for me to have taken up the intimidating task of the helping professions, to have had the courage to raise children and ask my family to share in my calling, to have courageously continued the work of both through the very heavy sledding typical of the field, and to have been able to live with myself while looking back on it all if I could not have believed that in, under, and through it all stood God's unconditional grace to me. I was sure that with its guarantee, we could not lose. I learned early that I could not sin myself out of his grace. However, adequate or inadequate to the task, I could not fall, or inadvertently squirm, out of God's long embrace.

I am sure that it was that profound assurance that kept me focused well enough, strong and courageous enough, integrated and sure enough to carry on in mental health and psychospiritual well-being. In fact, the years in his grace get better and surer as they unfold. Each step is a clearer view for me of the reality that God is for us and not against us, in all things, unconditionally, and that he accepts us where we are, just as we are at any given moment in our pilgrimage of growth, with affirmation and joy.

CHAPTER 14

GRACE THEOLOGY IN PSYCHOTHERAPY

We have come to that point in this volume at which we will summarize and more specifically finalize the application in clinical operations of what has been discussed thus far. That will require some recollection of ideas treated earlier and discussion of their relevance to the actual treatment of persons suffering psychological illness.

Johann von Goethe observed that everybody wants to be somebody, but nobody wants to grow. That is not a universally applicable principle, fortunately, but it is what the therapist is often up against at the clinical level; that is, healing, education, maturation, and wholeness are each a growth process, and there is a profound sense in which illness, ignorance, immaturity, and counterproductive forms of spirituality are states or postures produced by obstruction of the needed growth. Likewise, wholeness, wisdom and knowledge, and maturity and wholesomeness are the final integrated achievements to which growth brings us.

The process of growth hinges on insight. It requires the application of insight (1) to the state of our illness or need and (2) to the possibilities and methods for growing or inciting growth. That principle is true whether the obstruction to growth or resistance to the change is psychological, physiological, intellectual, theological, or a combination of these. As I have explained in previous chapters, I make that assertion against the backdrop of a Christian view of human personhood, structured in terms of the biblical theology of unconditional, radical, and universal grace.

That is to say, I am assuming that God has imputed an inviolable status to humans. That status of companion and compatriot of God means that

humans have a significant role and status in life. We are more than merely
servants or children of God. It is a status and role of being, among other
things, colaborers with God in the development in this world of his reign of
grace that works and love that heals. As persons, God created us in his image,
and we share his essential qualities and characteristics: communication, creativity, generativity, memory, self-conceptualization or self-consciousness,
decisiveness, rationality, power, self-actualization, love, and the like. This assumption, moreover, includes the perception that God *will not* and *cannot*
abrogate that status.

This Christian view of the living human document implies that the nature
of humans is shaped by an identifiable set of magnificent potentials for psychological, physical, intellectual, and spiritual growth. Such a Christian view
further conceives the destiny of humans to be the achievement of wholeness
and integration through total actualization of all the potentials inherent in
humanness, namely, inherent in the status of God-compatriot and carrier of
the divine image. Facilitating that is the task of the psychologist and pastor.

A PSYCHOTHEOLOGY OF HEALTH

So, viewed psychologically and theologically, a complete understanding of
human beings centers in a sense of the purpose of human existence, our destiny
before God's face and in his grace; that is, a biblical psychotheology of human
nature conceives of us as being born for and moving toward a purposive destiny. That purpose is the achievement of wholeness and self-fulfillment or self-
actualization through growth. That is not only true of humans but of the entire
material universe. Thus health is the state of having achieved wholeness or being
in the process of achieving it and having gained that degree of it appropriate to
one's stage of psychospiritual maturity at any given point in time.

Christian psychologists, theologians, and other clinicians, therefore, must
develop clinical criteria for assessing the process of psychospiritual healing
and wholeness and of a person's stage in it. Secular psychology, insofar as
it represents unimpeachable truth about its field, provides Christians with
much ready-made equipment and insight for this endeavor. Those secular information resources must be received gratefully and seriously as a gift from
God's general revelation through the natural and social sciences. Christian
healers can wisely employ it in a psychotheological framework.

The principles for wholeness and health stated previously apply equally
to physiological, psychological, intellectual, emotional, and spiritual spheres.
They are equally true with regard to sickness of body, mind, and spirit and
apply as much to treatment of clinical pathology as to spiritual dysfunction,
sinfulness, and religious disorder. Christians have a high motivation driving
our concern for a dialogue between psychology and theology in this quest
to understand wholeness and the process of healing that leads to it. That

motivation arises from the sense that there is a necessary, and not merely accidental, relationship between our being a reflection of God's nature, celebrating God's grace, and being a psychological scientist, therapist, or pastoral counselor.

There are difficulties inherent in this matter, one of which is the difficulty of basic definition. In his fine book *Mind and Madness in Ancient Greece*, Bennett Simon declared that the difficulty in talking about psychology is that of getting a commonly agreed on definition, even among the specialists in psychology.[1] It is important, therefore, that we further clarify our main concepts.

A PSYCHOTHEOLOGY OF ILLNESS

As previously observed, the subconscious posture of persons in Western culture, professional healers and laypersons alike, is surprisingly negative and stereotyped with regard to those who are ill. We often unconsciously feel that those who are ill did not take proper care of themselves. God, fate, aging, irresponsibility, or destiny finally caught up with them. We must admit that the ill are often seen as second-class citizens. They are too easily handled as objects. We, of course, are somehow superior, even morally superior, since we are not ill.

That psychotheology of illness will not square with our Christian understanding of the nature of human personhood and with the theology of divine and human grace. A sound psychotheology of illness must operate from the perspective that mentally or physically ill persons are, despite their deficits, God-compatriots of infinitely and inviolably worthy status, whose growth toward their divinely destined self-actualization has somehow been obstructed. That state of obstruction to and loss of growth is, by definition, illness. We infrequently think of their illness as a gift to them and that they may be growing from their pain.

The obstructive illness may be a genetic distortion, a foreign organism, an imbalance in nutrition, a malfunction of metabolism, a disrupted socialization, a failure of appropriate instruction and guidance, inappropriate fear, ineffective worship, unchanneled assertiveness, bad biochemistry, or the like. Whatever is the case, insight on the part of the patient and understanding applied by the healer is necessary to free the patient for growth, health, and wholeness. Sickness has no moral import, but is simply an existential condition. The only moral issue is whether we promote healing if and where it is possible.

A PSYCHOTHEOLOGY OF HEALING

It is predictable, then, that a psychotheology of healing deals with the method and substance of reducing obstructions to growth and health and enhancing growth's vitality. This is the immediate level of concern to the clinician and pastor. It is imperative that the clinician's model of humanness is comprehensively shaped by a dynamic Christian anthropology, that is, a concept of human nature structured in terms of a thoroughgoing theology of grace. Only then can a psychotheology of healing be sound.

Moreover, the healer's Christian anthropology must be dynamic, not constrained by dogma. It must be interacting constantly with real clinical and pastoral experience as well as with the work of the research scientists so that the healer's Christian view of human nature is constantly being reshaped and refined. Only then will it progressively mature honestly and relevantly.

MODELS OF PSYCHOPATHOLOGY AND PSYCHOTHERAPY

Siegler and Osmond provided interesting insights and useful foci for the field of clinical psychology. In their book *Models of Madness, Models of Medicine*, they presented a table of eight current models of psychopathology.[2] For each model, they described 12 typical clinical functions, including diagnosis or definition, etiology, subject behavior, treatment, prognosis, therapy setting, types of therapists, rights of the patient and of the patient's social unit, and goals of therapy.

They described current models and the definitions of psychopathology characteristic of each. The *medical model* assumes that a physician will diagnose the illness, rule out other pathologies, inform the patient, and determine treatment and prognosis. Natural causes are assumed to be the sources of the disorder. The goals of the process are to (1) prevent worsened illness; (2) cure the symptoms; (3) if possible, eliminate the sources; (4) accumulate medical knowledge in the process; and (5) do no harm. The *moral model* assumes that a moral practitioner will determine the nature and extent of the dysfunction or inappropriate and hence immoral behavior. The specific etiology is assumed to be unimportant but has to do with learned bad behavior of some kind. Treatment modifies the bad behavior with discipline: positive and negative sanctions. Prognosis is considered good if the patient cooperates in the establishment of behavior change instructions and reinforcement of good behavior. The goal of therapy is to alter the patient's behavior with acceptable social norms.

The *impaired model* sees the patient as maimed and is unconcerned with most of the 12 functions, except diagnosis and institutionalization. The goal is to protect the patient from society, and vice versa. Anything short of permanent impairment is not identified as clinical pathology. The *psychoanalytic model* assumes that patients are somewhere on a continuum from mild neurosis to severe psychosis. Diagnosis is not significant; etiology is very important; therapy involves decoding the patient's symbolic systems and creating a transference base, enhancing the patient's move toward health. The patient has the right to sympathy, empathy, and progress toward health. The goal is to resolve the pathogenic conflicts, whether intrapsychic or psychosocial in nature.

The *social model* assumes that society is sick and that the patient's pathology is accidental to that. The sociopathology of the patient can be corrected by social change in the community. The rights and goals of society, the patient, and the therapist focus on creation of a healthy social environment for growth, especially for children. The *psychedelic model* sees psychopathology as a mind-expanding or distorting trip prompted by families or communities who drive patients crazy. Therapy involves breaking the family bond, providing a so-called guided trip to enlightenment, and so allowing the patient to develop the inner potential to change the self and his or her world.

The *conspiratorial model* assumes that pathology is a label given to the patient by others who cannot tolerate deviance. Treatment is brainwashing for the purpose of maintaining the status quo. The family *interactional model* assumes that patients are the index of family pathology. The patient's symptoms are enactments of the family's pathology. Family therapy is required, and if effective, the family will give up its pathological game pattern, and the index person can drop the personal symptoms. The goal of therapy is to understand family dynamics and restore pathological families to functional relationships.

It is evident that each of these models expresses some aspect of the truth with which psychologists and pastors must deal. It is difficult to critique all of the Siegler-Osmond categories in detail, but a few observations may be useful. First, the social model, though it embodies some reality, has thoroughly dysfunctioned in our society, as indicated by the hopeless ineffectiveness of the costly strategies for basic social change attempted over the last half century, from the individual and local level to the federal government and society level. Modifying the person by modifying the social setting does not work. That is further evident from recent acknowledgment that the long-standing strategies for rehabilitation of criminals have not worked and are financially, scientifically, and culturally bankrupt.

The impaired, psychedelic, and conspiratorial models offer no comprehensive usefulness at all. The medical model and family interaction model are much more comprehensively applicable, but both are deficient in their assessment regarding the seriousness of the general patient's depth and degree of disorder. The psychoanalytic model comes closest to appreciating the radical extent and depth of human pathology and dysfunction, but like the medical and family models, it fails to appreciate adequately the pathological state of human beings generally, the radical depth of our alienation from our real potentials and our destiny. It fails, therefore, to appreciate the extent of generalized pathogenic anxiety and dissonance, intrapsychic and psychosocial, which lie at the root of human pathology and are inherent to the current state of just being a human being. The self-perceived fallenness or brokenness, alienation, and isolation at the core of our humanness are underestimated. The spiritual side of all this is usually ignored as irrelevant or inaccessible.

CHRISTIAN CLINICAL APPROACH

Eight Principles

There are eight principals or concepts that may be taken into consideration to insure that in the work of psychotherapy and pastoral counseling, the whole person of the patient or parishioner is addressed, including the spiritual side. These have to do with the themes that need attention if the healer is to develop a role and style that incarnates divine grace into his or her person and work. These themes might be called *biblical principles*. They ring true to and illumine psychological theory and practice at numerous key points; that is, biblical anthropology, notions of human nature, illumines sound psychosocial research and practice. These principles have to do with the biblical notions of personhood, alienation, grace, sin or sickness, discipline, the woundedness of the healer as well as the patient, mortality, and celebration as a way of life. These principles reflect the main themes of the Hebrew Bible and Christian scriptures.

The *biblical theology of human personhood* is profound and has been alluded to repeatedly already in this volume. Their essence is the emphasis on unconditional grace from God to humans and from us to each other. Humans are unconditionally cherished by God in spite of themselves. God so loved the world that he created it and cherishes it, investing all of us with inviolable dignity and value. Our flaws and fracturedness, our sickness and inadequacy, have not prompted God to abrogate this commitment to us. In this nonnegotiable and inviolable status, each person has only two options. We can place ourselves in a posture that rings true to that God-given status and, therefore, be true to our real selves; or we can choose to be inauthentic to that relationship with God, in perspective, disposition, or behavior, and suffer the dissonance and dis-ease inherent to such a posture.

Nonetheless, God remains preoccupied with human *need*, not human *naughtiness*, with our failure of *destiny* more than of *duty*, and with our *potential* for healing, not with our flawed *past*. Since God confirms needy or suffering persons and their healers in that quality of personhood and that state of grace, Jewish and Christian psychological theory and practice must be based on it. Patients and parishioners are free to be what they are for the sake of what they can become, before the face and in the grace of God. The same must be said of authentic Muslim ministry in so far as the Qur'an is based upon the ancient Hebrew traditions.

The *biblical theology of alienation* starts, in the mythic faith system of most Christians, with the story of the Fall in Genesis 3, which we have already addressed in chapter 1. As noted there, while this ancient Mesopotamian myth, dressed up in the clothes of ancient Israel's God, is a symbolic report on human birth and adolescent maturation, it nonetheless expresses a deep truth about each human person who feels like a child that has lost touch with his or her father's hand. We readily respond with St. Augustine, "You have made us for yourself and our souls are restless until they rest, O God, in you."

That we are people who fall short of our own inherent potential and our God-designed destiny is obvious and requires no theological argument or persuasion. The psychological realities of that are evident every day, everywhere. The brokenness and disjointedness of the psyche of all humans is an empirical expression of human dysfunction of the primal anxiety permeating everything, and of the thirst for anxiety reduction as our main quest in life. The many psychospiritual compensatory strategies incited by all of that are frequently themselves inducers of further illness. Religion, particularly Judeo-Christian religions of divine grace, are designed to be significant, indeed the ultimate, anxiety reducers. The uniqueness of the authentic biblical theology of grace is that it reveals God as unconditionally gracious and accepting of us as we are, rather than being a threat to us. Religion that does not center in this insight, even much of distorted Judaism and Christianity, moves instead in the direction of legalistic self-justification. It is the strategy of forcing God's favor by means of correct performance of liturgical or ethical requirements, thus measuring up to some kind of religious or social standards. This is always self-defeating because no one ever believes he or she has adequately measured up, unless he or she is a pathological narcissist.

In authentic biblical religion, grace as unconditional positive regard for the inadequate or sick human is the exclusive anxiety reducer. That is reinforced by the opportunity for the healed person to live a spontaneously joyful life of gratitude for that healing insight. Anyone who really gets that point will spontaneously turn his or her life around and desire to be God's kind of person. So a proper biblical theology of human alienation or fallenness from our own ideal destiny is critically necessary to the Jewish and Christian healer's perception of self and others. Only this can generate the proper recognition of God's way of dealing with our brokenness as an analogue for how we handle our patients and parishioners.

The *biblical theology of grace*, therefore, is critical for shaping any sound psychological or psychotherapeutic concept or method. In the Bible, grace is unconditional, arbitrary, universal, exploitable, radical, and uncalculating. It is unconditional, as in the parable of the prodigal son. It is universal, as in the promises to Abraham in Genesis 12 and 17—a covenant for the healing of all nations—as well as in John 3:16–17 and numerous passages in Paul's

letters. It is radical in that, by an arbitrary act of God, it cuts through to
the center of human alienation, whether humans like it or not, as in Micah
7:18–20. Moreover, God's grace perpetually reaffirms the compatriot status
of all of us humans with God, in spite of ourselves. Throughout history,
that has been a difficult perception for the believing community to hold to.
As noted previously, it took the ancient Israelites about 1,000 years to lose
their grip on it and revert to legalistic religion. It took the early Christians
about 500 years to resort to the formalistic religion of scholasticism, with
its legalistic medieval atonement theories and ethics. It took the Protestants
about 250 years after the great Lutheran and Calvinist Reformation of the
sixteenth and seventeenth centuries to revert to a kind of medieval scholastic
Reformed theology.

We seem to be improving our pagan efficiency over time. Humans have a
native compulsive proclivity to try to get our own hands on the controls of
self-justification because accepting free grace is so scary and so nearly unbelievable for people who are somewhat neurotic and perceive themselves as
not OK children as well as for narcissists who are always sure they are the
only ones who are thoroughly OK. All of us fall, to some degree, in one of
those categories. Moreover, accepting free grace requires accepting the need
for it, and most of us do not recognize that our problem is as profound as it is.
We do not believe that we are inherently alienated from our true selves, our
true potential, our authentic destiny, and hence from wholeness.

The *biblical theology of sin* is likewise crucial to the perspectival model of
Christian healing therapy. Contrary to popular opinion, sin is a failure in
achievement of authenticity to self and of full-orbed personhood in God's
grace. It is a distortion and distraction to lesser achievements. It cannot be
compensated for. It can only be converted from. *Metanoia* is the only solution.
That is a Greek word for changing one's mind, life direction, and posture
toward God. That change from illness to health is possible only to the person who has heard the announcement that he or she is forgiven and accepted
unconditionally. Nietzsche said that "the courage to be," in this hopelessly
tragic world, is the ability to stand at the brink of the abyss of nothingness
and hear without flinching the announcement that God is dead.

The real story that he could have known is that the courage to be, in this
fractured and alienated world, is the ability to stand in the middle of the
hopelessness and helplessness of human alienation and hear the announcement that God has embraced us in spite of ourselves. That is the courage to
accept unconditionally God's unconditional acceptance of us: to realize that
since God is for us, no one and nothing can be against us (Rom. 8). Ultimately,
each person cannot even be against himself or herself as an obstruction to
divine grace and acceptance since, in the end, as St. Paul declares, every eye
shall see God, and every knee shall bow before God, and every tongue will
affirm God, to the glory of God and the healing of humankind.

Such an outlook comes from hearing the word that human destiny is the destiny of realizing in full-orbed personhood the palpable experiences of the secure status of compatriot of God, a status God has imputed to us in spite of ourselves, as his colaborers in extending his reign of forgiveness and love. God never abrogates that status. We cannot sin ourselves out of his grace, nor squirm out of his long embrace. He simply waits for us to achieve the self-actualization that expresses it. Our sin or sickness is merely a matter of falling short of that expectation.

God's law is not a threat in the sense that an infraction brings loss of favor. It is, rather, a constitution for the kingdom of peace and prosperity, of *shalom*, wholeness in every way. It is interesting that Jesus was oriented, as were the prophets, toward social and psychological wholeness, rather than merely toward private piety and personal purity. Religions of mere private piety and personal purity tend to be idolatry of the self, narcissistic, making of the self a kind of plastic doll to be cherished for its own sake. True religion is a celebration of the compatriot status grace establishes for us who are made in God's image. What we have tended to call sin, incorrectly I think, is a distraction to trying to be OK by measuring up to some standard and obsessively pursuing purity or some sort of perfection. This is a different sort of psychological business than maturity in the freedom God's grace brings to us. Thus Martin Luther, the great sixteenth-century Reformer, said, "Sin boldly. Since you are going to be a sinner in any case, step out boldly into the new day, living in the assurance of God's grace! Be preoccupied with God's grace, not with how you fall short of self-actualizing all our growth potentials."

The *biblical theology of discipline* is the theme of discipleship. Getting well and doing good is enacting grace. Discipline is the endeavor of beginning down the road of forgiving ourselves and others, of acceptance of ourselves and others, of unconditionally cherishing ourselves and others, and of reflecting in this way the nature of the divine analogue of delight in us as we are. The discipline of discipleship is a troth with self and with God to incarnate in ourselves God's divine grace dynamic that infuses the universe. It is the troth *to forsake all other preoccupations and keep ourselves only to that divinely ordered destiny.*

Jesus urged people to such discipline by the grace with which he handled them. To the adulterous woman (John 8) brought to him for judgment, he urged, "I do not condemn you. Go your way and do not hurt yourself anymore. It is untrue to your self." To the Samaritan woman (John 4), he gave the insight that spirituality, not religiosity, is the issue at the center of our psychological and spiritual health. Peter, the denier, Jesus ordained to ministry. Matthew reports that when Judas met Jesus in the Garden of Gethsemane to betray him to the authorities, Jesus embraced him, held on to him, and said, "Friend, how did it come to this?" The discipline of discipleship means to be bound to God and so to be free in his grace. It means to live toward what life can and will be. Since that is what life is designed to be, godly expectations for healers and their clients will be shaped by such a transcendent psycho-spiritual worldview.

Henri Nouwen has the finest word on the *biblical theological theme of the wounded healer*.[3] He takes the suffering servant notion of the Hebrew Bible, which is also epitomized in the messianic theology of the New Testament, and he points out metaphorically that there are five doors for God, and for the human healer, into the heart of human need. There are doors of the wound-edness of the world, the woundedness of any given generation, the wounded-ness of each individual, the wounds of Jesus Christ, and the woundedness of the human healer. By *woundedness* he means the fracturedness, inadequacy, distortion, dysfunction, and illness of a person: the way and degree in which we all fall short of our potential as God made us to be. Nouwen refers to all the ways in which we fall short of our own realistic ideals and goals.

Nouwen points out that this wounded healer theme implies that all grace, growth, and healing are communicated or incited by starting where the healer and the person to be healed are in the human journey. The humanness and brokenness of both must be affirmed. The healer's role is not to remove the pain of life from the sufferer, but to interpret or illuminate it. Moreover, the evidence in the healer of woundedness and pain, and of the transcen-dence or constructive endurance of it, helps to heal the patient. Carl Jung felt that half of the healing power of any healer lay in the notion of the archetype healer projected by the patient on the therapist.[4] Therefore the value of the healer sharing his or her own growth dynamics in therapy is relevant here. The wounded healer can become the model and the incarna-tion of the risk taking inherent to growth, healing, and wholeness, neces-sary for the patient or parishioner.

The *biblical theological theme of mortality* is directly related to the idea of the wounded healer. The Bible gives little impetus to the perfectionist no-tion that building God's reign of grace and love in this world will eliminate mortality and the brokenness of this world. Instead, it *affirms* our mortal-ity, and the world's fracturedness, and the terminal nature of life. The Bible emphasizes the strategies for making godly sense of things in that setting. That, after all, is what grace is all about. The brokenness, humanness, and sickness of the world are affirmed—as is the fact that we are dying men and women in a generation of dying men and women. It acknowledges both the magnificence and the malignancy in the universe.

The persistent malignancy is pathologically denied in our cultural ide-alization of the bigger and better. The Bible says that it is OK to vary from the idealized norm. It is acceptable to age, wrinkle, decrease, distort, weaken, become more dependent, and even die. In fact, to die can be a real gain, in the end, according to St. Paul. Youthfulness is not the focus of meaning in the biblical concept of mortality; maturation is. Patients need to feel in therapists the Christian realization that it is a supportable, and perhaps even a celebrat-able, condition to be a human, mortal, dying person, before the face of God.

The finest biblical illumination of what it means behaviorally to be Christian or godly in our work and world is the *biblical theological theme of celebration*. It is a revealing clinical and biblical fact that people who can be grateful can be healthy and people who are incapable of generating spontaneous and authentic gratitude are unable to be psychospiritually healthy. They do not have the interior machinery or dynamics for it. The German Reformers knew that 450 years ago, when they wrote it into the warm, humane document of the Heidelberg Catechism, with its focus on gratitude as the godly way of life.

They said we must know three things for a life of wholeness: the size of our need, the nature of our healing, and the life of gratitude appropriate to that healing. Celebration as gratitude may take the form of worship, or the childlike posture before our father that we call prayer, or just the satisfied joy of living. Celebration may be exhilarated joy for the providence of God in life or for a specific deliverance from a specific suffering or dysfunction. To be godly means to be like children celebrating their father's beneficence. A Christian therapist or pastor who sees life as that kind of enterprise will incarnate for the patient crucial elements of celebration in the clinical spirit and process that he or she provides during illness, healing, and the achievement of wholeness.

A PSYCHOTHEOLOGICAL MODEL OF PSYCHOTHERAPY

So it should be clear that a Christian, or at least a godly, psychotheological model of pathology and healing interventions is essential. It must incorporate an adequate appreciation of our real sense of universal dysfunction and lostness, expressive of the distance between our destiny and our daily function, between our potential and our problematic state of underachievement and underevolvement, between our imagination and our performance, between our reach and our grasp. It must take into consideration the physical stress and distress, the sickening effects, and the psychospiritual defeat reflected in and generated by that distance between God's realities for us and our own realities in us.

We are all rational, emotional, relational, and biological persons. To be whole, we need to function with coherent thought, freely expressed emotions, mutually gratifying and empowering relationships, and medically sound bodies. These are the basic concerns of the healer. To develop a godly healing strategy that adequately reflects a biblical view of human nature and a thoroughgoing grace theology will involve 10 essential factors, as suggested in previous chapters. First, the healer must incarnate in his or her person unconditional acceptance of the needy person, accepting him or her just where he or she is in life's journey, no matter how sick or well. Second, the healer must evince the kind of empathy that places him or her inside the psychospiritual frame of reference of the patient's or parishioner's pathology.

This will greatly assist the healer in the endeavor to determine the sources and nature of the obstructions to health as well as the possibilities for growth and healing inherent in the suffering person. In this set, the healer can affirm the sufferer as a person, not just as a patient, as God affirms all of us in our psychospiritual dysfunction. God takes our dysfunction or illness seriously and reinitiates growth *by means of it*. Verbal and nonverbal mediation of God's unconditional acceptance of persons, sick and well, is a crucial baseline for the needy person's recovery of a sense of self-worth, power, and a worthwhile destiny that rings true to his or her real nature and potential as a whole person.

Third, the godly healer will provide the suffering person a sense of mutuality with the healer in the quest for wholeness on which the patient-therapist team has embarked. Fourth, it will be evident in the therapy process that the healer, too, is wrestling with his or her own humanness, in its pathology and its potential for health. Fifth, within this sound strategy, it will become evident that the psychologist's or pastor's worldview includes a real ambition for the wholeness of all humans and that this particularly needy person is embraced within that larger concern. Sixth, the possibilities and expectations for the patient or parishioner inherent in that worldview will become overtly apparent. Seventh, the grace-imputed status of the suffering person as a colaborer or compatriot with God in the healing of himself or herself and in the healing of the whole world of humankind will be seen by the patient or parishioner as the underpinning of his or her real life and world.

Eighth, soundly established techniques for countering defensive patterns in the patient or parishioner will be used to defeat obstructions of growth to wholeness. Ninth, the needy person's physical, intellectual, psychological, and spiritual needs and states will be taken seriously as functions of a whole-person concern for wholeness and wholesomeness. Tenth, the effectiveness of this healing intervention will be measured in relative terms at each level of increased functionality—physical, psychological, intellectual, emotional, and spiritual—in the light of the expectation that the ultimate achievement of health will be the arrival at psychospiritual maturity. This entire process assumes, of course, that the healing by both psychologist and pastor expresses an assiduous commitment to sound scientific criteria of diagnosis and clinical intervention.

Some Christian professionals active in the pastoral care movements, such as Thomas C. Oden, when commenting on the helping professions have severely denigrated the clinical perspective and psychotheological models of healing. They are reverting to what Wayne Oates used to call a pseudo-classical style of pastoral counseling.[5] Oden's approach is not theological nor psychological but moralistic, much like that of Jay Adams was three decades ago. Oden has resorted to a primitive and antipsychology notion. This approach will be of no service to the godly concern for and dialogue about authentic psychotheology or psychospiritual psychotherapy. It is, rather, a return to a directive form of ecclesiasticism in the helping professions that Oden attempts to shore up by mining the ancient notions of the Church Fathers of 17 centuries ago. This resort to moralism and conditional notions of grace is unbiblical and fails to help in providing a useful new model of Christian healing. It is a trivial shortcut that undermines the hard-won progress of the last half century. That regression is to be assiduously avoided. Both psychology and theology have managed too well and come too far to warrant an anticlinical and anti-grace-theology iconoclasm at this point.

EIGHT RESULTS FOR PSYCHOTHERAPY AND PASTORAL CARE

The consequences of the above for psychotherapy are eight obvious operational results. To operate clinically from the point of view that humans image the nature of God and are given by God an inviolable status and role as God's coworkers in the kingdom of grace and love (1) leads the healer first to communicate to the suffering person how much the healer appreciates the sufferer's infinite worth, dignity, and esteem as God's person. It is necessary for needy persons to realize that, in spite of themselves and their dysfunction, they have this preestablished identity that cannot be taken away from them and that sets the course for their growth to wholeness. The point of therapy is to recover and enhance that sense of identity. Though it may never be overtly explained in therapy, it will shape the healer's affirmation of the needy person and hence that person's experience of being affirmed by the healer. The psychologist or pastor is in that sense a priest of God for that needy person. This unconditional positive regard for the patient is equally the imperative of good scientific psychotherapy and grace theology.

This perspective, taken from the biblical themes we discussed above, (2) implies for the suffering person a certified and secure destiny, infused with a clear sense of purpose and psychospiritual self-realization. This (3) can insure for the needy person the certainty of receiving the kind of acceptance in society that is the analogy derived from the analogue of God's unconditional grace. Administered with responsible psychotherapeutic interventions, this will defuse neurotic guilt, unproductive remorse, hopelessness, unresolved grief, self-pity, compulsivity, fear, guilt, and shame as well as some of the need for schizoid ideation. That biblical perspective also potentially decreases the need for the defeating processes of masked denial, self-justification, self-affliction, and the conversion reactions so often produced by these. Moreover, the insight afforded by these biblical themes frees one for informed and con-structive self-acceptance.

This (4) can provide the patient or parishioner the foundation for a lifestyle of dignity, of being cherished and affirmed, rather than of self-abnegation and demeanment. Such a sense of self will be reinforced by the corollary insight that the dysfunction of the sufferer is a failure of destiny and not of duty: illness is not a moral issue. Moreover, (5) this biblical outlook on things can take the panic out of the therapy process for the psychotherapist and the pastoral counselor. Since God is God and grace is grace, even when we are not experiencing it, the therapist need not feel as though the weight of the world is on him or her and as though the therapist's own personhood or destiny hangs on the outcome of this case. As a result, the therapist's anxiety will be reduced, and the dysfunction of the therapist with which the patient must deal will be decreased.

That frees the healer to make the godlike decisions often necessary in the healing process. This clinical model should effect meaningful, constructive anxiety reduction for the suffering person, who perceives that he or she does not need to get well to be accepted and cherished, certified and honored, by the healer or by God. Thus the patient is free to get well in a naturally unfolding, unpanicked growth process. The patient will be led to recognize that his or her worthiness is inherent, not earned by measuring up to the therapist's expectations, his or her own expectations, or God's.

Such a process (6) provides a setting of trust, healthy transference, and increased potential for the risk taking necessary to growth as well as reduced injection of the therapist's pathology into the growth framework of the pa-tient. The suffering person can know from the experience with the therapist that he or she is affirmed and certified as a worthy person who may therefore develop a sense of worth and worthiness that is inherent to him or her as a person, rather than earned by approvable behavior or by getting well.

To work out of such a perspective (7) makes it possible for the healer and the person in need of healing to be usefully humorous about themselves, each other, their pathologies, and their potentials. It makes possible also a good sense of humor about God and about our limited ability to figure God out in relation to us or his world. We can laugh about our presumption of knowing a lot more about God than we do. The (8) relief from constraints that dis-tract patients from godly self-actualization and self-esteem afforded by this outlook empowers the sufferer to a sense of freedom he or she never knew before or believed was possible. This freedom makes possible our acceptance of our moral limitations and our inevitable mortality, the freedom to die well, for when we fall off the edge of this mortal coil, we fall into the hands of the God of grace. That relief attacks the ultimate panic that stands as a specter behind all our pathology.

CONCLUSION

Theology and faith are cognitive-emotive processes. Therefore their function for ill or good is most relevant and applicable to disorders that are cognitive or emotive in source. That means that healthy dynamics and perspectives in theology and faith will affect the potential health of the psychologist and pastor as well as their patients and parishioners who suffer such psychosocial disorders. Religious or spiritual dynamics may be somewhat less relevant in psychopathology that has biochemical sources, though even then, healthy theology and faith may be invaluable in management of the symptoms.

However, as previously noted, with the increasing evidence for the two-way switching function of the hypothalamus in channeling or controlling the impact of endocrine disorders on the psychological field and psychic disorders on the endocrine function, the role of healthy or pathological theology, faith, or spirituality becomes increasingly interesting with regard to their role in or impact on even those psychopathologies that appear to root in distortions of body chemistry. Therefore concerns about theological perspective, faith commitment, religious experience, and spiritual maturity are becoming increasingly vital therapeutic issues. The concern to be a godly or Christian professional in the helping professions really is a crucial one.

For me, the godly enterprise of a biblical perspective on healing people holds out one additional and overriding dimension: the incomparable encouragement and delight that, though I may never see my patients again, in their need and quandary, I shall with certainty celebrate with them and all the saints of God our mutual ecstasy of gratitude one great and glorious morning when faith has become sight, when we shall see reality whole and face-to-face, and know and affirm God as thoroughly as God now knows and affirms us (I Cor. 13).

NOTES

1. Bennett Simon (1980), *Mind and Madness in Ancient Greece: The Classical Roots of Modern Psychiatry*, Ithaca, NY: Cornell.

2. Miriam Siegler and Humphrey Osmond (1974), *Models of Madness and Models of Medicine*, New York: Macmillan.

3. Henri Nouwen (1972), *The Wounded Healer: Ministry in Contemporary Society*, Garden City, NJ: Doubleday.

4. Carl G. Jung (1958), *Undiscovered Self*, trans. R.F.C. Hull, Boston: Little, Brown.

5. Wayne E. Oates (1958), *What Does Psychology Say about Religion?*, New York: Association Press; Oates (1987), *Behind the Masks: Personality Disorders in Religious Behavior*, Philadelphia: Westminster; Oates (1978), *The Religious Care of the Psychiatric Patient*, Philadelphia: Westminster; Oates (1973), *The Psychology of Religion*, Waco, TX: Word; and Oates, ed. (1959), *An Introduction to Pastoral Counseling*, Nashville, TN: Broadman.

Conclusion: Summing Up—Grace and Health

As I indicated at the outset, it was my intent in writing this work to express a specific perspective on the field of the helping professions. I wished thereby to illumine as wide a range of conceptual issues as possible in the fields of psychology, theology, and spirituality. The outlook I have expressed is that of human personhood fashioned in the nature and for the work of God and viewed in terms of the biblical notion of God's radical, unconditional, and universal grace. To accomplish that, I have attempted to produce an interface and mutual illumination between psychology and theology. Psychology brings with it all the natural and social sciences that apply to it. Theology, likewise, carries with it the historical, philosophical, linguistic, and literary sciences that apply to it. I have brought them to bear on some of the main themes and current problems of the helping professions so as to lead the earnest reader across some new psychospiritual frontiers of insight and vision.

The objective of this work has been to emphasize the urgent need for a thoroughly holistic and integrated model of people care, in all facets of the helping professions. Human health and wholeness require a unity in body, mind, and spirit. In that psychospiritual direction lies the future of all healing ministry and the only hopeful future for humankind.

SERIES AFTERWORD

J. Harold Ellens

The interface between psychology, religion, and spirituality has been of great interest to scholars for a century. In the last three decades, a broad popular appetite has developed for books that make practical sense out of the sophisticated research on these three subjects. Freud expressed an essentially deconstructive perspective on this matter and indicated that he saw the relationship between human psychology and religion to be a destructive interaction. Jung, on the other hand, was quite sure that these three aspects of the human spirit—psychology, religion, and spirituality—were constructively and inextricably linked.

Anton Boisen and Seward Hiltner derived much insight from both Freud and Jung as well as from Adler and Reik while pressing the matter forward with ingenious skill and illumination. Boisen and Hiltner fashioned a framework within which the quest for a sound and sensible definition of the interface between psychology, religion, and spirituality might best be described or expressed.[1] We are in their debt.

This series of general interest books, so wisely urged by Praeger Publishers, and particularly by its editors Deborah Carvalko and Suzanne I. Staszak-Silva, intends to define the terms and explore the interface of psychology, religion, and spirituality at the operational level of daily human experience. Each volume of the series identifies, analyzes, describes, and evaluates the full range of issues, of both popular and professional interest, that deal with the psychological factors at play (1) in the way religion takes shape and is expressed, (2) in the way spirituality functions within human persons and shapes both religious formation and expression, and (3) in the ways that spirituality is shaped and expressed by religion. The interest is psychospiritual. In terms of the rubrics of the disciplines and the science of psychology and spirituality, this series of volumes investigates the *operational dynamics* of religion and spirituality.

The verbs *shape* and *express* in the above paragraph refer to the forces that prompt and form religion in persons and communities as well as to the manifestations of religious behavior (1) in personal forms of spirituality, (2) in acts of spiritually motivated care for society, and (3) in ritual behaviors such as liturgies of worship. In these various aspects of human function, the psychological and/or spiritual drivers are identified, isolated, and described in terms of the way in which they unconsciously and consciously operate in religion, thought, and behavior.

The books in this series are written for the general reader, the local library, and the undergraduate university student. They are also of significant interest to the informed professional, particularly in fields corollary to his or her primary interest. The volumes in this series have great value for clinical settings and treatment models, as well.

This series editor has spent an entire professional lifetime focused specifically on research into the interface of psychology, religion, and spirituality. These matters are of the highest urgency in human affairs today, when religious motivation seems to be playing an increasing role, constructively and destructively, in the arena of social ethics, national politics, and world affairs. It is imperative that we find out immediately what the psychopathological factors are that shape a religion that can launch deadly assaults upon the World Trade Center in New York and murder 3,500 people, or a religion that motivates suicide bombers to kill themselves and murder dozens of their neighbors weekly, or a religion that prompts such unjust national policies as preemptive defense, all of which are wreaking havoc on the social fabric, the democratic processes, the domestic tranquility, the economic stability and productivity, and the legitimate right to freedom from fear in every nation in the world today.

This volume is an urgently needed and timely work, the motivation for which is surely endorsed enthusiastically by the entire world today, as the international community searches for strategies that will afford us better and deeper psychological and religious self-understanding as individuals and communities. Careful strategies of empirical, heuristic, and phenomenological research have been employed to give this work a solid scientific foundation and formation.

For 50 years, such organizations as the Christian Association for Psychological Studies and such graduate departments of psychology as those at Boston University, Fuller, Rosemead, Harvard, George Fox, Princeton, and the like, have been publishing significant building blocks of empirical, heuristic, and phenomenological research on issues dealing with religious behavior and psychospirituality. In this project, the insights generated by such patient and careful research are synthesized and integrated into a holistic psychospiritual worldview that takes the phenomenology of religion and spirituality with the utmost seriousness.

Some of the influences of religion on persons and society, now and throughout history, have been negative. However, most of the impact of the great religions on human life and culture has been profoundly redemptive and generative of great good. It is urgent, therefore, that we discover and understand better what the psychological and spiritual forces are that empower people of faith and genuine spirituality to give themselves to all the creative and constructive enterprises that, throughout the centuries, have made of human life the humane, ordered, prosperous, and aesthetic experience it can be at its best. Surely the forces for good in both psychology and spirituality far exceed the powers and proclivities toward evil that we see so prominently demonstrated in the name of religion in our world today.

This series of Praeger volumes is dedicated to the greater understanding of psychology, religion, and spirituality and thus to the profound understanding and empowerment of those psychospiritual drivers that can help us transcend the malignancy of our earthly pilgrimage and enormously enhance the humaneness and majesty of the human spirit, indeed, the potential for magnificence in human life.

NOTE

1. LeRoy Aden and J. Harold Ellens, eds. (1990), *Turning Points in Pastoral Care: The Legacy of Anton Boisen and Seward Hiltner*, Grand Rapids, MI: Baker.

BIBLIOGRAPHY

Aden, LeRoy, and J. Harold Ellens, eds. (1990), *Turning Points in Pastoral Care: The Legacy of Anton Boisen and Seward Hiltner*, Grand Rapids, MI: Baker.

Allport, Gordon W. (1937), *Personality: A Psychological Interpretation*, New York: Henry Holt.

Allport, Gordon W. (1950), *The Individual and His Religion: A Psychological Interpretation*, New York: Macmillan.

Allport, Gordon W. (1960), *Personality and Social Encounter: Selected Essays*, Boston: Beacon.

Allport, Gordon W. (1961), *Pattern and Growth in Personality*, New York: Holt, Rinehart, Winston.

Arapura, J. G. (1973), *Religion as Anxiety and Tranquility*, Paris: Mouton.

Beker, J. Christiaan (1980), *Paul the Apostle: The Triumph of God in Life and Thought*, Philadelphia: Fortress.

Berry, C. Markham (1980), "Entering Canaan: Adolescence as a Stage of Spiritual Growth," *Bulletin of CAPS* 6(4), 110–14.

Betz, Hans Dieter (1975), *Plutarch's Theological Writings and Early Christian Literature*, Studia ad corpus Hellenisticum Novi Testamenti 3, Leiden, Netherlands: Brill.

Betz, Hans Dieter (1978), *Plutarch's Ethical Writings and Early Christian Literature*, Leiden, Netherlands: Brill.

Blanton, Smiley, and Edward Robinson (1957), *Love or Perish*, New York: Simon and Schuster.

Blum, H. I. (1974), *Planning for Health: Developmental Application of Social Change Theory*, New York: Human Sciences Press.

Boman, Thorlief (1960), *Hebrew Thought Compared with Greek*, trans. Jules L. Moreau, New York: W. W. Norton.

Bonhoeffer, Dietrich (1965), *The Cost of Discipleship*, New York: Macmillan.

Brister, C. W. (1964), *Pastoral Care in the Church*, New York: Harper and Row.

Capps, Donald (1993), *Reframing: A New Method in Pastoral Care*, Minneapolis, MN: Fortress.

Capps, Donald, and Janet Jacobs, eds. (1995), *The Struggle for Life: A Companion to William James' Varieties of Religious Experience*, Society for the Scientific Study of Religion Monograph Series 9, Newton, KS: Mennonite Press.

Carnell, Edward J. (1965), *The Burden of Soren Kierkegaard*, Grand Rapids, MI: Eerdmans.

Carter, John D., and Bruce Narramore (1979), *The Integration of Psychology and Theology: An Introduction*, Grand Rapids, MI: Zondervan.

Childs, Brevard S. (1979), *Introduction to the Old Testament as Scripture*, Philadelphia: Fortress.

Clark, Walter H., H. Newton Malony, James Daane, and Alan R. Tippett (1973), *Religious Experience, Its Nature and Function in the Human Psyche: The First John G. Finch Symposium on Psychology and Religion*, Springfield, MO: Charles C. Thomas.

Clinebell, Howard J. (1966), *Basic Types of Pastoral Counseling*, Nashville, TN: Abingdon.

Clinebell, Howard J. (1979), *Growth Counseling: Hope-Centered Methods of Actualizing Human Wholeness*, Nashville, TN: Abingdon.

Clines, David J. A. (1968), "The Image of God in Man," *Tyndale Bulletin* 19, 53–99.

Daane, James (1973), *The Freedom of God*, Grand Rapids, MI: Eerdmans.

Dever, G. E. Alan (1976), "An Epidemiological Model for Health Policy Analysis," *Social Indicators Research* 2, 455–468.

Dicks, Russell L. (1949), *Pastoral Work and Personal Counseling*, New York: Macmillan.

Dicks, Russell L. (1980), *Toward Health and Wholeness*, New York: Macmillan.

Eliade, Marcea (1958), *Yoga: Immortality and Freedom*, New York: Pantheon.

Ellens, J. Harold (1975), "Anxiety and the Rise of Religious Experience," *Journal of Psychology and Theology* 3(1), 11–18.

Ellens, J. Harold (1976), "Psychological Process and Christian Experience in Psychotherapy," in *Research in Mental Health and Religious Behavior*, ed. W. J. Donaldson Jr., Atlanta, GA: Psychological Studies Institute.

Ellens, J. Harold (1982), *God's Grace and Human Health*, Nashville, TN: Abingdon.

Ellens, J. Harold (1987), *Psychotheology: Key Issues*, Johannesburg: UNISA.

Ellens, J. Harold (1988), "The Psychodynamics of Christian Conversion," in *The Church and Pastoral Care*, ed. LeRoy Aden and J. Harold Ellens, Grand Rapids, MI: Baker.

Ellens, J. Harold, ed. (2004), *The Destructive Power of Religion: Violence in Judaism, Christianity, and Islam*, 4 vols., Westport, CT: Praeger.

Ellis, Peter (1968), *The Yahwist: The Bible's First Theologian*, Notre Dame, IN: Fides.

Erikson, Erik H. (1963), *Childhood and Society*, 2nd ed., New York: W. W. Norton.

Erikson, Erik H. (1980), *Identity and the Life Cycle*, New York: W. W. Norton. First published 1959 by International Universities Press.

Erikson, Erik H. (1982), *The Life Cycle Completed: A Review*, New York: W. W. Norton.

Finch, John G. (1976), *The Message of Anxiety*, taped lecture, CAPS-WACPS Convention, Santa Barbara, CA.

Fowler, James W. (1976), "Faith Development Theory and the Aims of Religious Socialization," in *Emerging Issues in Religious Education*, ed. G. Durka and J. Smith, New York: Paulist.

Fowler, James W. (1980), "Moral Stages and the Development of Faith," in *Moral Development, Moral Education, and Kohlberg: Basic Issues in Philosophy, Psychology, Religion, and Education*, ed. B. Munsey, Birmingham, AL: Religious Education Press.

Fowler, James W. (1981), *Stages of Faith: The Psychology of Human Development and the Quest for Meaning*, San Francisco: Harper and Row.

Fowler, James W. (1984), *Becoming Adult, Becoming Christian: Adult Development and Christian Faith*, San Francisco: Harper and Row.

Frankl, Victor E. (1962), *Man's Search for Meaning: An Introduction to Logotherapy*, Boston: Beacon.

Frankl, Victor E. (1963), *Man's Search for Himself*, New York: Washington Square Press.

Frankl, Victor E. (1964), *The Heart of Man*, New York: Harper and Row.

Frankl, Victor E. (1969), *The Doctor and the Soul*, London: Souvenir Press.

Frankl, Victor E. (1973), *The Anatomy of Human Destructiveness*, New York: Scribner's Sons.

Frankl, Victor E. (1975), *The Unconscious God: Psychotherapy and Theology*, New York: Simon and Schuster.

Frazer, James G. (1959), *The Golden Bough*, ed. Theodore Gaster, New York: Criterion.

Fromm, Eric (1950), *Psychoanalysis and Religion*, New Haven, CT: Yale University Press.

Fromm, Eric (1973), *The Anatomy of Human Destructiveness*, New York: Holt, Rinehart, Winston.

Fuller, Robert C. (1988), *Religion and the Life Cycle*, Philadelphia: Fortress.

Gerkin, Charles V. (1984), *The Living Human Document, Re-visioning Pastoral Counseling in a Hermeneutical Mode*, Nashville, TN: Abingdon.

Groddeck, G. (1977), *The Meaning of Illness: Selected Analytic Writings*, New York: International Universities Press.

Groeschel, B. J. (1984), *Spiritual Passages: The Psychology of Spiritual Development "for Those Who Seek,"* New York: Crossroad.

Hauerwas, Stanley (1974), *Vision and Virtue*, Notre Dame, IN: University of Notre Dame Press.

Hauerwas, Stanley (1975), *Character and the Christian Life: A Study in Theological Ethics*, Notre Dame, IN: University of Notre Dame Press.

Hauerwas, Stanley (1977), *Truthfulness and Tragedy*, Notre Dame, IN: University of Notre Dame Press.

Hauerwas, Stanley (1981), *A Community of Character: Toward a Constructive Christian Social Ethic*, Notre Dame, IN: University of Notre Dame Press.

Hiltner, Seward (1949), *Pastoral Counseling*, Nashville, TN: Abingdon.

Hiltner, Seward (1972), *Theological Dynamics*, Nashville, TN: Abingdon.

Hiltner, Seward, and Karl Menninger, eds, (1963), *Constructive Aspects of Anxiety*, Nashville, TN: Abingdon.

Horney, Karen (1937), *The Neurotic Personality of Our Time*, New York: W. W. Norton.

James, William (1956), *The Will to Believe*, New York: Dove.

James, William (1958), *Varieties of Religious Experience*, New York: Morrow.

Jaynes, Julian (1976), *The Origin of Consciousness in the Breakdown of the Bicameral Mind*, Boston: Houghton Mifflin.

Joy, D. M. (1983), *Moral Development Foundations: Judeo-Christian Alternatives to Piaget/Kohlberg*, Nashville, TN: Abingdon.

Jung, Carl G. (1958), *Undiscovered Self*, trans. R.F.C. Hull, Boston: Little, Brown.

Jung, Carl G. (1964), *Man and His Symbols*, Garden City, NJ: Doubleday.

Kerr, Hugh T., and John M. Mulder (1983), *Conversions: The Christian Experience*, Grand Rapids, MI: Eerdmans.

Kim, Wonil, Deborah Ellens, Michael Floyd, and Marvin A. Sweeney (2000), *Reading the Hebrew Bible for a New Millennium: Form, Concept, and Theological Perspective*, 2 vols., Harrisburg, PA: Trinity International.

Knierim, Rolf P. (1995), *The Task of Old Testament Theology: Method and Cases*, Grand Rapids, MI: Eerdmans.

Kohlberg, L. (1963), "Development of Children's Orientation toward a Moral Order," *Vita Humana* 6, 11–16.

Kohlberg, L. (1973), "Continuities in Childhood and Adult Moral Development Revisited," in *Lifespan Developmental Psychology: Personality and Socialization*, ed. P. Baltes and K. Shaic, New York: Academic Press.

Kohlberg, L. (1974), "Education, Moral Development and Faith," *Journal of Moral Education* 4(1), 5–16.

Kohlberg, L. (1976), "Moral Stages and Moralization," in *Moral Development and Behavior: Theory, Research, and Social Issues*, ed. T. Likona, New York: Holt, Rinehart, Winston.

Kubler-Ross, Elizabeth (1969), *On Death and Dying*, New York: Macmillan.

Lalonde, M. (1974), *A New Perspective on the Health of Canadians*, Ottawa: Office of the Canadian Minister of National Health and Welfare.

Levenson, D. J. (1978), "The Anatomy of the Life Cycle," *Psychiatric Opinion* 15, 29–48.

Levenson, D. J. (1978), *The Seasons of a Man's Life*, New York: Knopf.

Lewis, Edson T. (1981), "The Story of Medicine and Theology: A Context for Ministry," dissertation, Trinity Lutheran Seminary, Columbus, OH.

Loder, James E. (1981), *The Transforming Moment*, New York: Harper.

Maddi, Salvatore R. (1980), *Personality Theories: A Comparative Analysis*, Homewood, IL: Dorsey Press.

Malony, H. Newton, ed. (1980), *A Christian Existential Psychology: The Contributions of John G. Finch*, Lanham, MD: University Press of America.

Malony, H. Newton, ed. (1983), *Wholeness and Holiness: Readings in the Psychology/Theology of Mental Health*, Grand Rapids, MI: Baker.

Malony, H. Newton, ed. (1988), *Spirit Centered Wholeness: Beyond the Psychology of Self*, Lewiston, NY: Mellen.

Malony, H. Newton (1995), *Win-Win Relationships: 9 Strategies for Settling Personal Conflicts without Waging War*, Nashville, TN: Broadman.

Massey, Morris (1972), *What You Are Is Where You Were When*, Series on Life Cycle Development, video tape, Boulder: University of Colorado.

May, Rollo (1950), *The Meaning of Anxiety*, New York: Ronald Press.

May, Rollo (1969), *Love and Will*, New York: W. W. Norton.

McNeill, Robert (1975), *God Wills Us Free*, New York: W. W. Norton.

Mertz, Barbara (1966), *Red Land, Black Land*, New York: Coward, McCann, Geoghegan.

Morris, J. N. (1975), *Uses of Epidemiology*, 3rd ed., Edinburgh: Churchill Livingstone.

Nouwen, Henri (1972), *The Wounded Healer: Ministry in Contemporary Society*, Garden City, NJ: Doubleday.

Nouwen, Henri, and Walter Gaffney (1976), *Aging: The Fulfillment of Life*, Garden City, NJ: Image.

Oates, Wayne E. (1958), *What Does Psychology Say about Religion?*, New York: Association Press.

Oates, Wayne E., ed. (1959), *An Introduction to Pastoral Counseling*, Nashville, TN: Broadman.

Oates, Wayne E. (1973), *The Psychology of Religion*, Waco, TX: Word.

Oates, Wayne E. (1987), *Behind the Masks: Personality Disorders in Religious Behavior*, Philadelphia: Westminster.

Otto, Rudolph (1958), *The Idea of the Holy*, trans. John W. Harvey, New York: Oxford University Press.

Outler, Albert C. (1963), "Anxiety and Grace: An Augustinian Perspective," in *Constructive Aspects of Anxiety*, ed. Seward Hiltner and Karl Menninger, Nashville, TN: Abingdon.

Phillips, J. B., trans. (1958), *The New Testament in Modern English*, London: William Collins.

Piaget, J. (1967), *Six Psychological Studies*, New York: Random House.

Piaget, J. (1969), *The Psychology of the Child*, New York: Random House.

Piaget, J. (1977), *The Development of Thought: Equilibration of Cognitive Structures*, trans. A Rosin, New York: Viking.

Punt, Neil (1980), *Unconditional Good News: Toward an Understanding of Biblical Universalism*, Grand Rapids, MI: Eerdmans.

Restak, R. M. (1979), *The Brain, the Last Frontier*, New York: Warner.

Restak, R. M. (1984), *The Brain*, New York: Bantam.

Ridderbos, Herman (1958), *Paul and Jesus, Origin and General Character of Paul's Preaching of Christ*, trans. David H. Freeman, Grand Rapids, MI: Baker.

Ridderbos, Herman (1962), *The Coming of the Kingdom*, trans. H. de Jongste, ed. Raymond O. Zorn, Philadelphia: Presbyterian and Reformed. Distributed by Baker.

Ridderbos, Herman (1975), *Paul: An Outline of His Theology*, trans. John R. De Witt, Grand Rapids, MI: Eerdmans.

Rogers, Carl (1951), *Client Centered Therapy*, Boston: Houghton Mifflin.

Ryan, Regina, and John Travis (1981), *Wellness Workbook*, San Diego, CA: Ten-Speed Press.

Sagan, Carl (1974), *Broca's Brain*, New York: Random House.

Schaeffer, Francis A. (1971), *True Spirituality*, Wheaton, IL: Tyndale House.

Schleiermacher, Friedrich (1963), *The Christian Faith*, ed. and trans. H. R. Mackintosh and J. S. Stewart, 2 vols., New York: Harper and Row.

Sheehy, Gail (1976), *Passages: Predictable Crises of Adult Life*, New York: Dutton.

Shirley, H. B. (1983), *Mapping the Mind*, Chicago: Nelson Hall.

Siegler, Miriam, and Humphrey Osmond (1974), *Models of Madness and Models of Medicine*, New York: Macmillan.

Simon, Bennett (1980), *Mind and Madness in Ancient Greece: The Classical Roots of Modern Psychiatry*, Ithaca, NY: Cornell.

Smedes, Lewis (1984), *Forgive and Forget: Healing the Hurts We Don't Deserve*, New York: Harper and Row.

Smith, Wilfred C. (1963), *The Meaning and End of Religion: A New Approach to Religious Traditions of Mankind*, New York: Macmillan.

Springer, S. P., and G. Deutsch (1981), *Left Brain, Right Brain*, San Francisco: W. H. Freeman.

Tillich, Paul (1948), *The Protestant Era*, trans. James Luther Adams, Chicago: University of Chicago Press.

Tillich, Paul (1951), *Systematic Theology*, 2 vols., Chicago: University of Chicago Press.

Tillich, Paul (1957), *The Meaning of Persons*, trans. Edwin Hudson, New York: Harper.

Tournier, Paul (1962), *Guilt and Grace*, trans. Arthur W. Heathcote, New York: Harper and Row.

Tracy, David (1975), *Blessed Rage for Order: The New Pluralism in Theology*, New York: Seabury.

Van Leeuwen, Mary Stewart (1983), *The Sorcerer's Apprentice*, Grand Rapids, MI: Baker.

Van Leeuwen, Mary Stewart (1985), *The Person in Psychology: A Contemporary Christian Appraisal*, Grand Rapids, MI: Eerdmans.

Weatherhead, Leslie D. (1952), *Psychology, Religion, and Healing*, Nashville, TN: Abingdon.

Westberg, Granger E. (1979), *Theological Roots of Wholistic Health Care*, Hinsdale, MI: Wholistic Health Centers Inc.

Westerhof, John (1976), *Will Our Children Have Faith?*, New York: Seabury.

Whitehead, E. E., and J. D. Whitehead (1984), *Seasons of Strength: New Visions of Adult Christian Maturing*, Garden City, NJ: Doubleday Image.

Wiesenthal, Simon (1976), *Sunflowers, with Symposium*, New York: Schocken.

Williams, J. F. (1946), *Personal Hygiene Applied*, 8th ed., Philadelphia: Saunders.

Wolterstorff, Nicholas (1984), *Reason within the Bounds of Religion*, Grand Rapids, MI: Eerdmans.

Wulff, David M. (1991), *Psychology of Religion: Classic and Contemporary Views*, New York: John Wiley.

Yancey, Philip (1986), *What's So Amazing about Grace?*, Grand Rapids, MI: Zondervan.

INDEX

About the Author

J. HAROLD ELLENS is a Research Scholar at the University of Michigan Department of Near Eastern Studies, a retired Presbyterian theologian, an ordained minister, a retired U.S. Army Colonel, and a retired Professor of Philosophy, Theology, and Psychology. He served 15 years as Executive Director of the Christian Association for Psychological Studies and was Founding Editor and Editor-in-Chief of the *Journal of Psychology and Christianity*. He has authored, co-authored, or edited more than 75 books, including *The Destructive Power of Religion* (Praeger, 2004) and *Sex in the Bible* (Praeger, 2006).